Strategic Market Planning

Wiley Series in Practical Strategy

Published titles

Business Unit Strategy
Segev

Forthcoming titles

The Turbulence Concept: Strategic Management for Difficult Times
Ansoff

Virtual Organizations and Beyond
Hedberg

Strategic Market Planning

A Blueprint for Success

Patrick McNamee

JOHN WILEY & SONS

Chichester • New York • Weinheim • Brisbane • Singapore • Toronto

Copyright © 1998 by John Wiley & Sons Ltd,
Baffins Lane, Chichester,
West Sussex PO19 1UD, England

National	01243 779777
International	+(44) 1243 779777

e-mail (for order and customer service enquiries): cs-books@wiley.co.uk
Visit our Home Page on   http://www.wiley.co.uk
or http://www.wiley.com

Other Wiley Editorial Offices

John Wiley & Sons, Inc., 605 Third Avenue,
New York, NY 10158-0012, USA

Weinheim • Brisbane • Singapore • Toronto

Library of Congress Cataloging-in-Publication Data
McNamee, Patrick B.
Strategic market planning : a blueprint for success / Patrick McNamee
p. cm. — (Wiley series in practical strategy)
Includes biographical references and index.
ISBN 0-471-97932-5 (cloth)
1. Marketing—Management. I. Title. II. Series.
HF5414.13.M3695 1998   97–41435
658.8—dc21   CIP

British Library Cataloguing in Publication Data
A catalogue record for this book is available from the British Library

ISBN 0-471-97932-5

Typeset in 11/13pt Times by Stephen Wright-Bouvier of the
Rainwater Consultancy, Faringdon, Oxfordshire.
Printed and bound in Great Britain by Bookcraft (Bath) Limited,
Midsomer Norton, Somerset.
This book is printed on acid-free paper responsibly manufactured from sustainable forestation, for which at least two trees are planted for each one used.

Contents

Series Foreword

The aim of this series is to provide managers with books on strategy, strategic management and strategic change, which are helpful, practical, and provide guidance for the application of sound concepts in real situations.

In the mid-1960s when the subject of planning began to emerge, the whole literature could have been listed on one or two sheets of paper. It was easy to decide which books to read, because so few were available. This state of affairs changed rapidly, and the scope of the subject has moved from a focus on formal planning to a broader view which merges with the literature of leadership, change management, strategic analysis and organization. Modern writing sees the organization and its strategies in an integrated way, and there are many, often conflicting, theories about the 'right way' to formulate strategies and practise strategic management.

Management does not take an academic interest in theories, but is concerned about what works best in the situation in which it operates. Hence this series. Each book is conceptually sound, and gives proper acknowledgement to the originators of concepts and ideas, but the emphasis is on using the concepts or methods, rather than academic argument.

Business school faculty and students are also concerned with the application of theories and will find much in these books to supplement the more academic texts.

In this series the aim is to give readers clear guidance on how to make the subject of the book work in their own situation, while at the same time taking care to ensure that the books do not oversimplify situations. Checklists and questionnaires are included when they aid the aims of the book, and examples are given. The experience of the author in actually applying the concepts, rather than just knowing about them, is intended to show through the writing.

The series will make complex matters understandable. We hope that it will become a catalyst that helps managers make a difference to the strategic performance of their organizations.

David Hussey
David Hussey & Associates
Editor of *Journal of Strategic Change*

Preface

The title of this book – *Strategic Market Planning: A Blueprint for Success* – reflects its purpose: to persuade managers that enduringly successful firms are those that understand most clearly and then serve most effectively the markets in which they operate. Such firms will draw their commercial nutrition from their markets more effectively than rivals and enjoy sustained, superior and more bountiful returns. Expressing this more simply: exceptionally successful firms will be those which are exceptionally successful in their markets. Consequently this book aims to provide managers with a blueprint that will enable them to develop and implement strategies which will make them and their firms exceptionally successful.

This book reflects my experiences in working closely with managers in large firms. A repeated observation which I have made is that the firm and its managers are much more important than the industry in which it is operating. Thus, exceptionally successful firms become so not because of lucky industrial circumstances, but because of the drive and strategic vision of their managers. A complementary observation is that industries are not 'special': there are generic strategic rules that enable those firms which follow them to enjoy exceptional success irrespective of the industry in which they operate. This is good news for managers; it means that being in a relatively poor industry is not a sentence to a dismal career. As illustrated in Chapter 1 there are many relatively poor industries in which firms and their managers have enjoyed exceptional success.

These observations come from experiences with firms operating in diverse industries: banking, financial services, retailing, cigarette retailing, coin-operated vending, contract catering, meat production, oil distribution, industrial chemicals, aircraft manufacturing, professional accounting, food manufacture and distribution, computer manufacturing, construction, building insulation, building materials, DIY, and luxury consumer goods. These firms were relatively large and operated in different European locations at both national and multinational levels. This is not the usual list of superior industries that is feted in the business press – industries which appear to receive most attention tend to be 'glamorous' ones such a high tech, rapid growth, and spectacularly innovative ones – yet within the list there are many firms that enjoy exceptional success. This book sets out the agenda, or the blueprint, which such firms have followed in achieving this success.

One area frequently neglected in the strategic planning process is the necessity of seeing it as essentially creative in nature and building the supporting organizational humanity which is essential for such creativity to flourish. Firms that are exceptionally successful tend to have a sense of humanity stimulated by the senior management and sustained at all levels which helps every member of staff to work as a united and committed coalition towards common goals. In such circumstances not only is superior performance realized but, more importantly, the self-esteem and confidence of the participating managers are enhanced. Such a cultural atmosphere develops an esprit de corps that predisposes all managers to revisit and improve their strategic market planning: a process which when continuously pursued builds enduring success.

Another, less important, observation is that most managers claim that 'the data' for strategic market planning, particularly at the market level, are not available. In one sense this is true: often detailed market share figures are indeed not available. However, this problem is often a virtue in disguise. The lack of data forces managers to think deeply and often creatively about their market positions relative to other competitors in the industry. Such forced thinking often yields deep insights, creative strategic ideas and, ultimately, surprisingly good data.

As the first paragraph of the Preface indicated, this book reflects my experiences working with firms and it is appropriate that I should now thank formally the many managers with whom I have enjoyed working. So, in alphabetical order, with apologies to any I have omitted, I would like to thank the following people: Paul Carty, Des Crowley, Paul Davidson, Pat Dineen, Bill Hayes, Richard Hewat, David Keen, James

Lancaster, Hugh Lavery, James Leonard, Sean Kehoe, Gareth McClay, Pat and Brian McColgan, Ian McFarlane, Leo Martin, Gerard Murphy, Pat McGrath, Gerry O'Doherty and John Wright. Included in this list must be, of course, all the students with whom I have had the pleasure to work since I started this book. I would also like to thank the staff of PIMS Europe in London, particularly Keith Roberts, Mike Clayton and Graeme Turner, for their help. Finally, I would like to thank my family, Brid, David and Stephen, for all their encouragement.

I feel it is appropriate to write something about the audience at which this book is aimed and about what a typical reader ought to be able to achieve after reading it. The primary audience is practising managers and students of business, particularly at the post-graduate level. The book aims to be useful to managers at all levels and especially useful for those who wish to integrate a strong strategic dimension into their firms and their own professional lives. Although the book mainly reflects experiences with larger firms, the lessons are generic and can be applied easily to smaller firms and to public sector organizations. Indeed, it should be particularly useful for managers in firms which have recently become privatized and are seeking insights on how to develop and implement the strategic market planning process.

On completion of this book the reader should have gained the following insights:

* a personal belief in his or her ability to build their own career and to build the strategic strength of their firm;
* a personal belief in the power of strategic market planning and its attendant human dimensions to confer competitive advantage upon any firm, almost irrespective of the industry conditions in which it operates;
* a blueprint for developing and implementing a strategic market plan irrespective of the industry;
* a knowledge of strategic market thinking and its associated techniques which will provide insights denied to others;
* a knowledge of the rules of strategic market planning that when applied will build any firm into one that habitually achieves superior results;
* a register of the language of strategy that will foster communication, creative debate and ultimately sustained superior performance.

Patrick McNamee
Belfast, 1998

How to Use this Book

This book is for practising managers and students of strategic market planning. It is set out in two parts with which all readers ought to be able to identify.

4 The Skeleton   A generic approach to strategic
   Strategic Market   market planning, i.e. a blueprint
   Plan   and an overview of the book.

5 Alban Chemicals   A real-life example of a
                         completed strategic market plan.

PART II DEVELOPING A STRATEGIC MARKET PLAN

This is the major section of the book and shows how a strategic market plan can be developed for any organization. In the book the organization will always be a private sector firm. However, readers with a public sector orientation ought to be able to apply the private sector methodology to the public sector. Part II is set out in a series of logical and discrete steps with a chapter for each.

Section A provides the background to the plan and is written after Sections B and C and D have been completed. It comprises two chapters: A1 and A2.

A1 Introduction and Background

A2 Executive Summary

Section B assesses the current strategic position. This provides an historical analysis of the firm up to the date of development of the strategic market plan. It comprises five chapters: B1 to B5.

B1 Defining the Business

B2 The Product Market

B3 Analysing the Environment

B4 Analysing the Firm

B5 Key Strategic Issues

Section C covers the future strategic market plan. This provides the future strategic market plan for the firm from the date of the strategic market plan. It comprises three chapters: C1 to C3.

C1 Future Mission, Goals, Targets and Portfolios

C2 Gap Analysis

C3 Building on the Messages of the Market

Section D deals with implementation. This provides the future detailed tactics and actions necessary to implement the strategic market plan. It comprises two chapters: D1 and D2.

D1 Tactics and Implementation

D2 Resources for the Strategic Plan

Thus, this book is both a text which develops the manager's knowledge of strategic market planning as well as a handbook for the actual development of such plans within any organization.

Part I
Background Information

1
The Market is the Message

After a certain age, most managers asked to reflect upon their business will often reply with words such as:

> 'Don't talk to me about this business. I'm sorry I ever went into it. When I consider what I could have achieved if I had started working in the . . . well some other industry.'

> 'Times are bad. They have been bad for years. I don't really know how anyone can see a future in this business.'

> 'I can't stand the stress. You've no idea just how hard we have to work just to stand still.'

Often these negative sentiments are complemented by wry observations:

> 'Funny old business this. Not like any other. You need to be in this business for years, and even then you still don't understand it.'

> 'Ours isn't like any other business. There's a lot of cowboys in this industry that others don't have to contend with.'

These are not unusual sentiments, even in industries which are enjoying good or reasonable growth rates. Why is this so? Why should managers who usually start in their careers with such enthusiasm and hope ultimately become filled with supine apathy?

These are important questions because such attitudes mitigate against success. Indeed, it could be argued that a lack of success causes such attitudes. This is a vicious cycle. As shown in Figure 1.1, a lack of success leads to negative attitudes which foster even less success. It is as though work is an abrasive which, over time, rasps off the manager's husk of self-esteem and personal belief.

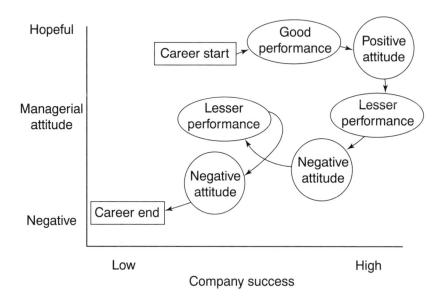

Figure 1.1 A lack of success fosters even less success

A fundamental assertion of this book is that such attitudes develop, then fester and cause greater infection because the firms in which these managers work are often relatively unsuccessful and the managers are relatively unsure of their futures. The firms are not growing and healthy. If only they could become so then such attitudes are likely to be less prevalent. This is the thrust of this book – it is about managers growing their careers through growing strong healthy firms. These firms will draw their sustenance from the market. The market is the medium in which they will grow. In other words: The Market is the Message.

Stating this more comprehensively, an underlying premise of this book is that the success of all firms is ultimately determined in the marketplace:

- Firms which fail to satisfy their customers will fail.
- Firms which satisfy their customers in an average manner will have an average performance.
- Firms which satisfy their customers in a superior manner will enjoy superior performance.

Additionally, all markets continuously send signals or messages to firms and the most successful will be those whose managers are adept at interpreting and then acting upon these messages.

Industry characteristics don't matter: It's structural position that counts

Many managers often look enviously at industries which appear to enjoy superior returns. They are often seen as glamour industries in exotic locations which have extraordinary resources, electrifying growth rates and an aura of continuous joy and excitement. Indeed, in more popular business magazines it is not unusual to read accounts of firms couched in terms such as the following:

> Californian based Zylomicrotec Corporation which is just three years old has revealed its twentieth world beating high tech product which the twenty five year old chairman and CEO says will increase their phenomenal annual compound earnings growth of 400 per cent.

There may be firms like this, but for most managers they are a far remove from their working lives and experiences which are set in more pedestrian firms and in less exciting industries. However, being in a non-glamorous industry ought not to be an impediment to strategic success. Indeed, so-called glamorous industries often offer no better opportunities than more pedestrian and less publicized ones. Thus, a number of studies, (1,2) has shown that there is more variation in profit performance within industries than between industries. This implies that for managers to be successful it is much more important to be a member of a successful firm rather than to be in a successful industry. In other words, the strategy and structure of the firm is more important than the industry. More precisely, not all firms in dismal industries are dismal and unsuccessful and not all firms in buoyant industries flourish.

The rest of this chapter is concerned with illustrating the viewpoint that true strategic victories occur when firms win against the odds: *the industry characteristics don't matter; it's the structural position of the firm that counts.*

This viewpoint is illustrated through examining a number of firms that, when faced with apparently insuperable difficulties, enjoyed outstanding strategic success. These firms could be described as unexpected winners or rather that their success had been achieved by 'winning against the odds', where this phrase means that the firms had achieved one or more of the following:

- superior results irrespective of the industry;
- superior results with inferior resources;
- superior results in both bad and good economic circumstances;
- superior results irrespective of the country.

EXAMPLES OF FIRMS WINNING AGAINST THE ODDS

Four well-known firms that have 'won against the odds' are now examined. The rationale behind this section is that when managers feel that the odds stacked against them are immense they may take inspiration from these firms. Each will be examined in two stages:

- *Stage 1* examines the industry conditions and circumstances in which the firm operated.
- *Stage 2* reveals the performance of the firm, its name and strategy.

The industries are: brewing and distilling, luxury consumer goods, tyres, and bananas and were chosen on two bases:

1. Diversity: they range from consumer goods to industrial goods. This diversity illustrates that strategic success is not dependent upon a particular industrial sector, but can be found in a great variety of diverse industrial circumstances.
2. Reader familiarity: most readers will be familiar with the industries and the firms.

CASE STUDY 1 BREWING AND DISTILLING INDUSTRY

Stage 1 Industry Characteristics and firm circumstances[1]

* *Time period*: 1980s–90s.
* *Average annual industry growth rate*: declining market.
* *Number of major competitors*: increasing concentration – by 1996 there were just five major players.
* *Imports*: increased in both the expensive and inexpensive segments.
* *Location*: UK.
* *Comments on industry situation*: prospects looked poor; not only was the overall market contracting, but it was being further eroded by imports (3,4).

Stage 2: Firm performance

The firm's performance over this period is shown in Figure 1.2.

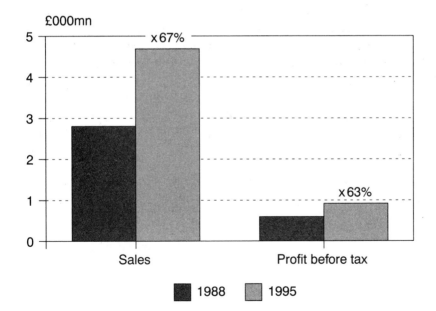

Figure 1.2 Guinness plc performance, 1988–95

Firm details

The firm is Guinness plc which shows an outstanding performance over this period. How did it achieve such results? It did so by responding to the messages from the markets – by tailoring its strategic market planning to its markets.

The message from the market for Guinness appears to have been that to continue to rely heavily on the UK market for sales would almost certainly cause Guinness to decline because the market was in decline. Guinness adopted a strategy that had some of the following characteristics:

> Our approach to acquisitions is to seek opportunities to strengthen core activities, provided that we can do so at an acceptable price and within the constraints of our financial and management resources. We only make acquisitions where we can add value. We have disposed of interests which are considered peripheral to our primary focus and do not plan to become involved in unrelated activities (5).

- *Core strategy*: high growth in the core activities of brewing and distilling to be achieved mainly by foreign acquisition and the building of global brands.
- *Product strategy*: concentrate on the core business of brewing, distilling and closely related activities. Sell off non-core businesses. Reduce the number of brands and concentrate building global scale in the remaining ones.
- *Geographical strategy*: As the UK market is insufficient for Guinness, to develop a truly global presence through building the core brands.

It would seem to be the case for Guinness at the time that: *the industry characteristics don't matter; it's the structural position of the firm that counts.*

CASE STUDY 2 LUXURY CONSUMER GOODS

Stage 1 Industry characteristics and firm circumstances

- *Time period*: 1975–93.
- *Strategic problems:* 75 per cent of sales came from one product; therefore vulnerable to the fortunes of this product.

  Of sales 91 per cent were from outside the UK; therefore vulnerable to exchange rate volatility.

  Highly dependent upon one country for sales and profits; therefore vulnerable to changes in the economy or consumer taste changes in that country.

  The market for this main product was in serious and unstoppable decline. Its only assets were a famous brand name and really not much else.
- *Comments on the industry situation*: prospects looked extremely poor for this firm; its main market was disappearing (4,5).

Stage 2 Firm performance

The firm's performance over this period is shown in Figure 1.3.

Firm details

The firm is Dunhill Holdings plc which had an outstanding performance over this period. How did it achieve such results? It did so by responding to the messages from the markets, by tailoring its strategic market planning and its operations to its markets.

In 1975 Dunhill sales comprised just lighters (75 per cent of sales) and pipes (25 per cent of sales) and these products relied very heavily on just one market – Japan. To continue to rely on this product–market configuration would have been disastrous for Dunhill. Instead, the new Managing Director, Tony Greener, redefined the business of Dunhill, not in terms of products but in terms of its customer services. Dunhill changed from being in the business of quality lighters, tobaccos and pipes to supplying high quality branded consumer merchandise on a global basis. Thus, the Dunhill brand was extended to include the following businesses:

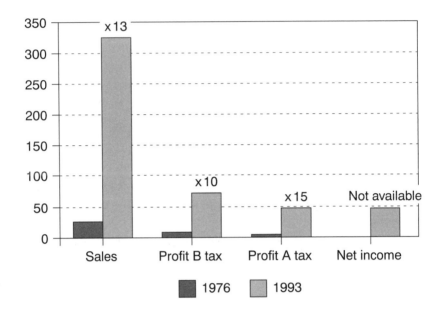

Figure 1.3:   Dunhill Holdings plc performance, 1976–93

- Chloe (ladies fashion and perfume);
- Karl Lagerfeld (ladies fashion);
- Hachett (menswear);
- Lane (tobacco);
- Mont Blanc Simplo (writing instruments);
- Alfred Dunhill (fashion, jewellery, smoking products, fragrances).

This strategic redirection enabled the firm to expand its range to include clothing, luggage, writing instruments, watches and perfume and can be clearly seen in the firm's mission statement:

> The business of the Dunhill group will be to utilise and develop brand names to sell high quality personal consumer merchandise and services. The group will seek to concentrate its main resources on those brand names which are capable of development internationally, and on merchandising and marketing as its prime activities.

It will not invest in manufacturing per se, and will seek generally to reduce investment in manufacturing except where essential to safeguard or develop a core activity which is fundamental to a brand name (6).

Clearly for Dunhill the key to success is marketing: developing and promoting brands and subtly placing them in the heads of prospective buyers in such a way that they were prepared to pay the proper premium price to have the satisfaction which the product and its associated cachet of distinctive luxury provided.

- *Product strategy*: Confine activities to core business while extending the brand to new products.
- *Geographical strategy*: Global niche markets. Growth through concentric diversification around the core brands.

Clearly for Dunhill: *the industry characteristics don't matter; it's the structural position of the firm that counts.*

CASE STUDY 3 TYRES

Stage 1 Industry characteristics and firm circumstances

This case study concerns a UK firm in a mature and declining industry. The firm was performing extremely poorly, much worse than the industry average (see Table 1.1).

Stage 2 Firm performance

When taken over, despite the fact that there had been no improvement in the industry and the previous management and workforce continued to be employed, this firm became outstandingly successful within three years of takeover (see Table 1.2).

Firm details

The industry is the UK tyre industry and the firm is Dunlop. Dunlop's performance has been outstanding. This represents the transformation of a classic, old-established firm with anarchic traditions that many

Table 1.1   Industry characteristics and firm circumstances prior to takeover

Industry characteristics prior to takeover	Firm circumstances prior to takeover
• Depressed – in decline	• Losses >£20m per year
• Ravaged by low price	• Nine unions: discordant relations
• Ravaged by imports	• History of redundancies
• Huge buyer power	• Terrible quality
• Low or no profits	• Terrible productivity
• Economy in decline	• Low price
	• Losing market share
	• Disastrous internationally
	• Everyone unhappy: managers, operators, shareholders, banks and customers

Table 1.2   Industry characteristics and firm circumstances after takeover

Industry characteristics after takeover	Firm circumstances after takeover
• Worse than before	• In two years breakeven
	• Profitable since
	• Sales on quality not price
	• Wastage in continuous decline
	• Productivity in continuous increase
	• Industrial relations harmonious
	• Union agreement
	• Happiness
	• A model firm in less than three years

believed could not be changed. The transformation was developed when Dunlop was taken over by Sumitomo Rubber Industries (SRI) in 1985 and a new strategy was adopted and implemented. This new strategy was based upon the relentless pursuit of superior quality and superior industrial relations. The essence of the new strategy is probably best appreciated from written comments made by the pre-takeover and post-takeover Managing Director G.D. Radford.

SRI identified communication as being a critical weakness . . .
There had typically been poor communication previously with

Board members rarely speaking even to their senior managers. Factory visits were like royal occasions and about as frequent . . . Management had only communicated bad news in the past, and worse still had relied on the union representative to communicate with the rest of the workforce.

The investment and production efficiency drive were backed up by a policy of improving the working environment . . . the whole working environment was transformed and became a more cheerful place. For the first time we could take visitors round our plants without fearing for their welfare, and without being ashamed of what they might see.

It is evident from our experience that success depends not so much on investment in machines as in people – caring about them, training them and motivating them by helping them to realize their full potential (7).

For Dunlop a key to success was relative product quality improvement achieved by superior human relations and culture. Clearly for Dunlop: *industry characteristics don't matter; it's the structural position of the firm that counts.*

CASE STUDY 4 BANANA INDUSTRY

Stage 1 Industry characteristics and firm circumstances

- *Time period*: 1980-95.
- *Comments on the industry situation*: Prospects are average or below average for a firm based in Ireland. Ireland is incapable of growing bananas so commonsense would indicate that this is a rather poor industry for any Irish company (8).

Stage 2 Firm performance

The firm's performance over this period is shown in Figures 1.4 and 1.5.

Firm details

The firm is Fyffes plc the Irish owned and based major distributor of bananas. Figure 1.4 shows that the firm has had an outstanding performance over this period. In 1995 it was the number four world distributor of bananas (see Figure 1.5). How did it achieve such results? It did so by responding to the messages from the markets, by tailoring its strategic market planning to its markets.

- *Core strategy*: very high growth to be achieved mainly by acquisition with a view to becoming a key player in the European fresh produce market with particular emphasis on bananas. This emphasis to be reflected in controlling the sourcing, shipping and distribution.
- *Product strategy*: concentrate on the core business of fruit distribution with particular reference to bananas.
- *Geographical strategy*: become a key player in Europe.

Thus, it can be seen once again that irrespective of the industry conditions – Ireland's inability to grow bananas is legendary and its small

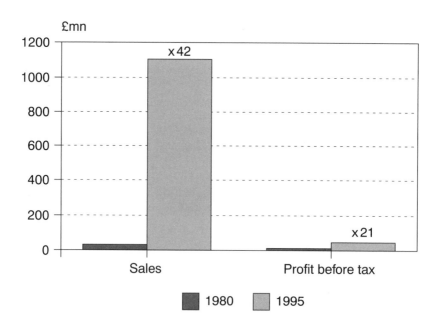

Figure 1.4   Fyffes Group plc performance, 1980–95

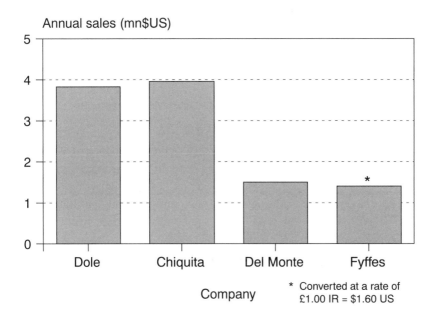

Annual sales (mn$US)

* Converted at a rate of
£1.00 IR = $1.60 US

Figure 1.5   Fyffes' position as a world heavyweight banana player, 1994

domestic market is evident – the firm has won against the odds and demonstrates the assertion that: *the industry characteristics don't matter; it's the structural position of the firm that counts.*

WHY IS THE MARKET THE MESSAGE?

The market is the message because firms will not succeed unless they tailor their activities to be responsive to (and indeed on occasions to lead) the wants and needs of their existing and new customers. Reflect again upon each of the case studies which are repeated again in Table 1.3.

Table 1.3 clearly shows that success is not dependent upon industry, product, country or stage in the economic cycle. Rather it is dependent upon the firm or more correctly the strategies of the firm. Each of these successful firms has, in a different fashion and in different circumstances, used their marketing antennae to take weak signals from the markets, amplify them and then translate them into strategic market plans which ultimately led to superior performance.

Table 1.3 Success is not dependent upon the industry

Industry	Nature of product	Company
Brewing and distilling	Fast-moving consumer goods	Guinness plc
Luxury consumer goods	Luxury consumer goods	Dunhill plc
Tyres	Industrial goods	Dunlop plc
Fresh produce distribution	Food distribution	Fyffes plc

CONCLUSION

This chapter and Figure 1.6 illustrate the subject of this book: it is about managers growing their careers through developing strategic market plans which reflect the sentiment that the market is the message.

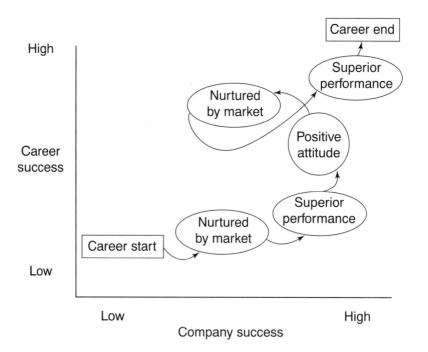

Figure 1.6   Success fosters even greater success

NOTES

1. It should be noted that in each case study there will be the following variations in the figures used:

    *   Time period: this will vary from company to company and industry to industry and has been determined by the availability of data.
    *   More than one annual industry growth rate: these reflect volume growth rates and value growth rates.
    *   The type of data has been selected to reflect the strategy adopted by each firm.

    The cases are set a number of years ago in order to illustrate sustained strategic success (i.e. over many years) following a previous period of severe difficulties.

REFERENCES

(1) How to think about the shape of your business (1992). *PIMS Letter on Business Strategy*, 47. PIMS Europe Ltd.
(2) Rumelt, R. (1991). How much does industry matter?. *Strategic Management Journal*, 12, March.
(3) Extel Financial Ltd.
(4) Keynote reports.
(5) Annual company reports.
(6) White, J. (1987). *Dunhill Holdings Plc, Case study.* Case Clearing House of Great Britain and Ireland, Cranfield Institute of Technology.
(7) Radford, G. D. (1992).How Sumitomo transformed Dunlop Tyres. In Toyohiro Kono (ed.), *Strategic Management in Japanese Companies, The Best of Long Range Planning*, pp. 167–171. Pergamon Press, Oxford.
(8) Annual company reports.

2

The Concept of Strategy

This book is concerned with strategic market planning, not just market planning. The word strategic is crucial to the content of this book and this chapter will examine the characteristics of strategic management which distinguish it quite clearly from other types of management.

WHY DO PROFIT LEVELS VARY?

National performance levels

Table 2.1 shows changes in gross domestic product (GDP) for seven nations.

Table 2.1 Changes in GDP for seven nations

Country	GDP 1985 (US$bn)	GDP 1996 (US$bn)	Change %
Mexico	241.8	294.9	4.0
USA	4,738.2	6,296.8	2.4
Japan	2,368.9	3,282.9	3.6
Germany	1,420.8	1,807.5	1.1
Ireland	36.2	64.5	7.0
Switzerland	197.0	225.3	-0.3
UK	828.2	1,058.6	2.4

Source: (1)

As can be seen there is great variation both in the value of the GDP and the growth rates and these variations pose the question: Why should such variation occur? One answer is that it is due to luck or just fortunate circumstances. If this is the case, then those people who work in more commercially unfortunate countries appear to be condemned forever to more meagre prospects than those who work in commercially favoured countries. A cardinal theme of this book, however, is that this supine view of economic prospects is erroneous and that it is the strategies pursued by countries and their constituent firms that determine economic performance. For example, Ireland will in the future see its GDP continue to rise relative to the other nations in Table 2.1 because of the strategic views and practices which prevail in business and government circles in that country.

Profit levels in different industries

Table 2.2 shows the average levels of pre-tax profits in four UK industries over the period 1989 to 1994–5.

Table 2.2 Average levels of profitability in four UK industries

Industry	1989–90	1992–3	1994–5
Pharmaceutical manufacturers	22.5	23.3	16.0
Brewers	13.1	14.9	11.0
Commercial vehicle manufacturers	5.0	-4.1	N/A
Leather manufacturers and processors	1.5	-2.6	1.0

Sources: (2,3,4,5,6)

As can be seen there is considerable variation in the average levels of profitability in each industry. Why should such variations occur?

Once again, a possible answer is that it is due to luck or fortunate circumstances and once again this view is rejected. Although industries differ in the competitive pressures they face, nonetheless, it is the strategies pursued by the constituent firms in an industry that affect the industry's overall level of profitability and the profitability of individual firms.

For example, in the UK, consistently, year after year, the pharmaceutical manufacturing and developing industry achieves higher returns than the brewing industry,[1] as illustrated in Table 2.3.

Table 2.3 Profit levels in UK pharmaceutical manufacturing and developing industry and brewing industry in the UK, 1992–3 to 1994–5

	1994–5	1993–4	1992–3
Pharmaceutical manufacturers and developers			
Sales (£k)	208,745	190,607	160,642
Pre-tax profit (£k)	34,088	37,368	31,983
Capital employed (£k)	130,516	125,051	96,695
Number of employees (000)	1,651	1,567	1,531
Sales per employee (£k)	126.4	121.6	104.9
Pre-tax profit per employee (£k)	20.6	23.8	20.8
Brewers			
Sales (£k)	187,758	179.019	171,515
Pre-tax profit (£k)	21,134	20,128	15,755
Capital employed (£k)	219,793	215,840	199,536
Number of employees (000)	4,196	4,041	3,909
Sales per employee (£k)	44.7	44.3	43.8
Pre-tax profit per employee (£k)	5.0	5.0	4.0

Sources: (3,4)

Profit levels in different firms in the same industry

Table 2.4 shows the profit margins for the top five UK pharmaceutical firms (by turnover) for the period 1992–3 to 1994–5 plus the firm with the highest profit margin.

This variation in profit levels is even more intriguing when the pharmaceutical industry is ranked in terms of profits rather than sales, as shown in Table 2.5. This table shows the profit margins for the top five UK pharmaceutical firms (by profit margin) for the period 1992–3 to 1994–5.

As can be seen there is great variation in the profit levels within the industry and profit margin does not seem to be related to sales volume. Why should such variation occur? Once again, the answer that it is due to luck or fortunate circumstances is rejected. The strategies pursued by the firms determine their profitability.

The economist versus strategist

These illustrations of profit variation at national, industry and firm level reflect the philosophical orientation of this book: namely that a firm's profit destiny is not pre-ordained by outside forces, but rather it is determined by the vision, strategic skills and drive of its managers, especially its senior managers. The senior managers determine the firm's commercial destiny. This conviction reflects a strategist's view of the firm rather than that of the economist.

Table 2.4 Levels of profitability for top five UK pharmaceutical firms (by turnover) for the period 1992–3 to 1994–5 plus firm with highest profit margin

		Profit margin (%)		
Firm	Sales rank	1989–90	1990–1	1991–2
SmithKline Beecham plc	1	10.6	19.8	20.9
Glaxo Wellcome plc	2	32.4	4.0	34.8
Zeneca Group plc	3	14.7	14.2	2.61
Fisons plc	4	-36.0	-0.1	9.6
AAH Pharmaceuticals	5	1.8	1.5	2.0
McCarthy's Laboratories	72	75.9	33.6	11.7

Source: (3)

Table 2.5 Top five UK pharmaceutical manufacturing firms (by profit margin) for period 1992–3 to 1994–5

		Profit margin (%)		
Firm	Sales average (£mn) 1994–95	1994–5	1993–4	1992–3
Mc Carthy's Laboratories	10.2	75.9	33.6	11.7
Pfizer	206.8	36.0	24.4	77
CV Laboratories	8.9	35.3	33.9	22.8
Synpac Pharmaceuticals	36.9	32.5	34.4	26.2
Glaxo Wellcome plc	5,656.0	32.4	34.0	34.8

Source: (3)

THE ECONOMIST'S VIEW

One of the starting points of the subject of strategic market planning lies in the discipline of industrial economics.[2] This discipline has as a central tenet the relationship between a firm's Structure, Conduct and Performance (S–C–P). This tenet, as illustrated in Figure 2.1, holds that all industries have particular given structures which cause their constituent firms to engage in certain types of conduct (i.e. strategies), ultimately leading to particular levels of individual firm performance (i.e. levels of profitability).

Driving this model is the underlying economist's view that competition should be fair, should be free and, assuming that there are sufficient safeguards to ensure that such fair and free competition takes place, then the industry as whole will tend towards equilibrium – the economist's ideal.

In addition, this view also assumes that the firm's strategies and

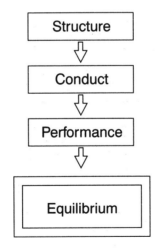

Figure 2.1 The economist's view of conduct, structure and performance leading to equilibrium

performance are very largely determined by the industry structure, which cannot be changed through the strategies of an individual firm. Thus, the firm is regarded as a culture-free, inanimate unit which can only influence its commercial future through price changes, with its fate largely determined by industry structure.

THE STRATEGIST'S VIEW

In contrast to the economist's view, the strategist's central tenet could be described as Conduct, Structure and Performance (C–S–P). This view maintains, as illustrated in Figure 2.2, that firms can engage in particular types of conduct (i.e. strategies) to influence the structure of their industry and the performance (i.e. levels of profits) of their firm.

Furthermore, driving the strategy model is the underlying assumption that, far from seeking equilibrium, the firm is striving for competitive advantage over rivals which will be reflected in superior

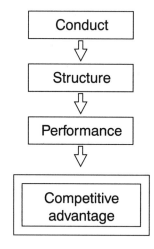

Figure 2.2   The strategist's view of conduct, structure and performance
leading to competitive advantage

profits. Thus the goal of the strategic market planner could be described as building sustainable superior profit performance. In addition, this view also assumes that the firm's strategies can influence or rather change the structure of the industry. This view, which is central to this book, accords the firm, that is, the managers, a much more active role in determining its commercial future and destiny. Thus, each firm is regarded as a unique and active unit in which managers impose their own particular mission, goals, culture, value systems, structures and strategies, all of which collectively determine the future of the firm (strategies, scope of activities, growth rates, profits) and also influence the structure of the industry.

ORGANIZATIONAL DECISIONS

Although all firms are unique and unique managers make unique decisions in response to the unique circumstances in which they operate, it is possible to look at the decisions which are made in all firms in a generic manner.[3] Table 2.6 shows the types of decisions that tend to be made in most large divisionalized firms.[4]

As can be seen, most decisions can be categorized for most firms.

Table 2.6 also illustrates the main levels of focus of this book. It concentrates on strategic decisions at the divisional or strategic business unit (SBU)[5] level with a limited emphasis at the operational or functional levels. Thus the book is concerned with the strategic market planning of a given division within a larger divisionalized corporation.

Characteristics of strategic decisions

In addition to classifying the decisions of organizations according to type and level, it is also possible to characterize the nature of decisions according to whether they are strategic, administrative or operational. This is illustrated in Table 2.7.

Thus strategic decisions are very different in nature from operational ones. The following examples illustrate the distinctive nature of strategic decision-making.

Table 2.6 Generic decisions taken in most firms

Level	Typical issues	Main stakeholder	Scope	Time span	Risk
Corporate Corporate strategy decisions	Overall corporate direction Growth rate Financial returns Market positions Risk Portfolio balance of business Internal and environmental appraisal	Shareholders Directors Banks Top management Employees Buyers Suppliers Society Government	Company wide	Long run: many years	Very high
Divisional/SBU Strategic decisions	Overall divisional direction Growth rate Financial returns Market positions Risk portfolio of products Marketing, financial, production and personnel strategies Internal and environmental appraisal	Directors Top management Employees Buyers Suppliers Society Government Banks	Division wide	Many years	High
Operations/product market Operational/funct-ional decisions	Overall departmental direction Growth rate Financial returns by product Market positions Marketing, financial, production and personnel budgets Market segment appraisal Competitor appraisal	Top management Employees Buyers Suppliers Local community	Department wide	Less than one year	Relatively low

Table 2.7 Characteristics of strategic, administrative and operational decisions

Strategic	Administrative	Operational
Company wide		Department wide
Highest level in firm		Low level in firm
Long run, perhaps many years		Short time scale, perhaps days
Largely irreversible		Easily reversible
Visionary	Somewhere in between	Vision not needed
Infrequent		Frequent
Unique		Repetitive, therefore programmable
Risky		Low risk

Department or company wide

Strategic decisions tend to affect the whole company or firm because they are fundamental to the nature of its existence and operations. For example, the decision of the Japanese steel producer, Sumitomo Metal Industries, in the early 1990s to diversify into electronics and herbal medicines clearly affected the entire company: it was a strategic decision.

Highest level

Strategic decisions tend to be taken at the highest level, by the most senior managers. Indeed, if senior managers do not take strategic decisions they will be taken by someone else, perhaps lower in the firm, or by senior managers in a rival firm which is being managed more successfully. For example, the decision of Ford motor company in 1993–4 to restructure its operations on a truly global scale was taken at the highest level: it was a strategic decision.

Long run

Strategic decisions tend to be long run. Just how long this is depends upon the industry. For example, the time horizon for strategic decisions in the fashion or popular music industries tends to be relatively short run, perhaps one year or more, whereas strategic decisions in extractive industries such as oil may span decades. Thus, the decision of the major oil companies to exploit the North Sea for oil was made in the 1960s and the effects are still apparent more than 30 years later: it was a strategic decision.

Irreversible

Strategic decisions tend to be very difficult if not impossible to reverse. They often involve the commitment of dedicated fixed assets[6] and it may be impossible to employ these assets in any other way. For example, the decision of the UK store group Marks and Spencer in the 1980s to build large numbers of out-of-town shopping centres would have been difficult to reverse: it was a strategic decision.

Visionary

Although not an absolute requirement, it is often the case that really significant strategic decisions are the result of some visionary perspective being on a quite pedestrian topic. For example, the decision of Dunhill to redefine its business in terms of luxury consumer goods for men rather than pipes and tobacco was visionary: it was a strategic decision.

Infrequent

Strategic decisions, because of the magnitude of change which they engender, tend to happen infrequently. For example, the decision by the German car maker Daimler-Benz in the 1990s to change its method of design and manufacture from cost plus to target pricing was one of a number of infrequent decisions: it was a strategic decision.[7]

Unique

Although this is not always the case – for example, a strategic decision could be to continue operations over the next five years in the same way as they were conducted over the last five years – when strategic decisions lead to real and enduring superiority and involve a break with the past they tend to be unique. For example, in the 1990s many UK building societies changed status from mutual societies into banks. These were new and unique decisions for the management of those societies: they were strategic decisions.

Risky

Strategic decisions tend to be risky for two reasons. First, they are difficult to reverse; second, they involve the commitment of substantial resources. For example, the decision of the Boeing aircraft company to manufacture its first jumbo jet was a most risky decision: such a commercial aircraft had not been built before and the market was far from proven: it was a strategic decision.

Summary

When managers are trying to categorize decisions into whether or not they are strategic it can be useful for them to ask whether the decision has most of the following characteristics:

- company wide;
- highest level;
- long run;
- irreversible;
- visionary;
- infrequent;
- unique;
- risky.

If the decision has a high component of these elements then it is likely to be strategic.

A MODEL FOR STRATEGIC MARKET PLANNING

Strategic market planning can be defined as the process by which the firm achieves a sustainable good fit with its marketing and broader environment. Each word in this definition is important and each is discussed below.

- *Strategic market planning.* The planning is concerned not with day-to-day issues but with marketing issues which are: company wide, high level, long run, irreversible, visionary, infrequent,

unique and risky.
- *Process.* It is an iterative process which takes time to develop, amend and finally complete. It is not a mechanical task such as ensuring that a budget balances: in developing a strategic market plan the final result, after revisits etc., may be substantially different from the initial plan.
- *Firm.* In this book the organization under consideration will be a firm or a division within a large private sector company.
- *Achieves a sustainable good fit.* It is the firm that ought to react to its environment and not try to change its environment.[8] A sustainable good fit means that the firm adapts its shape, i.e. its strategies, structure and operations so that it achieves superior returns, not just in a transitory fashion, but for many years.
- *Marketing and broader environment.* It is generally insufficient, at a strategic level to respond to the marketing environment alone. All firms, irrespective of the markets they are addressing, are buffeted by other and perhaps stronger environmental forces. Any strategic market plan must take cognisance of these forces.

Finally, this process of strategic market planning can be made more explicit through the use of a diagrammatic model of strategic market planning as shown in Figure 2.3.

True strategic victories

A true strategic victory occurs when a firm implements its strategic market plan and then enjoys returns which are superior to other competitors for many years, i.e. it achieves a sustainable good fit with its marketing and broader environment.

Dramatic true strategic victories abound and are well publicized: for example, Matsushita's introduction of the video cassette recorder or Sony's development of the Walkman. What are less well publicized are the more important and more frequent non-dramatic true strategic victories. These are more important because, in reality, for most firms, dramatic victories based upon a revolutionary invention such as the VCR or the Walkman will never occur. Most firms tend to lead a much more pedestrian existence and yet, over time, there will arise individual firms which in subtle and undramatic ways will enjoy true strategic victories. Generally such true strategic victories will involve the following characteristics.

A MODEL FOR
STRATEGIC MANAGEMENT

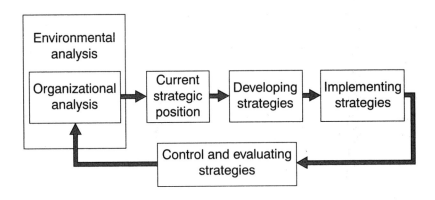

Figure 2.3 A model of the strategic market planning process

New ways of doing business in familiar markets with familiar products

Most real victories do not come from dramatic inventions. These tend to be the exception. Yet there are many examples of firms which have had great strategic success undramatically, for example, the introduction of telephone banking in the UK by First Direct. This is a clear demonstration of success being predicated upon a new way of doing business in familiar markets with familiar products. There is a key lesson here for managers in all industries.

Managers of firms who wish to enjoy robust[9] superior returns must continuously and creatively reflect on how they define their business in terms of meeting the needs (often unexpressed) of their customers and developing products and their associated services which more than fulfil these needs (to build customer loyalty and the permit premium pricing) and position their firm's products and services in the heads of their customers as providing unrivalled value for money.[10]

Superior performance with inferior resources

Managers often look somewhat enviously at other major high profile, high performance firms and observe that, unlike their own firm, the majors have been endowed with such glittering resources that their own rather poorly endowed firm will never be able to compete successfully. They feel that the competitive game is rigged in favour of the majors. This is not true. Indeed, if it were true it would mean that the major corporations of today are set in their superior positions like stars in the firmament. They will never change from being the leaders and all the existing hierarchies in all industries are impervious to change. Casual observation shows this to be untrue. For example, in the computer industry the recent relative fortunes of IBM and Compaq demonstrate this. Examples of leaders being overtaken can be found in almost all industries.

The firm's strength against competitors' weaknesses

Having made the observation that small firms can indeed wrest victory from majors it is important to recognize that this is rarely if ever achieved by a head-on competitive confrontation. Rather it will normally be achieved through the use of a unique strength of the smaller firm being employed against a weakness of the major. For example, executive car manufacturer BMW's successful assault on the giant Mercedes-Benz was based upon providing a unique product – an expensive, relatively small, very high performance executive saloon car for the executive car market segment – with which Mercedes-Benz could not compete

CONCLUSION

This chapter developed a concept of strategy and showed that it is possible to distinguish three types of decisions – strategic, administrative and operational – which are taken in all firms. The distinctiveness of strategic decisions was examined and a model of strategic market planning was developed. Finally some key determinants of true strategic victories were examined.

NOTES

1. Why this should be is discussed in detail in Chapters B3 and B4.
2. For a comprehensive exposition on industrial economics and associated economic subjects see: Branson, W.H. (1989). *Macroeconomic Theory and Practice*, 3rd edn. Harper and Row, London.
3. This generic view of firms is a recurring theme of this book. It implies that when considering strategic recipes for the commercial development of a firm one does not need detailed knowledge of the industry, i.e. there are generic rules for success in all industries.
4. This type of firm is considered because it is the one with which most readers are likely to be most familiar. Readers who work for other structures – say public sector or small business – may amend this section so that it reflects their particular organization.
5. SBU means strategic business unit, see page 110 for further details.
6. Although it is easier to think of irreversibility when applied to major fixed assets, there are many other types of strategic decisions which do not involve physical assets. For example, deciding upon the computer operating system is increasingly a strategic one and is often difficult to reverse, not for hardware reasons but because of the retraining that would be necessary to adopt a new system.
7. This is in contrast to frequent decisions such as changing the daily/weekly/monthly/annual production schedules which are taken continuously in most manufacturing firms.
8. This may not always be true. Some firms have been able to change their environments.
9. By 'robust' is meant that they will endure for many years, i.e. the superior returns are strong.
10. A product or service which is value for money usually has the characteristic that although it has a premium price, its attributes are such that the customer is happy to pay the extra cost. Such products often have remarkable customer loyalty. Examples of consumer goods in this category include Coca-Cola and Waterford Crystal.

REFERENCES

(1) Organization for Economic Cooperation and Development (1997). *Main Economic Indicators*. OECD, Paris.
(2) ICC (1993). *UK Industrial Performance Analysis*. ICC, Hampton.
(3) ICC (1966). *Pharmaceutical Manufacturers and Developers, Business Ratios Plus*, 24th edn. ICC, Hampton.
(4) ICC (1996). *The Brewing Industry, Business Ratios Plus*, 23rd edn. ICC, Hampton.
(5) ICC (1994). *Commercial Vehicle Manufacturers, Business Ratios Plus*, 16th edn. ICC, Hampton.
(6) ICC (1994). *Leather Manufacturers and Processors, Business Ratios Plus*, 21st edn. ICC, Hampton.

3

Communicating the Strategic Market Plan

A written strategic market plan is inert. Generally it is not an influential object. For it to become effective it must become influential; it must influence other managers, often more senior managers, who may not have been involved in its development. This influence is most effective when it is exercised by the managers who have developed the plan. Consequently developing and writing a strategic market plan is not sufficient, it must also be communicated. The authors of the strategic market plan must communicate the blueprint for success by breathing life into it.

COMMUNICATION: TRANSMITTING THE MESSAGE

Of all the skills required by senior managers, perhaps the most important is that of communication, or more precisely verbal communication. How often do we hear managers express sentiments such as:

> 'A more successful rival doesn't know more than me. In fact he knows less. He just has the gift of eloquence.'

> 'My proposal hasn't been accepted, not because it wasn't good, but a rival proposal was more slickly presented.'

> 'He [a rival] has the chairman in his pocket.'

Most managers have spoken, often ruefully, in this manner. What these sentiments express is the often held view that it is not the quality of a proposal or a plan that determines its acceptability but the powers of persuasiveness of the manager making the proposal. It is difficult to overstate how important verbal communication is. It is essential. Indeed, research of the characteristics of outstandingly successful managers repeatedly shows this to be the case.

The researches of Pfeffer (1) (others) have concluded that there are four main characteristics that determine the power, i.e. the degree of influence of managers:

1. *Verbal skills and articulateness.* Generally the most influential managers tend to be most skilful in this area.
2. *Diagnostic skills.* Managers who are able quickly and accurately to diagnose problems and power relationships in organizations tend to be most influential.
3. *Understanding the rules of the organization.* Managers who understand and follow the rules of the organization tend to be most influential.
4. *Personal belief in oneself.* The more confidence one has, the more influential one is likely to be.

This chapter reflects the importance of communication. It aims to help managers, who often have had no formal training in communication, to develop these skills through the medium of their strategic market plans.

PRESENTATION OF THE STRATEGIC MARKET PLAN

It is assumed that the plan will be presented by a manager who has relatively little experience of such an exercise. Accordingly, the following suggestions convey a number of basic rules which seem to apply to all presentations.

Elements in a presentation

There are five principal elements in any presentation:

- the presenter (henceforth known as you);
- the structure of the presentation;
- the material (henceforth known as the strategic market plan);
- the audience (henceforth known as your colleagues);

- the venue and layout.

How each of these elements can be combined into a persuasive entity is now set out.

The presenter

The primary condition necessary for an effective presentation is belief in yourself and the consequent confidence that such belief confers. If you do not believe in yourself and your ability no one else will believe in you and certainly no one will believe in your strategic market plan. Self-esteem and confidence are fundamental. For success you must have this attitude or you must develop it.

Flowing from confidence in yourself is belief in your strategic market plan. Such overt and confident belief tends to be infectious and can compel your colleagues to support your plan. You must portray yourself, and your team, as being totally committed to it. Such commitment is reflected during a presentation by the following:

- unstoppable enthusiasm reflected in your voice and your body language;
- interesting dialogue with your colleagues during your presentation which will tend to make them active participants whom you can lead to supporting your plan;
- very high quality acetates or 35mm slides to support your verbal enthusiasm;
- very high quality documentation of the strategic market plan.

To achieve this effect you must develop your skills of presentation. These skills are now considered.

Skills of presentation

There are no absolute guidelines for the complete range of skills of the effective presenter, nor can these skills be learnt from a book. However, there is a number of skills that are the most common to be observed in effective presenters.

Sense of presence

Sense of presence is difficult to define, but managers are certainly aware of it. Most managers know of people who, when they address an audience, have them 'in the palm of their hand'. Once again, there are no rules for developing a sense of presence but there seem to be a number of essentials which include the following.

Knowledge

You must be knowledgeable about your plan. You must convey to your colleagues the impression that you and your team have made a very serious effort to develop it and you are completely familiar with every aspect. If you are not knowledgeable, a precise and pointed question will quickly deflate your ego and demolish your presentation.

Eye contact

You must look directly into the eyes of your audience. At small group presentations you must lock your eyes sequentially on to the eyes of each person in the room and send your message directly. No one should escape the intensity of your eyeballing. In larger group presentations this is not possible, but you should still be able to have direct eye contact with a number of your colleagues. Remember that to address the screen on which your messages are displayed rather than looking and fixing your colleagues' eyes with yours is to inhibit communication. If your colleagues are not looking at you, you have probably lost their attention.

Reading versus presenting

There is a world of difference between reading a strategic market plan and presenting it. Anyone can read such a plan. They do not have to have been involved in its development. Reading a plan is simply giving the audience the words. In presentation you should face your audience without notes, using the information on the screen as an aide memoir, and capture their attention with your voice, eyes, body language and above all your sincerity.

Body language

Your words are only part of your language. Your body also speaks to the audience. Therefore, it is important that your posture, how you use your hands, how you react to questions and where you sit all contribute to the presentation. Generally, presenting from behind a table, with notes on the table and the screen some distance away, will tend to convey a sense of defensiveness and a lack of sincerity. Get out and face your audience.

Sincerity

Sincerity and demonstrable belief in your plan are key ingredients in a successful presentation. If you do not have this sincerity you will not convince your colleagues. In passing, it should be noted that for most audiences even an inferior presentation will be redeemed if the presenter exudes sincerity.

Verbals

Voice variety

Try to have some voice variety when addressing your colleagues. This variety can be manifested in:

- voice volume, louder perhaps to emphasize a point and softer to draw a logical conclusion;
- speed of delivery, quicker to convey excitement and enthusiasm and slower for reflection.

Sentence variety

Try to have a variety of types of sentences in your presentation. For example, although the bulk will be concerned with the transmission of essential facts through standard factual sentences, you can nonetheless provide variety through questioning your audience. Remember that questions may or may not demand an answer. For example, the question:

'What was our unit's net operating income last year?'

demands an answer. Whereas the questions:

> 'I wonder how many of us can predict the scale of our unit's business over the next three years?'

> 'When we reflect upon our past performance should we be satisfied?'

do not necessarily demand answers. You can pose such rhetorical questions without expecting an answer from your audience. The answers to each of these questions provided by you could be:

> 'I wonder who could predict it? I wonder how many of us could have predicted the last three years? Or even the last two years? I couldn't predict the next three years. I am just going to try and develop a sense of whether they will be better than this year or worse.'

> 'Undoubtedly some people will be satisfied and some people will not. We who were promoted and received bonuses may, at that level be satisfied. However our board and also our shareholders may be less satisfied. So I would submit that the answer is some satisfaction, but not enough.'

Dialogue development

Most people, and certainly a majority of managers, prefer to speak rather than to listen. So you ought to give your audience opportunities to voice opinions during your presentation. Not only will this add variety and interest, but it will also give the audience a sense of co-ownership of your plan. It will build support.

Ask questions and simultaneously give signposts to the desired answers. Remember that you should structure your questions so that no one responding will ever give an unsatisfactory or a wrong answer. All questions ought to induce correct answers which reinforce your message and give the respondent a feeling of success. How this approach can be used is illustrated now. Consider how the information in Figure 3.1 could be communicated.

Projected growth rates
in 5 markets

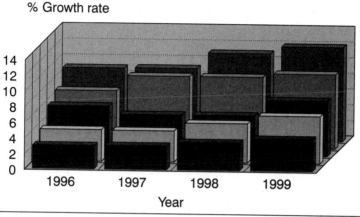

Figure 3.1 Typical slide of a typical presentation

This slide could be communicated as follows:

'Our projected sales in Germany are highest, the United States are next, followed by France, followed by Scandinavia and finally followed by the United Kingdom.'

This certainly transmits the message but it is dull; it is unlikely to intrigue and it certainly does not involve the audience.

An alternative and more active way of simultaneously transmitting the same message and involving the audience could be the following chain of linked questions:

'With our limited funds in which markets should we make our greatest efforts?'
'Why?'
'Is this certain?'
'What are the particular problems associated with each of these markets?'
'In what circumstances might a lower growth market be superior to a high growth one?'

After each question there should be a response from your colleagues. These responses foster dialogue and help to make them active participants in the presentation and give them a sense of ownership. The responses may also, as a bonus, give you valuable additional information. A chain of such questions is invaluable in building your position.

Visuals

Normally the quality of the visual material will have a major effect upon a presentation. Good visual displays will reinforce your messages and ensure that the audience is aware of the core themes of your plan. Today managers have a choice of three media: acetates, 35mm slides and personal computer (PC) displays. There are no absolute rules on which medium should be used, but personal preference will often play a part. Table 3.1 indicates some of the advantages and disadvantages of each medium.

THE STRUCTURE OF THE PRESENTATION

There is no single correct structure for a presentation. However, the author has found the following methods to be effective in a variety of companies.

1 *Start: conclusions.* Start with the conclusions. Briefly describe the kernel of the strategic market plan to your colleagues. Then proceed to how you and your team developed this plan.

2 *Middle: detail.* Present the detail of the strategic market plan using the skeleton structure provided in Part II and reproduced below. There will normally be one or more acetates for each section.

Section A: Background to division's strategic plan

A1 Introduction and background
A2 Executive summary

Section B: Current strategic position

B1 Defining the business
B2 Current product market portfolio
B3 Environment analysis: external prospects

Table 3.1 A comparison between acetates and 35mm slides and PC displays

Issue	Acetates	35 mm slides	PC displays
Audience size	Best for a smaller audience, say less than 50 people.	Good for all sizes of audience and best for largest audiences.	Good for all sizes of audience and best for largest audiences.
Flexibility	Flexible, can be changed before and during the presentation. Running order of acetates may be changed. First acetates may be revisited easily.	Inflexible. Prepared well in advance and cannot be amended. Also difficult to change the running order once started.	Some flexibility – can revisit slides and change the running order.
Dynamic qualities	Dynamic, can be written on and changed.	Static, cannot be amended.	Some flexibility – can have movement and also can write on slides.
Quality of image	Less dramatic.	Highest quality.	Highest quality.
Amount of information	Higher.	Lower.	Lower.
Colour	Perhaps, but usually black and white.	Yes.	Yes.
Development	Development in company or by a professional agency	Developed by a professional agency.	Developed in the company or by a professional agency.

B4 Analysing the firm: internal appraisal
B5 Key issues for the strategic plan

Section C: Strategic plan for next three years

C1 Missions, goals and targets
C2 Gap analysis
C3 Future strategies

Section D: Tactics, implementation and resources

D1 Tactics and implementation
D2 Resources

3. *End: conclusions.* This will be a repeat of, or at least be very similar to, the start.

4. *Duration.* There is no optimal duration for a presentation. However, few presentations should last more than thirty minutes with twenty minutes, being a more realistic target time. Generally, the shorter the presentation, the better. Remember that your colleagues, just like yourself, have a limited attention span.

MATERIAL

The material for the presentation is developed during the strategic market plan workshop (typical example is shown in Chapter 5). Remember, however, that most audiences cannot absorb a large number of facts and figures. In your presentation you should have one or two key themes to which you keep returning to ensure that your colleagues are in absolutely no doubt about the few major issues on which you wish them to concentrate.

As an illustration of the effectiveness of keeping your audience keenly aware of just a small number of key issues, consider how the process of continuous reinforcement benefits the most successful communicators of all: successful preachers. They tend to have a single and universal theme, the prospect of going to hell. In their presentations this spectre is raised at the start, detailed in the middle and confirmed at the end. The effectiveness of these preachers can be measured in terms of congregation size.

Written material

The quality of your written material should match the quality of your presentation. Generally, apart from being a record of your plan, the written material should provide detail which would be difficult to present, for example, the detailed projected cash flows from individual product lines. It is relatively easy for the audience to read and analyse these figures if provided in the written plan.

Written plans will probably be read without you being present so they must have compelling clarity. This is achieved by using simple non-jargon language to which the readers can instantly relate. Chapter 5 provides an example of a strategic market plan which attempts to do this.

Audience

Irrespective of your colleagues' predisposition, by the end of your presentation they will either support or reject your strategic market plan. They cannot be neutral. If after your presentation the prevailing view is one of neutrality, then this is actually rejection; it is failure to give active support. An important question therefore arises: what is likely to kindle such support?

Conventional textbook wisdom would assert that the sheer logic and rationality of your presentation ought to be the key. This, however, is not sufficient. It may engender support or it may not. What is needed, in addition to the logic of following your strategic plan, is the development of such rapport with your colleagues that they become predisposed to support you, even if your ideas are contrary to previously held beliefs.

Venue and room layout

The most appropriate location for the presentation of a strategic market plan will probably be in an hotel. This will not only help to minimize interruptions, but also alter the normal room – power relationships that prevail in most firms. The hotel will be seen as a relatively neutral venue.

Room layouts depend upon the size of the audience. For larger audiences, say of fifty people and above, there is probably little that can be done to further communication. Generally, the layout will be as shown in Figure 3.2. However, with smaller groups the layout shown in Figure 3.3 is advocated. This arrangement has the advantage of promoting closeness between presenter and audience.

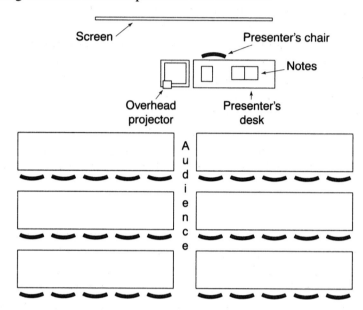

Figure 3.2   Typical room layout for a large group presentation

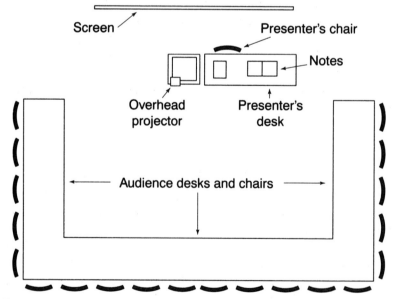

Figure 3.3   Typical room layout for a small group presentation

THE RESULTS OF THE PRESENTATION

Both company and personal results should arise from a successful presentation:

1. *Company results*

   • After debate, a robust strategic market plan which will guide the company over the next planning horizon.
   • A vehicle for further development.
   • A means of communicating with the various levels of management.
   • The development of a companywide approach to thinking strategically.

2. *Personal results*

   • A feeling of achievement after the event.
   • The acquisition of an additional and valuable managerial skill.
   • Progression or promotion either within the company or elsewhere.

NOTE

1. The rules of an organization may not of course be the official rules. Most organizations have official rules, which are often written, and unofficial rules, which are generally unwritten but are the actual practice. For example, it may be an official rule that 'the chairman's door is always open'. However, the practice may be that entering this open door will normally incur the wrath of the chairman. In such a situation it is the unofficial rule that prevails.

REFERENCE

(1) Pfeffer, J. (1981). *Power in Organization*. Pitman, London.

4

Skeleton Strategic
Market Plan

The key to ensuring that the winning against the odds lessons of Chapter 1 become infused into any firm is the development and implementation of an effective strategic market plan: 'making the market the message.'

There is no such thing as a standard strategic market plan which all firms can employ. Rather, effective strategic market plans can vary from the informal unwritten aspirations of an owner–manager to the weighty planning volumes of a large multinational corporation. Neither approach is superior. Each is addressing a different set of challenges. The appropriateness of a particular approach can only be judged by the long-run results that it achieves.

In practice it is often the case that when managers are required to develop and write a strategic market plan they feel the need for guidance. Questions they often ask include:

- Just what is a strategic market plan?
- In what way is it different from a normal planning exercise?
- What is its structure?
- What are the topics?
- How do I start?

With this need for guidance in mind, we now set out is an approach which has been used successfully with many managers who had little formal knowledge of strategic planning and were writing their first strategic plan.

The approach sets out a generic structure – the skeleton strategic market plan – which should enable managers to write a plan. The skeleton strategic plan is the 'bones' on which managers should be able to flesh out their plan so that it takes on the identity of the firm, irrespective of the industry, structure and size, to become an effective planning instrument. The skeleton consists of the major headings that ought to appear in a strategic market plan. Each heading makes reference to the relevant chapter or chapters in this book.

Before examining the skeleton strategic plan there are a number of core assumptions that must be made.

CORE ASSUMPTIONS

Firm structure

It is assumed that the strategic market plan is being developed for a discrete business unit within an firm which is subdivided into a number of such units. Figure 4.1 shows the type of structure for which this type of plan would be developed. In this case there are three distinct business units, XXX, YYY, and ZZZ. Corporate headquarters or group is known as XXXYYYZZZ. It gives broad general direction and monitors the activities of each business unit but does not become involved in the day-to-day decisions of a business unit. These decisions are the domain of the general manager of each business unit. In the skeleton strategic market plan given below, strategic market decisions are assumed to take place at the business unit level. Finally, although the only business unit that will be considered is XXX, similar plans can be developed for YYY and ZZZ.

Personnel involved

It is assumed that the plan is being developed by a senior management team which would normally comprise general manager of the business unit, other key managers and representatives from group.

Time horizon

This will vary from industry to industry, with industries with the longest lead times having the longest time horizons. In the case of the skeleton plan the time horizon is three years.

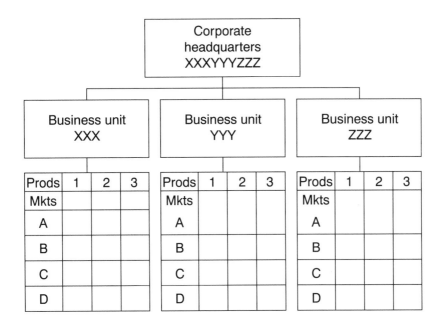

Figure 4.1   The structure in which the strategic market plan is assumed to be developed

Presentation of the strategic market plan

The plan will be presented, initially, to staff from business unit **XXX** who developed it and then, ultimately, it will be presented to group.

Time required to develop the plan

If the participating managers are familiar with the concepts set out in this book, then the first time that the exercise is undertaken a draft plan would be developed through the team working on it over a period of five days. A final plan would require several more days effort by a dedicated project team of around three managers. Plans in subsequent years would take less time to develop.

Plan frequency

A new plan will be developed each year unless circumstances change so dramatically that the existing plan loses touch with reality. In such circumstances, a new plan with genuinely different assumptions, expectations and strategies would be developed when the new circumstances are perceived.

Material

The material for the plan will be drawn from two principal sources:

- *This book.* This will provide the structure for the plan plus the language and the concepts necessary. In the skeleton plan set out below, it should be seen that each section has supporting reading.
- *Information from the firm.* Information about the business unit, group and the external: this will provide the figures and actual detail of the plan.

THE SKELETON STRATEGIC MARKET PLAN

The skeleton plan has four major sections: A, B, C, D.

- **A: Background to division's strategic plan**
  This is written after the plan has been completed and sets out how it came into existence.
- **B: Current strategic position of division**
  This provides a comprehensive historical view of the firm's operations up until the date of the plan.
- **C: Strategic divisional plan for the next three years**
  This provides a comprehensive view of the firm's future strategy and operations up until the end of the planning period.
- **D: Tactics, implementation and resources**
  This provides a detailed schedule of activities and tasks which must be carried out to ensure that the plan is actually implemented and also the resource implications.

The skeleton strategic plan is now considered in more detail.

A: Background to division's strategic plan

A1 Introduction

- The recent history and performance of the division.
- The substance of this strategic plan: a distillation of the views of the decision-makers of the division.

Reading: company documentation.

A2 Executive summary

- Summary of the main issues to be covered in the plan.

Reading: all chapters.

B: Current strategic position of division

B1 Defining the business

- Defining the division's current business and its likely future businesses in terms of products, markets, customers, technology and competitors.

Reading: Chapter B1.

B2 Current product market portfolio

- The division's current product market portfolio.

Reading: Chapter B2.

B3 Environmental analysis: external prospects

- An assessment of the business environment – markets, competition, economy, social, legal and technological – in which the division operates today and how that environment is likely to change in the next three years.

Reading: Chapter B3.

B4 Internal analysis of firm

- A strategic view of the areas in which the division excels and those in which it needs to be strengthened.

  Reading: Chapter B4.

B5 Key issues for strategic plan

- Key issues to be addressed in the strategic plan.

  Reading: none.

C: Strategic divisional plan for the next three years

C1 Future mission, goals, targets and portfolios

- The division's mission goals, targets and portfolios over the next three years. Qualitative and quantitative measurement.

  Reading: Chapter C1.

C2 Gap analysis

- A gap analysis for the division to be carried out at the following levels: sales; PBIT.

  Reading: Chapter C2.

C3 Future strategies

- The fundamental and detailed marketing strategies that the division will follow over the next three years.

  Reading: Chapter C3.

D: Tactics, implementation and resources

D1 Tactics and implementation

- The detailed tactics, programme for implementation and measurement of achievement.

  Reading: Chapter D1.

D2 Resources

- The resource implications of following the chosen strategies and tactics.

  Reading: Chapter D2.

CONCLUSION

This skeleton plan can be used, with amendment, in most organizations as a framework to enable managers to build their own strategic market plans. Finally, an example of a completed, or fleshed out, skeleton strategic plan is provided in Chapter 5.

5
Alban Chemicals:
A Completed Strategic
Market Plan

INTRODUCTION

This chapter sets out a completed strategic market plan for an imaginary firm called Alban Chemicals. Although the firm's managers, its performance and activities are imaginary, they represent fairly typical issues which the author has encountered in dealing with a wide range of firms. Consequently this strategic market plan could be considered as representative of the types of strategic market plans developed after working with a firm.

The plan follows the skeleton framework set out in Chapter 4 and the manner in which it is reproduced in this chapter reflects, fairly accurately, how a real strategic market plan would be set out.

For reasons of confidentiality no real data have been used – the products are referred to as Chemical A to Chemical E – and in addition any connection between Alban Chemicals and any existing firm is purely coincidental.

Finally, when readers of this book have completed all the chapters they should be able to develop a similar strategic market plan.

Alban Chemicals
Strategic Market Plan: 1998–2001
Developed by the Senior Management Team
December 1998

_____

CONTENTS

A: Background to strategic market plan

- A1 Introduction and background
- A2 Executive summary

B: Current strategic position

- B1 Business definition
- B2 Product market portfolio for 1998
- B3 Environmental analysis
- B4 Internal analysis
- B5 Key strategic issues

C: Strategic market plan, 1998–2001

- C1 Mission, goals and targets
- C2 Gap analysis
- C3 Future strategies

D: Tactics, implementation and resources

- D1 Tactics and implementation
- D2 Resources for the strategic plan

A: BACKGROUND TO STRATEGIC MARKET PLAN

A1 Introduction and background

Alban Chemicals is a Scottish based and owned independent manufacturer and distributor of industrial chemicals which principally serves the Scottish market. Although the firm's prospects look healthy, its senior management have decided that they are not taking a sufficiently strategic view of the firm's long-term future. Accordingly, using the skeleton strategic market plan, they have developed a strategic market plan for the years 1998 to 2001.

Recent performance of Alban Chemicals

The recent performance of Alban Chemicals is shown in Table 5.1.

Table 5.1 Sales, profit and productivity performance of Alban Chemicals

	1996	1997	1998	Annual % change
Sales (£k)	10,157	11,040	12,650	12
Gross profit (£k)	2,100	2,184	2,565	11
PBIT (£)	1,200	1,284	1,565	15
ROS (%)	12	12	12	0
ROI (%)	13	12	13	0
Employees	53	54	57	4
Sales/employee (£k)	192	204	222	8
Value added/employee (£k)	68	71	75	5
Value added/employee real (£k)	68	68	69	0
Average market growth rate (%)	5	5	5	5
Number of products	4	4	4	0
Percentage of sales in Scotland	90	89	89	0

Comments on recent performance

- *Sales*: rising well and growing at a faster rate than average market.
- *Gross profit*: less satisfactory.
- *Percentage profit measures*: static.
- *Productivity*: static £68,000 (real) value added per employee last year.

Major strategic marketing challenges

- Existing markets almost saturated so any substantial new growth only from taking market share from competitors.
- For profitable future growth need additional products/geographical market with greater profit potential.
- Existing markets not addressed in an optimal fashion.
- Product range has been static for the past three years at four products.
- Not enough growth through acquisition.

Future growth

This will be based upon the following principles:

- *Existing products*. Building customer loyalty through the provision of superior quality services.
- *New products and markets*. Continuous searching for new related product market segments with acceptable profit growth potential.
- *New firms*. Continuous searching for suitable acquisitions.
- *Productivity*. Relentless pursuit of profitable volume combined with unit cost reduction.

A2 Executive summary

Current performance is satisfactory although there is need for future strategic adjustment for the following reasons.

A2.1 Market forecasts

By 2001 the future of Alban's markets is mixed:

- Chemical A will decline by 7 per cent.
- Chemical B is static.
- Chemicals C and D will grow at 5 per cent and 8 per cent.
- Chemical E must enter aggressively this market. Competition is benign; should sell around £6mn p.a. by 2001.
- Heavy industry customer base will decline; make this up from other groups.
- Must diversify into England – 23 per cent of sales by 2001.
- Product development to keep ahead of competition.

A2.2 The strategy

Rapid and profitable growth through a generic strategy of differentiation to be achieved.

1. *Organic*: an additional £4,725k p.a. by 2001.
2. *Acquisition*: an additional £2,025k p.a. by 2001.

   - Main driver of growth: Product E supported by B and D.
   - Broaden customer range.
   - Major quality enhancement programmes.
   - Unit cost reduction programme.
   - Staff development programme.

A2.3 Future performance

A summary of future performance is given in Table 5.2.

B: CURRENT STRATEGIC POSITION

B1 Business definition

Currently Alban Chemicals has defined its business in terms of:

- *Products*: manufacture, market and distribute four chemicals, A to D.
- *Customer groups*: three types: major local companies, major multinationals and major heavy industry.
- *Territories*: mostly Scotland.
- *Technology*: patented the technology for a number of its processes. Further subdivision.

Table 5.2 Forecast performance for Alban Chemicals

Year	1998	1999	2000	2001	Average %
Sales ratios					
Sales (£k)	12,650	14,950	17,250	19,230	17
Gross profit (£k)	2,565	3,200	3,900	4,800	29
PBIT (£k)	1,565	1,800	2,240	2,690	24
Return on sales (%)	12	12	13	14	1
ROI (%)	13	13	14	15	1
Number of employees	57	65	66	67	6
Sales/employee (£k)	222	230	261	282	9
Value added/employee (£k)	75	84	98	108	15
Value added/employee real terms (£k)	75	81	91	94	8
Average market growth rate (%)	5	3	2	3	N/A
Number of products	4	5	5	5	N/A
Percentage of sales to Scotland	89	83	78	77	N/A
Percentage of sales to England	11	17	22	23	N/A

Table 5.3 shows the firm's view that it is both market led and also customer led. In addition, business can be considered in terms of:

- geographical markets;
- technology;
- competitors.

Geographical markets

- 89 per cent of sales from Scotland.
- 11 per cent to England.
- This balance to be altered.

Technology

State of the art process technology: produces superior grade products.

Table 5.3 Alban Chemicals current product market configuration (tonnes)

	Markets/customer groups			
Products	Major local companies	Major multinational chemical manufacturers	Major heavy industry manufacturers	Total
Chemical A		8,200 (45%)	10,200 (55%)	18,400
Chemical B	6,000 (23%)	12,000 (46%)	8,000 (31%)	26,000
Chemical C	10,000 (23%)	24,000 (54%)	10,000 (23%)	44,000
Chemical D	1,000 (67%)	500 (23%)		1,500
Totals	17,000 (19%)	44,700 (50%)	28,200 (31%)	89,900

Continuous upgrading to:

- preserve market position;
- provide premium prices;
- permit low unit costs.

Competitors

Major much larger multinational chemical companies. Alban can compete because of:

- superior technology;
- transportation cost;
- customer service;
- marketing agility.

B2 Product market portfolio for 1998

The data for Alban Chemicals's 1998 product market portfolio are shown in Table 5.4 and the actual product market portfolio is shown in Figure 5.1.

Table 5.4   Data for Alban Chemicals product market portfolio, 1998

Products	Alban Chemicals sales volume (tonnes)	Largest rival sales volume (tonnes)	Alban Chemicals RMS	Alban Chemicals annual sales (£mn)	Market growth rate %
Chemical A	18,400	5,000	3.7	3.1	-2
Chemical B	26,000	9,000	2.9	4.1	0
Chemical C	44,000	140,000	0.31	5.0	10
Chemical D	1,500	4,000	0.37	0.4	12
Chemical E	0	0	N/A	0	3
Total	89,900	158,000	N/A	12.6	N/A

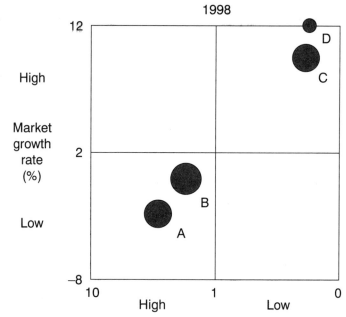

Figure 5.1   Alban Chemicals product market portfolio, 1998

Comments on 1998 portfolio

- *Chemicals A and B.* Dominance and cash cows but markets have zero or negative growth.
- *Chemical C.* Excellent market growth rate of 10 per cent: should continue to be a major contributor to the firm for many years.
- *Chemicals C and D*: Low relative market shares.
- *Chemical E.* Not in portfolio, but Alban will enter because will provide substantial profit growth, lack of intense competition and can overcome entry barriers.
- *Portfolio balance.* Need new high growth product or products.

B3 Environmental analysis

Alban Chemicals has analysed its environment under the following segments: competitive, marketing, customer group, economic, government/legal, social and technological. Each is now considered.

B3.1 The competitive environment: positive

Table 5.5 illustrates the competitive environment of Alban Chemicals.

B3.2 Marketing: negative

- Poor to average growth in major current markets.
- New entrants will seek to enter each market.
- Market forecasts for each product are given in Table 5.6.

The major issues in each market niche are as follows:

1. *Chemical A*

- In decline.
- Not attractive to new entrants due to Alban's dominance. Strong strategic position and prices, unlike many rivals, at a value for money level and so achieve superior returns.

Table 5.5   Summary of competitive forces faced by Alban Chemicals

Competitive force	Threat	Response
Threat of entry	Low switching costs. Low capital requirements.	Geographical proximity. Superior service.
Buyer power	Make large purchases.	Continuity and quality of supply. Production 24 hours per day 365 days per year.
Supplier power	Highly concentrated: very large user of electricity supplied by monopoly utility.	Monopoly supplier of electricity is a major cost issue. Energy study to supply own power.
Substitute threat	Low because of their high cost.	Substitutes are higher priced.
Rivalry	Many competitors. Slow industry growth. Lack of switching costs.	We communicate with customers. Discipline in the market-place. Only manufacturer which is generating customer loyalty.

2. *Chemical B*

- Poor growth.
- Alban relatively well placed: mature so unlikely to see new entrants.
- Buyers buy largely on lowest price.

3. *Chemical C*

- Growing relatively quickly so attractive for existing players to invest heavily in it and for new entrants to join.

- Competition severe and Alban a follower in the market.
- Sales are on the basis of price, but Alban will try to redress this.

4. *Chemical D*

- Same comments as for Chemical C.

5. *Chemical E*

- Not currently in this market.
- However, it is a very attractive market and the company will make a major move. Reasons:
  - — Growth rate moderate.
  - — Strongly related to existing product range.
  - — Competition relatively low: one lethargic major player and a substantial number of small fragmented players.
  - — Production technology used by rivals much inferior to what Alban has available.
  - — Product quality low; many complaints from buyers.
  - — Buyers very demanding in terms of product quality and service, willing to pay premium prices for premium products and services.
  - — Number of suitable acquisitions available.

Table 5.6 Forecast sales for Chemicals A to E

Year forecast volume sales (tonnes)	1998	1999	2000	2001	Annual growth rate (%)
Chemical A	92,000	84,000	77,800	71,600	-7
Chemical B	109,200	110,000	108,000	109,000	0
Chemical C	420,000	441,000	463,000	486,000	5
Chemical D	24,000	25,900	28,000	30,000	8
Chemical E	400,000	412,000	424,000	437,000	3
Total	1,045,200	1,072,900	1,100,800	1,133,600	3

B3.3 Customer groups: positive

Changes in customer groups are shown in Table 5.7.
  The major changes in each customer group are:

- Major heavy industry customers: declining

  — But increase in Chemical B.

- Multinational chemical manufacturers: remaining static

  — Decrease Chemical B.
  — Increase in Chemical E.

- Major local companies: increasing

  — Increase in Chemical B.

B3.4 Economic: positive

- Scottish economy will behave similarly to 1995 in 1998.
- Inflation will average around 4.0 per cent.

B3.5 Government/legal: negative

- Environmental legislation will make it more expensive to operate a chemical facility, but this will also make it more difficult for new entrants.

B3.6 Technological: positive

- Firm's technology most modern and environmentally friendly production system. Will remain so.

Conclusions on future environment

Positive with major opportunities for Chemical E.

B4 Internal strengths and areas for development

These are analysed under the headings behavioural, structural, and functional analysis.

Table 5.7 Alban Chemicals's forecast sales by customer group in 2001 (tonnes)

| | Markets/customer groups | | | |
Products	Major local companies	Major multinational chemical manufacturers	Major heavy industry manufacturers	Total
Chemical A		5,200 (40%)	8,280 (60%)	13,800
Chemical B	12,900 (43%)	5,080 (17%)	12,020 (40%)	30,000
Chemical C	12,000 (25%)	26,400 (55%)	9,600 (20%)	48,000
Chemical D	4,200 (70%)	1,800 (30%)		6,000
Chemical E	6,900 (15%)	33,200 (72%)	5,900 (13%)	46,000
Totals	36,000 (25%)	72,000 (50%)	35,800 (25%)	143,800

B4.1 Behavioural analysis

*   *Leadership: strength.* Strong and effective.
*   *Culture: strength.* Creative atmosphere good communication at all levels. Sharing of responsibilities.
*   *Power process: strength.* Decentralized power system: consensus driven.
*   *Behavioural areas for development.* Although successful the firm needs the development of managerial creativity. Needs more time for standing back from the day-to-day operations and taking a more strategic view.

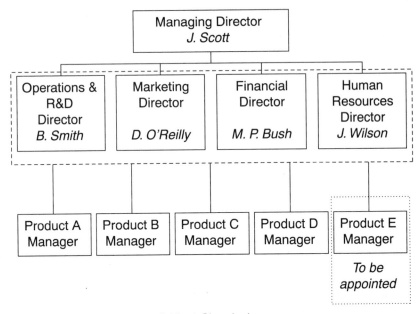

Figure 5.2   The structure of Alban Chemicals

B4.2 Structural analysis

Current structure is shown in Figure 5.2 and considered appropriate. New product manager will be appointed for Chemical E.

B4.3 Functional analysis

Marketing and sales

- Strengths

    — Good sales/marketing relationships.
    — Dominant market share in two products.
    — Good relationships with all customer groups.

- Weaknesses

    — IT capabilities.
    — Too functionally focused.
    — Speed of response to market developments.
    — Limited portfolio.

— Huge dependency on multinational chemicals.

R&D and operations

- Strengths

  — Good technical knowledge.
  — High quality products.
  — Flexible workforce and facilities.
  — Spare capacity.
  — Prepared to take risk/change.
  — Quality culture.

- Weaknesses
  — Cost of storage of products.
  — Management skills underdeveloped.
  — Customer focus.

Finance

- Strengths

  — Ready adoption of new techniques/technology.
  — Excellent first-hand knowledge of customer base.
  — Integrity of information.

- Weaknesses

  — Succession management.
  — IT resources.
  — Communication with sales managers.

Training and development

- Strengths

  — Resources available.
  — Leading edge.

- Weaknesses

  — Pool of players too small.

— Development viewed as reward in past.
— Need longer term perspective.
— Losing some good managers.

Personnel

- Strengths

  — Tight control.
  — Computerized.
  — Low labour turnover.
  — Good clear systems.

- Weaknesses

  — Knowledge base not evenly spread.
  — Backup.
  — Personnel staff leaving.

Current financial performance and key strategic ratios.

Recent financial performance and key strategic ratios are shown in Tables 5.8 to 5.12
—   Greater interdepartmental communication.
—   Succession planning.

B5 Key strategic issues

This section summarizes the key issues – external and internal – considered in detail in B5.1 to B5.5.

B5.1 Key external issues

The markets

- Overall market

  — Growth.
  — Increasing segmentation.
  — Scottish market becoming saturated, so need new markets.
  — Pricing pressures.

— Environmental issues will increase.

The markets by product

- Chemical A
  - In decline.
  - No new opportunities apparent.

- Chemical B
  - Static.
  - No new opportunities apparent.

- Chemical C
  - Good growth but Alban weak share: build and invest.
  - Very large size: scope for development.

- Chemical D
  - Small but 'good for Alban': strong local interaction. Build.

- Chemical E
  - Great new opportunity: poor competitors and a huge market. Enter and build.

Table 5.8 Alban Chemicals income statement

	1996	1997	1998	Annual % change
Sales (£k)	10,157	11,040	12,650	12
Purchases (£k)	6,553	7,206	8,375	14
Value added (£k)	3,604	3,834	4,275	9
Manufacturing costs (£k)	1,200	1,300	1,350	6
Depreciation (£k)	304	350	360	9
Gross profit (£k)	2,100	2,184	2,565	11
Other expenses (£k)	900	900	1,000	6
PBIT (£k)	1,200	1,284	1,565	15

Table 5.9   Alban Chemicals percentage income statement

Year	1996	1997	1998
Sales (%)	100	100	100
Purchases (%)	65	65	66
Value added (%)	35	35	34
Manufacturing and distribution (%)	12	12	11
Depreciation (%)	3	3	3
Gross profit (%)	21	20	20
Other expenses (%)	9	8	8
PBIT (%)	12	12	12

Comment: satisfactory.

Table 5.10   Alban Chemicals balance sheet

	1996	1997	1998	Annual % change
Current assets (£k)	3,889	4,200	4,400	7
Fixed assets (£k)	7,019	8,020	8,800	13
Goodwill (£k)	0	0	0	0
Creditors (£k)	(1,422)	(1,190)	(944)	17
Total invest (£k)	9,486	11,030	12,256	15

Comment: significant increase in total investment.

Table 5.11   Alban Chemicals cash flow

	1996	1997	1998	Annual % change
Net income (£k)	1,200	1,284	1,565	15
Depreciation (£k)	304	350	360	9
Sources (£k)	1,504	1,634	1,925	14
Fixed assets and goodwill (£k)	1,000	1,231	1,140	7
Working capital (£k)	300	543	446	24
Uses (£k)	1,300	1,774	1,568	10
Net cash flow (£k)	204	(140)	357	38
Cumulative (£k)	204	64	421	53

Comment: satisfactory.

Customer group

• Major local companies becoming more important.
• Major multinational chemical companies maintaining importance: Alban too dependent.
• Major heavy industry: in decline.

Distribution

• Becoming faster.
• Night-time delivery.
• JIT and IT are increasingly important.

Competition

• Consolidation may make majors even larger.
• May be new entrants.
• Price is main competitive weapon.
• Becoming faster.
• Fragmenting.
• Must maintain technology/service superiority.

Table 5.12   Key strategic ratios for Alban Chemicals, 1996–8

Year	1996	1997	1998	Comment
Competitive position				
Sales (£000s)	10,157	11,040	12,650	Increase ahead of market
Market share (%)	30	30	30	Scotland only static
Rel mkt share	0.3	0.3	0.3	Scotland only, cannot grow much more
Market characteristics				
Market growth rate (%)	5	5	5	None
Capital and production structure				
Total invest (£000)	9,486	11,030	12,256	Continuous investment
ROI/PBIT/total inv (%)	13	12	13	Static
Invest/value added	2.6	2.9	2.9	Increasing; unsatisfactory
Invest/sales	0.93	0.99	0.97	Increasing; unsatisfactory
Productivity ratios				
Number of employees	53	54	57	Satisfactory
Sales/emp curr (£000)	192	204	222	
Sale/emp real (£000)	192	196	205	Not growing enough
Productivity current (£000)*	68	71	75	
Prod real (£000)	68	68	69	Static; unsatisfactory
Invt/emp curr (£000)	179	204	215	
Invt/emp real (£000)	204	196	198	Increasing; unsatisfactory
Profitability measures				
Gross profit (£000)	2,100	2,184	2,565	Increasing
Gross pro/sales (%)	21	20	20	Static; unsatisfactory
PBIT (£000)	1,200	1,284	1,565	Increasing
PBIT/sales (%)	12	12	12	Static; unsatisfactory
Cashflow (£000)	204	(140)	357	Satisfactory

* Measured by value added per employee.

Key internal issues

- Need clear definition of business.
- Need wider product and geographical range.
- Need to develop culture and skills.
- Must be increased productivity.
- Technology/production, invest to maintain leadership and differentiation for premium prices.
- Future capacity: must be increased.

C: STRATEGIC MARKET PLAN, 1998–2001

C1 Mission, goals and targets

Mission

We, Alban Chemicals, are the only indigenous Scottish chemical manufacturing company supplying its particular range of products to the Scottish market.

We will confine our activities to the manufacture and distribution of industrial chemicals or products directly related to them.

We will maintain our **leadership** in this market through working in partnership with our customers and being responsive to their needs. We will continue to resolutely pursue our **unit cost reduction** programme.

This dual mission will, we believe, enable us to maintain our market dominance against existing competitors and also erect strategic barriers which will deter new entrants.

From this strategic position of strength we will continuously achieve profitable growth.

We acknowledge that our responsibilities extend to the communities in which we operate and we will continue to be proactive in our response to the critical issues of health, safety and the environment.

Goals

Alban Chemicals has the following primary goals:

- Pursue profitable growth.
- Grow our existing market share by at least 10 per cent by 2001 to

total annual sales of £19mn.
- Strive for market dominance in all our market niches.
- Commence the manufacture and distribution of Chemical E in 1999.
- Reinforce the strategic position of the core business through the development of at least one supporting product by 2001.
- Pursue relative product and service enhancement to build margins.
- Reduce operating unit costs by 10 per cent in real terms by 1998.
- Establish a more balanced portfolio of products.
- Reduce the risk accruing from being 89 per cent dependent on the Scottish market by having 23 per cent of annual sales in the English market by 2001.

Targets

Targets are shown in Tables 5.13 to 5.16.

Product market portfolio for 1998 and 2001

The data for the 2001 product market portfolio are shown in Table 5.17 and the actual product market portfolio for 1998 and 2001 is shown in Figure 5.3.

Table 5.13 Alban Chemicals product sales targets

Sales (£k)	1998	1999	2000	2001	Annual change (%)
Total	12,650	14,950	17,250	19,230	17
Chemical A	3,100	2,850	2,620	2,300	-9
Chemical B	4,100	4,300	4,400	4,600	4
Chemical C	5,000	4,800	4,650	4,500	-3
Chemical D	400	800	1,200	1,500	92
Chemical E	0	2,200	4,380	6,300	NA

Table 5.14 Alban Chemicals customer groups sales targets

Sales (tonnes)	1998	1999	2000	2001	Annual change (%)
Total	89,900	108,290	129,000	143,800	20
Major local Companies	17,000	23,290	32,000	36,000	37
Major multinational chemical manufacturers	44,700	54,000	64,000	72,000	20
Major heavy industry manufacturers	28,200	31,000	33,000	35,800	9

Table 5.15 Alban Chemicals geographical sales targets

Sales (tonnes %)	1998	1999	2000	2001	Annual change (%)
Total	89,000	108,290	129,000	143,800	20
Scotland	80,000 (89)	90,900 (83)	101,000 (78)	110,800 (77)	13
England	9,900 (11)	18,290 (17)	28,000 (22)	33,000 (23)	78

Table 5.16 Alban Chemicals target sales by customer group and geographical region, 2001 (tonnes)

| | Customers | | | | | |
	Major local companies	Major multinational chemical manufacturers	Major heavy industry manufacturers	Scotland	England	Total
Chemical A		5,520 (40%)	8,280 (60%)	13,800 (100%)	0 (0%)	13,800
Chemical B	12,900 (43%)	5,080 (17%)	12,020 (40%)	30,000 (100%)	0 (0%)	30,000
Chemical C	12,000 25%	26,400 (55%)	9,600 (20%)	28,800 (60%)	19,200 (40%)	48,000
Chemical D	4,200 (70%)	1,800 (30%)		6,000 (100%)	0 (0%)	6,000
Chemical E	6,900 (14%)	33,200 (73%)	5,900 (13%)	32,200 (70%)	13,800 (30%)	46,000
Totals	36,000 (25%)	72,000 (50%)	35,800 (25%)	110,800 (77%)	33,000 (23%)	143,800

Notes:

• Reduction in sales to major heavy industry manufacturers.
• Increase in sales to major local companies.
• Increase in sales to the English market.

Comments on Alban Chemical 1998 and 2001 portfolio

• Overall balance will improve with Chemical E.
• Decline in growth rates of the firm's core products.

Projected financial performance and key strategic ratios

Projected financial performance and key strategic ratios are shown in
Tables 5.18 to 5.22 and a much stronger performance is predicted.

Comments on Alban Chemicals targets

An ambitious agenda has been set. All the projected measures: sales,
profitability and capital and productivity show healthy growth.

Table 5.17 Data for Alban Chemicals product market portfolio, 2001

Products	Alban Chemicals sales volume (tonnes)	Largest rival sales volume (tonnes)	Alban Chemicals RMS	Alban Chemicals annual sales (£mn)	Market growth rate (%)
Chemical A	13,800	2,900	4.7	2.3	-8
Chemcial B	30,000	7,500	4.0	4.6	0
Chemical C	48,000	140,000	0.34	4.5	5
Chemical D	6,000	3,000	2.07	1.5	8
Chemical E	46,000	98,000	0.46	6.3	3
Total	143,800	N/A	N/A	19.2	N/A

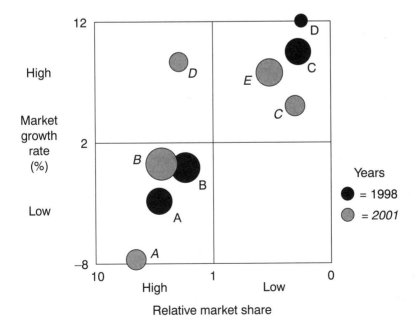

Figure 5.3 Alban Chemicals product market portfolio, 1998 and 2001

Table 5.18 Alban Chemicals projected income statement

	1998	1999	2000	2001	Annual % change
Sales (£k)	12,650	14,950	17,250	19,230	17
Purchases (£k)	8,375	9,500	10,800	12,000	14
Value added (£k)	4,275	5,450	6,450	7,230	23
Manufacturing costs (£k)	1,350	1,750	2,000	2,000	16
Depreciation (£k)	360	500	550	430	6
Gross profit (£k)	2,565	3,200	3,900	4,800	29
Other expenses (£k)	1,000	1,400	1,660	2,110	37
PBIT (£k)	1,565	1,800	2,240	2,690	24

Table 5.19 Alban Chemicals projected percentage income statement

	1998	1999	2000	2001	Annual % change
Sales (k)	12,650	14,950	17,250	19,230	18
Purchases (k)	8,375	9,500	10,800	12,000	14
Value added (£k)	4,275	5,450	6,450	7,450	23
Manufacturing costs (£k)	1,350	1,750	2,000	2,000	16
Depreciation (£k)	360	500	550	430	6
Gross profit (£k)	2,565	3,200	3,900	4,800	29
Other expenses (£k)	1,000	1,400	1,660	2,110	37
PBIT (£k)	1,565	1,800	2,240	2,690	24

Table 5.20 Alban Chemicals projected balance sheet

	1998	1999	2000	2001	% change
Current assets (£k)	4,400	5,200	6,000	7,200	21
Fixed assets (£k)	8,800	10,200	11,500	13,000	16
Goodwill (£k)	0	0	0	0	0
Creditors (£k)	(944)	(1,554)	(1,590)	(1,986)	N/A
Total invest (£k)	12,256	13,846	15,900	18,214	16
Working capital (£k)	3,456	3,646	4,410	5,214	17

Table 5.21 Alban Chemicals projected cash flow

	1998	1999	2000	2001	Annual % change
Net income (£k)	1,565	1,800	2,240	2,690	24
Depreciation (£k)	360	500	550	430	6
Sources (£k)	1,925	2,300	2,790	3,120	21
Fixed assets and goodwill (£k)	1,140	1,900	1,850	1,930	23
Working capital (£k)	428	190	764	804	27
Uses (£k)	1,568	2,090	2,614	2,734	25
Net cash flow (£k)	357	210	176	386	3
Cumulative (£k)	421	631	807	1,193	61

Table 5.22 Targets for Alban Chemicals, 1998–2001

Year	1999	1999	2000	2001	Average %
Competitive position					
Sales (£000)	12,650	14,950	17,250	19,230	17
Market share (%)	30	31	32	32	2
Rel mkt share (%)	0.3	0.3	0.35	0.35	1
Market characteristics					
Market growth rate	5	3	2	3	(13)
Market concentration (%)	85	85	86	86	0
Capital and production structure					
Total invest (£000)	12,256	13,846	16,000	18,214	16
ROI/(PBIT/total inv (%)	13	13	15	14	0
Invest/value added	2.6	2.5	2.5	2.5	0
Invest/sales	0.9	0.9	0.9	0.9	0
Productivity ratios					
Number of employees	57	65	66	67	6
Sales/emp curr (£000)	222	230	261	287	10
Sale/emp real (£000)	222	221	241	255	5
Prod current (000)	75	84	98	108	15
Prod real (£000)	75	81	91	96	9
Invt/emp curr (£000)	215	213	242	272	9
Invt/emp real (£000)	215	215	149	284	11
Profitability measures					
Gross profit (£000)	2,565	3,200	3,900	4,800	29
Gross pro/sales(%)	20	21	23	25	8
PBIT(£000)	1,565	1,800	2,240	2,690	24
PBIT/sales (%)	12	12	13	14	1
Cash flow (£000)	357	210	176	386	3

Table 5.23   Data for Alban Chemical sales gap analysis

	1996	1997	1998	1999	2000	2001
Forecast sales (£k)	1,000	11,040	12,650	12,750	12,425	12,480
Add org sales (£k)	0	0	0	1,750	3,480	4,725
Add acq sales (£k)	0	0	0	450	1,345	2,025
Total sales (£k)	1,000	11,040	12,650	14,950	17,250	19,230

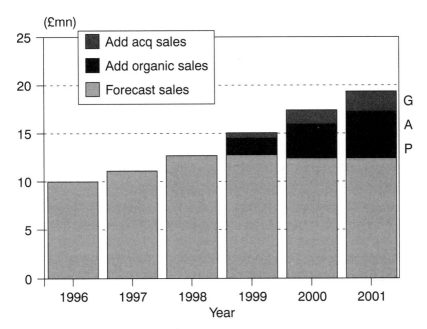

Figure 5.4 Sales gap analysis for Alban Chemicals, 1996–2001

C2 Gap analysis

Two gap analyses, one for sales (see Table 5.23 and Figure 5.4) and one for PBIT (see Table 5.24 and Figure 5.5), have been conducted.

C2.1 Sales gap analysis

Comments

To achieve the goals for 2001 Alban Chemicals must have:

- additional growth in organic annual sales of £4,725k;
- additional growth in annual sales due to acquisition of £2,025k.

C2.2 PBIT gap analysis

PBIT gap analysis is shown in Table 5.24 and Figure 5.5.

Comments:

To achieve the goals for 2001 Alban Chemicals must substantially increase the PBIT from organically derived sales.

Table 5.24   Data for Alban Chemicals' PBIT gap analysis

	1996	1997	1998	1999	2000	2001
Forecast PBIT (£k)	1,180	1,284	1,565	1,680	1,790	2,050
Add org PBIT (£k)	0	0	0	0	250	420
Add acq PBIT (£k)	0	0	0	120	200	220
Total PBIT (£k)	1,180	1,284	1,565	1,800	2,240	2,690

Figure 5.5   A PBIT gap analysis for Alban Chemicals, 1996–2001

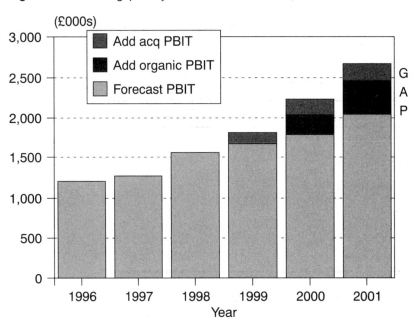

C.3 *Future strategies*

Major strategy of profitable and rapid growth will have two main elements:

* organic growth;
* growth through acquisition.

Organic growth

Additional organic sales from Product E, supported by products B and D, as shown in Table 5.25.

Table 5.25   Additonal sales from organic growth

	1999	2000	2001
Chemical A (£k)	0	0	0
Chemical B (£k)	0	0	50
Chemical C (£k)	0	0	0
Chemical D (£k)	0	100	–
Chemical E (£k)	1,750	3,380	4,675
Total additional sales (£k)	1,750	3,480	4,725

Means of achieving organic growth

*   Marketing initiatives

    — Relative quality.
    — Associated service.
    — Focus on promoting image of the only indigenous producer and the attendant knowledge of customers and flexibility.
    — Responsiveness to customer needs.
    — Value for money.

*   Other initiatives

    — Quality.
    — Unit costs.
    — Rationalization
    — Human relations.

Growth through acquisition

Suitable firms will be acquired to provide volume and additional customer groups. The schedule is shown in Table 5.26.

Table 5.26 Additional sales from acquisitions

	1999	2000	2001
Chemical A (£k)	0	0	0
Chemical B (£k)	0	0	0
Chemical C (£k)	0	0	0
Chemical D (£k)	0	345	400
Chemical E (£k)	450	1,000	1,625
Total additional sales (£k)	450	1,345	2,025

Portfolio balance and summary

Finally, Table 5.27 shows the overall balance of the firm's portfolio in 2001 and comments on each product area.

Table 5.27 The overall balance of Alban's portfolio, 2001

Product	RMS		Life cycle	Future prospects	Strategy
	1998	2001			
Chemical A	3.7	4.7	Cash cow	Decline	Harvest and defend position
Chemical B	2.9	4.0	Mature	Good but vulnerable	Defend
Chemical C	0.31	0.34	Mature/limited growth	Good but strong competition	More marketing: try to prevent price erosion
Chemical D	0.37	2.07	Small volume	Link to Chemical C	Acquire and build
Chemical E	0.0	0.46	New entrant	Good prospects	Mainly acquisition

D: TACTICS, IMPLEMENTATION AND RESOURCES

D1 Tactics and implementation

Tactics are considered under the following headings: products, customers, geographical spread, quality and service, productivity/unit
costs, people (see Tables 5.28 to 5.33).

Table 5.28

No	Task	Completion date	Action by
Major local companies			
1	One additional sales staff	1 July 1999	Marketing director
2	Quality and service improvement	Quality and service audit by September 1999	Marketing director
3	Develop related product	December 2000	R&D director/outside consultants
Major multinational chemical manufacturers			
4	Seek allliance with largest customer	After March 1999	Managing director
5	Negotiations on JIT and more flexible delivery	September 1999	Managing director and operations manager
6	Acquire two new customers: Company P and Company Q are targets	December 1999, December 2000	Marketing director
Major heavy industry manufacturers			
7	Maintain and build quality relationships	Continuous	All staff
8	Develop a higher margin replacement product	December 2000	R&D director

Table 5.29 Customer tactics and implementation schedule

No	Task	Completion date	Action by
Major local companies			
1	One additional sales staff	1 July 1999	Marketing director
2	Quality and service improvement	Quality and service audit by September 1999	Marketing director
3	Develop related product	December 2000	R&D director/ outside consultants
Major multinational chemical manufacturers			
4	Seek alliance with largest customer	After March 1999	Managing director
5	Negotiations on JIT and more flexible delivery	September 1999	Managing director and operations manager
6	Acquire two new customers: Company P and Company Q are targets	December 1999, December 2000	Marketing director
Major heavy industry manufacturers			
7	Maintain and build quality relationships	Continuous	All staff
8	Develop a higher margin replacement product	December 2000	R&D director

Table 5.30   Geographical tactics and implementation schedule

No	Tactic	Complete date	Action by
Scottish customers			
1	Quality and service improvements	Quality and service audit by September 1999	Marketing director and operations director
2	Retain agency to survey all Scottish customers to more fully ascertain needs	Commence August 1999	Marketing director
3	Retain agency to promote 'Scottishness' to existing and potential customers in Scotland	Commence after survey	Marketing director
English customers			
4	Quality and service drive	Audit by September 1999	Marketing director and operations director
5	Advertising/promotion campaign to win customers	Start in July 1999 and assess progress	Marketing director
6	Negotiations on JIT and more flexible delivery	September 1999	Marketing director and operations director
7	Acquire two new customers per year: Companies P and Q are targets	Start July 1999	Marketing director

Table 5.31 Quality and service tactics and implementation schedule

No	Tactic	Complete date	Action by
Strategic quality improvement programme			
1	Workshop series on strategic quality	Commence March 1999 and then repeated every four weeks for different groups for 1999	Human relations and marketing directors
2	Develop indices of strategic quality improvement in produce and service	Start April 1999 and complete by December 1999	All staff
Internal quality improvement			
3	Programme to improve process quality	Commence January 1999 and complete by June 1999	Operations director and outside consultants
4	Monitor speed and quality of deliveries	Commence January 199 and repeated every three months	Marketing director

Table 5.32 Unit cost and productivity tactics and implementation schedule

No	Tactic	Complete date	Action by
Unit costs			
1	Wastage study	Quality and service audit by September 1999	Marketing director and operations director
2	Benchmark study with best practice	December 2000	R&D director/ outside consultants
3	Introduce JIT	One in July 1999 and one in July 2000	Marketing director
4	Scrap and acquire state-of-art technology for product line B	After March 1999	Managing director

Table 5.33 Human relations tactics and implementation schedule

No	Tactic	Complete date	Action by
1	Develop cross-functional management through job rotation	Continuous	Human relations director plus senior managers
2	Course on quality development	May 1999 for four weeks	Human relations director
3	IT skills for all	Start in September 1999 and then continuous	IT manager and human relations director
4	Review of payment system with the development of productivity based schemes	Start February 1999 and implement June 1999	Human relations director

D2 Resources for the strategic plan

The overall additional resources and resources by product line needed to implement the strategic plan are shown in Tables 5.34 to 5.39.

Table 5.34 Overall resource implications of implementing the strategic plan

Alban Chemicals	1999	2000	2001
Staff (£k)	150	150	180
Fixed assets: plant and equipment (£k)	1,900	1,850	1,630
Current assets (£k)	800	800	1,200
Other expenditures (£k)	100	150	200
Total (£k)	2,950	2,950	3,210

Table 5.35 Chemical A resource implications of implementing the strategic plan

Chemical A	1999	2000	2001
Staff (£k)	0	0	0
Fixed assets: plant and equipment (£k)	0	20	50
Current assets (£k)	20	20	20
Other expenditures (£k)	0	10	10
Total (£k)	20	50	80

Table 5.36 Chemical B resource implications of implementing the strategic plan

Chemical B	1999	2000	2001
Staff (£k)	40	40	40
Fixed assets: plant and equipment (£k)	80	60	100
Current assets (£k)	50	50	50
Other expenditures (£k)	10	30	40
Total (£k)	180	180	230

Table 5.37 Chemical C resource implications of implementing the strategic plan

Chemical C	1999	2000	2001
Staff (£k)	0	0	0
Fixed assets: plant and equipment (£k)	20	20	50
Current assets (£k)	30	30	30
Other expenditures (£k)	10	20	30
Total (£k)	60	70	110

Table 5.38 Chemical D resource implications of implementing the strategic

Chemical D	1999	2000	2001
Staff (£k)	40	40	40
Fixed assets: plant and equipment (£k)	500	400	200
Current assets (£k)	100	100	200
Other expenditures (£k)	30	30	40
Total (£k)	670	570	480

Table 5.39 Chemical E resource implications of implementing the strategic plan

Chemical E	1999	2000	2001
Staff (£k)	70	70	100
Fixed assets: plant and equipment (£k)	1,300	1,350	1,230
Current assets (£k)	600	600	900
Other expenditures (£k)	50	60	80
Total (£k)	2,020	2,080	2,310

Part II
Developing a
Strategic Market Plan

A1

Introduction and Background to the Plan

INTRODUCTION

This section of the strategic market plan will be the first element which a reader will examine. Therefore it must be written in such a fashion that it catches the reader's attention and this will be most likely if it sets out the key areas in which the firm's recent performance has not been entirely satisfactory and also sets the scene for building the firm. Normally this section is written after the full detail of the plan has been developed.

CONTENT OF A1

Although it is impossible to be universally prescriptive about what this will contain, it will often include the following:

- How the plan came into being and the process of its development.
- The team of people involved in the plan's development.
- The structure of the planning document.
- The recent performance of the firm quantified in using marketing and financial measures.
- Comments on the recent performance of the firm, including areas such as:

  — Overall growth.

  — Growth by product niche, customer group and territory.

— Portfolio balance.

— Performance relative to competitors.

— Productivity.

— Issues in the firm that must be addressed if superior performance is to be achieved.

- Other unusual or special features of the firm, for example, proprietary technology, unique distribution system.

A2

Executive Summary

The executive summary is perhaps the most important part of the planning document – often readers will turn to this section first in order to gain immediate insights into where how the firm intends to develop. There may be some readers who read just this section. Consequently the executive summary needs to catch the reader's attention and communicate very effectively. Once again this section is written after the full detail of the plan has been developed.

CONTENT OF SECTION A.2

Although it is impossible to be universally prescriptive about the executive summary, it will often contain information such as the following:

- Major changes which will take place in the planning period
- Business definition in terms of products, customers, territories and competitors
- Portfolio balance and risk
- Position relative to main competitors
- The future strategy of the firm and key targets

- The planned future performance of the firm using standard performance measures such as sales, profitability and productivity.

B1

Defining the Business

INTRODUCTION

Derek Abell's book, *Defining the Business: The Starting Point of Strategic Planning* (1) outlines the crucial first step in developing a strategic market plan. Most managers engaged in strategic market planning would agree with this. Defining the business really is the starting point. The process of defining the business sets the strategic market agenda. It lays out the domain of activities in which the business will engage and automatically conjures up the true competitors so that the strategic position of the business can be assessed. Firms who clearly and often creatively, define their business in some unique manner often confer substantial strategic advantage upon themselves, which leads ultimately to enduringly superior profits (remember Dunhill in Chapter 1). Firms that are sloppy about their business definition or let it drift in an unquestioning manner will often suffer a much more haphazard commercial existence and almost certainly have inferior profits.

INDUSTRIES DON'T COMPETE:
COMPETITION TAKES PLACE IN NICHES

Only the most naive managers will define their business in terms of the generic name for the product or the service which they provide. For example, if a manager in a car showroom defines his business as selling cars, or a manager in a ship building firm defines his business as building ships, or a manager in an insurance company defines his business as providing insurance they are not defining any of these businesses. Such definitions are too broad and furthermore they are not driven by marketing or strategic considerations. Competition does not take place at the industry level, but occurs at the product market level. Even in the smallest business, with a very limited number of products and markets, the marketing needs for each product market grouping are often distinctively different. Knowing precisely and then fulfilling the needs of the customers in each product market group is the key to developing superior strategies. The case for this is unanswerable. Most businesses, even giant multinational corporations, compete in specific market niches which are occupied by rivals. Superiority in performance comes from having relative[1] power in the niche. This relative power can be manifested in many ways.

Relative market share

What is the firm's market share of the niche relative to the largest players in the niche? Generally the firm with the largest relative market share will have the lowest unit costs and will also be in a strong position to set prices for others to follow.

Relative product quality

What is the quality of the products and associated services offered by the firm relative to the other rivals in the niche? Generally the firm with the highest level of relative quality and associated service will have one of the highest and most sustained returns of all the players in the niche.

Degree of innovation

What is the firm's rate of innovation? Generally the firm which has the highest degree of innovation – where this is measured by the percentage of sales from products introduced, say, in the past five years – will enjoy stable and superior returns.

Homogeneous customer groups

What is the degree of homogeneity in the firm's customer groups? Generally the firm which is best able, relative to the other players in the niche, to have very similar customers will tend to enjoy superior returns. The logic is that if customers tend to have similar characteristics they can be served more effectively and with a greater degree of satisfaction than if they are quite dissimilar.

Common distribution channels

How well can the firm use common distribution channels for all its products? Generally firms which are able to use common distribution channels for many products should enjoy cost and quality advantages over rivals in the niche who have to use a variety of channels. These advantages often lead to superior returns.

Concentration to serve a specific geographical market

How well does the firm respond to the specific needs of a specific geographical market? When a firm is able to respond precisely to the particular needs of a specific geographical market then superior returns – based perhaps upon premium pricing through meeting customers' needs in a superior fashion – may accrue.

AGGREGATION LINES

It is now possible to consider the different levels of aggregation at which an industry can be examined. This is shown diagrammatically in Figure B1.1 which illustrates this type of classification for the automobile industry.

As Figure B1.1 shows, a number of levels of aggregation can be applied: industry, market segment and niches.

Automobile	Niche characteristics
Ferrari Testarossa Honda NSX Lamborghini Diablo Porsche 911 Toyota Supra	Very high performance, very expensive, highly exclusive
BMW M5 Jaguar XJS Mercedes SL 500	High performance, very expensive, luxurious, highly exclusive
BMW Z3 Mercedes SLK Porsche Boxster	High performance, prestige, expensive but not unreachable image
Ford Probe Toyota MR2	Good performance, more moderate pricing, less exclusive
Mazda MX5 Suzuki Cappuccino	Performance less important than looks and style, more moderate pricing, younger buyers

Figure B1.1   Different levels of aggregation in the automobile industry

Industry level

This is the broadest level and is of the least significance from a strategic marketing perspective. This is the level most often used by government economists to provide information on, say, the output of the automobile industry. It does not consider the characteristics of the individual products and their markets. It merely provides the number of units of output.

Market level

This is really the same as the industry level in that it is at the broadest level of aggregation and is also of minor significance from a strategic marketing perspective. Once again, this level is often used by government economists to provide information on, say, the market for automobiles in a particular country. It does not consider the characteristics of the individual products and their markets but merely provides the number of units sold.

Market segment level

Within all industries there are individual segments which have distinct and different characteristics. With the overall automobile market the following market segments exist:

- very cheap saloon;
- basic/standard saloon;
- luxury saloon;
- high-speed saloon;
- sportscar;
- hot hatchback;
- four-wheel drive;
- people carrier;
- small town car.

The market characteristics of each of these segments are different and having success in any segment requires that manufacturers and their retailers really understand and respond to segment buyers' needs. In addition to having different characteristics, each segment will tend to have different growth rates, different barriers to entry, different buyer power. Understanding the characteristics and dynamics of segments is strategically vital because not only does such knowledge enable a firm to address buyers' needs effectively, but also enables the firm to estimate its own strength, performance and uniqueness relative to its true rivals.

Niche level

Within the market segment an even finer level of aggregation is possible. This is to subdivide the segment into its constituent niches. To illustrate, in the UK, the following automobiles, in alphabetical order, apparently compete in the sportscar market segment.

- BMW M5
- BMW Z3

- Ferrari Testarossa
- Ford Probe
- Honda NSX
- Mazda MX5
- Lamborghini Diablo
- Jaguar XJS
- Mercedes SL 500
- Mercedes SLK
- Nissan 300ZX
- Porsche 911
- Porsche Boxster
- Renault Alpine
- Suzuki Cappuchino
- Toyota MR2
- Toyota Supra.

When the list of sportscars is examined, although it is true that they are all in the sportscar segment, they do not all compete with each other. To understand the dynamics of the genuine competition which each automobile faces it is necessary to refine the segment into the niches in which they compete as shown in Table B1.1.

Finally, although the automobile industry was taken to illustrate the distinction between an industry, market, segment and niche, these concepts are generic and apply to most industries. For example, even in an industry such as shampoo, where the product is often considered to be a commodity (although not by the managers in the industry), deeper reflection reveals that far from being a commodity industry, there are indeed many niches. For example, the shampoo market can be segmented by:

- *Purpose*: washing hair, washing hair and body, beautifying, making more healthy, male orientated, female orientated.
- *Convenience*: one rinse, conditioner included.
- *Price level*: premium to standard.
- *Promotion*: volume, channel, theme.

One of the major tasks facing strategic market planners in this industry is to continuously strive to redefine their products in unique ways to give them dominance (with the consequent financial superiority) in their niches

Table B1.1   Niches within the UK sportscar market segment

Automobile	Niche characteristics
Ferrari Testarossa Honda NSX Lamborghini Diablo Porsche 911 Toyota Supra	Very high performance, very expensive, highly exclusive
BMW M5 Jaguar XJS Mercedes SL 500	High performance, very expensive, luxurious, highly exclusive
BMW Z3 Mercedes SLK Porsche Boxster	High performance, prestige, expensive but not unreachable image
Ford Probe Toyota MR2	Good performance, more moderate pricing, less exclusive
Mazda MX5 Suzuki Cappuccino	Performance less important than looks and style, more moderate pricing, younger buyers

and so prevent their products from degenerating into commodities.

DEFINING THE BUSINESS: THE TRULY CREATIVE ACT

Defining the business in such a way as to provide strategic advantage ought to be a truly creative act. Managers should be involved in 'seeing into the soul' of their business and understanding just why existing and potential customers purchase their products. They should then meditate on how they could redefine their business to make it fresher and more appealing than the offerings from the other rivals in the niches in which it competes. The managers then need to develop and resolutely pursue those strategies, without deflection, to support this business definition.

In an ideal world a regular review and redefinition of the business would occur. However, in the real world, through pressure from operational or administrative tasks, redefining of the business is often ignored. This process should not be overlooked. Firms that burst ahead of rivals often do so through a redefinition of their business. These alert firms pre-emptively pick up and then amplify weak signals of change from the niches and broader environments in which they operate and then use these as the basis for redefining their business.

However, it often is the case that external events overtake businesses and redefinition then becomes a necessity for the maintenance of margins. For example, in recent years many businesses have suffered from the following types of strategic problems:

- low industry growth;
- overcapacity in the industry;
- many players of equal size;
- high fixed costs;
- standard products with little differentiation;
- crazy new entrants joining the industry and wrecking profitability for all.

All these problems lead to:

- profit stagnation or decline.

In such industry situations the managers of firms that take a supine view of their inability to alter these commercially dismal circumstances are likely to define their businesses so that they reinforce this perspective and contribute to the depressed, unhappy and low profit regime which they unfortunately inhabit. This dejected situation will continue for the majority of firms. The winners that escape from this bleak commercial landscape will be the minority of firms which creatively redefine their business and move to a superior strategic agenda.

The importance of creative redefinition of the business was illustrated clearly in the case of Dunhill in Chapter 1 and is reflected in its subsequent robust financial performance. A further example of the substantial benefits of redefining the business is now provided. Allied-Lyons, the UK-based food and drinks group, has an estate of 2,500 public houses. Unfortunately, since 1989, the pub industry has suffered severe competitive pressures. Allied-Lyons has sought to redress this negative influence by redefining its business (2). This quotation illustrates its approach.

Exactly what can be done to satisfy the more demanding, value-conscious consumers of the 1990s and improve the return on assets is an issue which pub operators are now concentrating their retail skills. Allied which earns an estimated 1.6 per cent of its profits from a directly-managed estate of 2,500 pubs, believes it has found several equally successful answers.

In an attempt to understand the demands of its varied customers, Allied classified its pubs in the mid-1980s according to the community they served, the dominant age and social class of customers, and their drinking habits.

McKeown (Retail services director of Allied-Lyons) has no doubt about what is needed to maintain the pub's place as a social centre.

'You have got to make a visit to the pub an occasion, provide an enjoyable experience that will persuade customers to stay a few hours, and provide the reassurance of consistent quality that will bring them back regularly,' he says.

Allied hopes to achieve these aims with three concepts, each designed to meet the need of a different niche market. Two in particular are transforming some of Allied pubs most threatened with closure.

Under the first concept, the company is converting into Firkin outlets local pubs which had little to offer their neighbourhood but convenience.

Firkin pubs appeal to young drinkers. They feature uncluttered floor space, at least one large table that a dozen people can sit around, young staff – and most of them have a micro-brewery in the cellar producing 10–12 barrels a week of rich brews with names like Dog Bolter.

Pubs that have already been converted – at an average cost of £150,000 – have achieved up to a fivefold increase in turnover.

Plans for Allied's second youth-appeal pub brand, Mr Q's are more ambitious. Pubs that have become stranded by population shifts, often on the edge of 1930s housing estates have been fitted with four or five pool tables, a wall of screens for MTV and video juke boxes.

Firkin and Mr Q's aim to buck the demographic and economic trends; but in the third part of this pubs strategy, Allied is trying to consolidate its position in the mainstream eating-out market for older couples and families.

Allied now seeks to fill a niche between the big pub-restaurant and the bar snacks trade with its Big Steak houses. 'A lot of people still feel uncomfortable in restaurants,' says McKeown. 'They don't like the ritual of ordering, and the waiter hovering around.' So Big Steak incorporates a dining area in the pub and links its service to the bar.

THE PROCESS OF DEFINING THE BUSINESS

Although it is difficult to promulgate precise guidelines for disaggregating a firm into appropriate strategic business units (SBUs), the Strategic Planning Institute (SPI) (3) has produced a methodology and process which can be applied universally to all businesses. This is set out in summary form below.

Step 1: Rationale for defining the business

In general firms do not compete. Rather, as was illustrated through the automobile industry, the firm's individual product market parts compete with rival product market parts of other firms in the niches which that firm occupies. Thus, considering how a firm ought to position itself in its marketplace is too broad a generalization. A firm ought to be broken down into smaller units. For strategic marketing purposes the question should be: Into what units should a firm be broken down so that it competes most effectively in its market niches?

Step 2: Characteristics of the units

The constituent units of any firm ought to be structured in such a way that:

1. They enable strategic marketing effort to be pinpointed. For example, in the case of Allied-Lyons the Firkin and Mr Q's business units enabled the strategic market planners to respond directly to the clear sets of customer groups who used each type of establishment.
2. They ought to be able to form a basis for resource allocation and also provide performance measures. Thus, once again, in the Allied-Lyons case each unit was capable of being treated as a discrete investment centre with measures to show resources allocated and returns received from each pub.
3. They ought to sell a well-defined range of products or services. Allied-Lyons had this.
4. They ought to have a homogeneous set of customers. Allied-Lyons had this.
5. They ought to be in competition with a distinct set of competitors. For Allied-Lyons there was a clear set of competitors, namely other local pubs and restaurants.
6. They ought to cover all phases of the business – design, procurement, manufacturing, marketing, selling and distribution. In the case of Allied-Lyons this was not quite true. However, the manager of each pub can regard it as a largely separate business under his or her control.

When all, or most of these conditions prevail, then the constituent business units ought to be considered not just as units but Strategic Business Units. Thus, in addition to the above, an SBU has the following characteristics:

• It is managed by an SBU manager, largely, as an independent unit. The SBU manager also acts as a link between the SBU and the board of directors.
• It has its own set of goals and strategies which are within broad parameters largely set by the corporate board of directors.
• Each SBU in a particular firm should be able to operate independently of any other SBU.

Although a firm may be segmented along a multitude of axes (for example, Allied-Lyons used clientele, services provided, product provided and location), SPI has suggested that the following approach is likely to be effective for all firms.

Start at the broadest possible level and then segment the firm according to what could be called its natural segments, as set out in Table B1.2.

Typically such a division which sells Products 1 to 7 in markets A to F ought to be able to define its business as a matrix such as shown in Table B1.3.

This segmentation represents the finest division of the business. As can be seen, in the matrix in Table B1.3 there are thirty separate product market configurations (shown by bullets). In a world where serving these markets was costless, obviously the product markets could be served in a really superior fashion if each of these thirty product market configurations were to be designated a separate strategic business unit. However, such a fine subdivision of any firm is likely to be rather expensive and impractical. Having made this initial very fine subdivision, the next step in the process is to recluster these units back into a smaller number of broader units. The advantages of the lower number of units ought to be lower costs and greater control.

At this stage, when managers recluster their firm back into new and unique configurations, they can be most creative and their inventiveness can give their firm a new orientation and provide it with new ways of conducting its business. It is difficult to overemphasize the importance of managers spending a substantial amount of time debating how their firm ought to be structured. Fundamentally, the question which managers must ask at this stage is: Which units should be kept separate or which should be combined? A well-known example of separating two related products because they demand different strategies was the decision by Toyota to have separate business units for the Toyota and Lexus brands.

Units that really do demand different strategies should be kept sepa-

Table B1.2 The natural segments in any business

The natural segments	Typical types of questions
Product families	How many clear families of products are in the business? List them.
Common technologies	How many distinct technologies are used in the manufacture of the product? List them.
Customer groups	How many clearly distinctive customer groups does the business have? List them.
Sales and distribution channels	Does the business need separate sales and distribution channels for each product and each customer group? List them.
Geography	How many different geographical regions are served? List them.

Table B1.3 A typical product market matrix after an initial segmentation

	Market A	Market B	Market C	Market D	Market E	Market F
Product 1	•	•	•	•	•	•
Product 2	•	•			•	•
Product 3	•	•			•	•
Product 4	•	•	•		•	•
Product 5	•	•	•	•	•	
Product 6	•	•		•	•	
Product 7	•	•				

rate while units that can be accommodated with common strategies should be combined. However, usually the situation is not as clear-cut as this. It will often be the case that the issue is fuzzy and there are choices to be made. Debate and disagreement will occur among managers about which units should be combined and which should be separated. In such a situation with, say, a team of ten managers decisions can be made using the SPI (3) criteria set out in Table B1.4. In this table the ten managers take two units at a time and then debate if the answer is yes or no to the five issues set out in the table. They then record their answers and if the number of yeses exceeds the number of nos then they should be kept separate. If the number of nos exceeds the number of yeses they should be combined. If the number of yeses

Table B1.4 SPI criteria for deciding which units to combine and which to separate

Does a pair of units?	Number of yeses	Number of nos	Score
Require different marketing skills?	6	4	Yes
Employ different basic technologies?	7	3	Yes
Exist at different maturity stages of the life cycle?	7	3	Yes`
Occupy different competitive positions?	5	5	0.5 Yes 0.5 No
Permit sensible accounting allocations to be made?	4	6	No

equals the number of nos (i.e. 2.5 each) then there should be further debate until a result is achieved. In Table B1.4 there are 3.5 yeses and 1.5 nos so for this pair of units the result is that they should be kept separate.

The true competitors

In view of the importance of measuring a firm's competitive position relative to its rivals in its niches, it is important for managers to be clear about who are their true competitors. There is no rigorous methodology for doing this but the following quick and dirty method can be informative and revealing. Simply ask the question: If my firm makes a major competitive move, say a price reduction of 10 per cent, which competitors will react?

Those that react are the firm's true competitors. For example, competitive battles between Ferrari, Honda NSX, Lamborghini, Porsche 911 and Toyota Supra are unlikely to have much effect upon the sales of Mazda MX5 and Suzuki Cappuchino.

CONCLUSION

Defining the business is indeed the starting point of strategic planning. It should be a truly creative act in which managers search for new ways of breaking up their firm and then reclustering it into some new and unique combination of units so that it becomes competitively distinctive in its niches and reaps the attendant benefits that such distinction can confer.

NOTES

1. The acquisition of relative power is crucial in giving a firm true strategic advantage. It is not the absolute power of a firm that is strategically important, but its power relative to its true competitors. For example, up until the mid-1990s IBM's absolute power in the computer industry was still immense in terms of measures such as assets, sales, technology, width of product line. However, this firm was severely damaged in the early 1990s because it lost its power relative to newer and much smaller rivals in the crucial PC niche. It lost its niche dominance.

REFERENCES

(1) Abell, D. (1989). *Defining the Business: The Starting Point of Planning*. Prentice-Hall, Englewood Cliffs.
(2) Rawsthorne, P. (1994). More than just a pint and a packet of crisps. *Financial Times*, 3 February, 12.
(3) *PIMS Introductory Briefing*. PIMS Europe Ltd.

B2
Product Market Portfolio

In Chapter B1 a methodology for breaking down any firm into its constituent strategic business units was developed. This methodology does indeed enable managers to see clearly how to address most effectively the niches in which a firm operates. However, the approach is incomplete in that it takes no account of the value or importance that each of the various subunits contributes. For example, if a firm addressed three distinct market niches and 95 per cent of its sales and profits came from one niche while the other two niches combined yielded the remaining 5 per cent of sales and profits, then clearly the greatest amount of managerial attention should be devoted to the firm's largest niche. This chapter will build upon B1 by providing a methodology for evaluating the current and potential contributions from each of the units into which the firm has been divided. This will be achieved by means of a technique known as the product market portfolio.

This technique asserts that to achieve appropriate strategic direction, which in the case of this book is considered to be long-run, robust and superior returns, a firm must continuously appraise itself in terms of:

- the growth balance of its product market niches. In addition to the current range of products that is generating acceptable returns, does the firm have new products for the future which will ensure that as contributions from current products decline they are more than replaced by contributions from new products?

- the competitive balance of its product market niches. How strong is the firm in each of its product market niches relative to its major rivals in each niche?
- the risk balance of its product market niches. How dependent is the firm on, say, just one or two product market niches?[1]

The product market portfolio is a technique which enables judgements about these issues to be made and strategies developed to provide appropriate strategic direction.

PORTFOLIO MANAGEMENT

The disaggregation of a firm into its constituent product market niches enables management to view the firm not as a single entity, but rather as a portfolio of product markets. Such a viewpoint enables managers to develop and implement appropriate strategies for each product market unit and combine this with an assessment of the firm's overall strategic position. Thus, the portfolio approach enables managers to take cognisance of each product market unit's strategic position in relation to:

- life cycle;
- sales volume and sales value;
- cash contribution;
- strategic position relative to its true competitors;
- strategic position in relation to the firm's overall portfolio;
- contribution to the overall risk profile of the firm.

Each of these dynamic[2] determinants of strategic position is now considered more fully.

LIFE CYCLE

In its simplest form the product life cycle concept maintains that, just like people, all commercial products have a certain life during which they pass through a series of stages. Taken together these form the product life cycle. How a product is managed ought to be influenced by the stage it has reached in its life cycle. The concept asserts that the life of a product can be divided into four distinct stages: development, growth, maturity and decline, as shown in Figure B2.1.

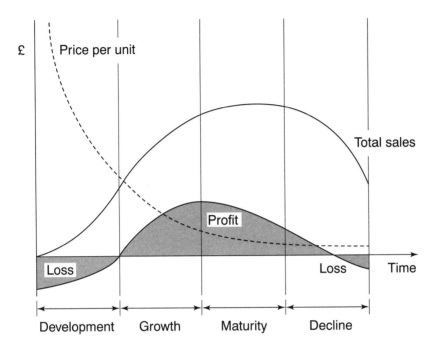

Figure B2.1 The product life cycle

Development stage

This is the stage at which a new product is introduced to the market. Typically in the development stage the following characteristics will be present:

1. There will be a single pioneering firm or a small number of pioneers.
2. The price of the product will tend to be high and sales volume will be low.
3. The introduction of the product will often be regarded as risky because:

   • As the product is new there is no certainty that consumers will purchase it in the required volumes and at the required price.

This fate befell the video disk when it was marketed as a rival to the video cassette recorder.

- The novelty of the product may mean that the competitive rules for success have not been established and consequently the fundamentals of potentially winning strategies have not yet emerged. For example, the winning strategies in the personal computer market have changed remarkably since the product was introduced in the 1980s.
- There is significant investment as production facilities must be constructed and personnel must be recruited and trained.

4. Pricing strategies are likely to be either a skimming or high price strategy or a penetration low price strategy. The merits of each of these strategies is considered in detail in Chapter C3.

Growth stage

At this stage the product has been accepted by the market and a very rapid increase in market size is likely. Typically, new firms (imitators who have seen the success of the pioneers) enter the now less risky market with similar products. Complementing the accelerating increase in sales is a rapid decrease in price levels which is often caused by two major factors:

- To gain market share the increased number of firms engage in price competition.
- Increases in the volume of production leads firms to effect unit cost reductions, through economies of scale and experience effects.[3]

Additionally in order to serve the rapidly expanding market, marketing expenditures, promotion and distribution all require increased resources. Finally, it is in this stage that profits tend to reach a peak.

Maturity

At this stage, although sales may be continuing to increase, they do so at a slower rate and prices and profits begin to decline. The importance of promotion also tends to reduce as consumers typically have adopted particular brands of the product and tend not to switch. The number of competitors may also decline as some firms leave the industry for more lucrative prospects elsewhere or, alternatively, takeovers or mergers may occur.

As the maturity stage proceeds and growth continues to decline consumer saturation develops. This further increases the downward pressures on prices as the competition among the remaining competitors intensifies in their efforts to maintain viable market shares. This competitive pressure may be further exacerbated by those competitors who wish to increase their share of the market – as there is no growth in the market the only source of growth is to take market share from existing competitors.

Decline

At this stage saturation of the market has occurred and absolute sales of the product decline. (On occasions demand for the product will even disappear completely as has happened with the demand for hand-held LED calculators and LED digital watches.) Because of the ensuing overcapacity in the industry there is severe competitive warfare which is manifested in promotion battles (using price competition and advertising), declining profits and withdrawal from the industry by the less successful competitors. This phase is also frequently described as the shakeout phase and is characterized by an increasing concentration of competitors as they form alliances in the hope of remaining viable.

In conclusion, these are the major stages of the product life cycle. A summary of the basic strategic and functional implications of the product life cycle for a leading product in a market niche is given in Table B2.1.

Sales volume and sales value

For effective portfolio management managers must be able to measure both the volume and the value of the sales of each product market unit. For each product market these measures show its contribution and enable judgements to be made about strategic position relative to rivals.

Table B2.1   The basic strategy and functional implications of the product life cycle for a leading product

Stage in life cycle	Development	Growth	Maturity	Decline
Basic strategy	Invest	Invest	Hold	Divest
Marketing				
No of Competitors	Few	Increasing	Decreasing	Fewer
Market size	Small	Growing	Subtle	Decline
Relative market share	Large	Growing	Large and stable	Large and stable
Price	High	High	Falling	Low
Expenses	High	High	Falling	Low
Research	Intense	Reducing	Minimal	None
Finance				
Liquidity	Low	Improving	Improving	High
Profitability	Losses	Greatest	Decreasing	Decreasing or losses
Cash flow	Negative	Improving	Improving	High stable
Leverage	High	High	Decreasing	Low
Dividends	None	Small and increasing	Large	Large
Production				
Volume	Low	Increasing	Stable	Declining
Unit costs	High	High and falling	Falling	Low and stable
Development	Continuing	Slowing	Mininal	None
Technology	New	New	Established	Becoming obsolete
Personnel				
Numbers	Few and increasing	Increasing	Stable or fewer	Fewer
Skills	Being developed	Developing	Developed	Developed
Risk	High	Lower	Lower	Low

Cash contribution

One of the fundamental assertions of portfolio management is that the value of the contribution of each product market unit to the firm should be made using cash as the numeraire.

Strategic position relative to true competitors

As already stated, in strategic marketing terms it is not the absolute position of a product market unit that is important, but rather its position relative to its true competitors which must be captured.

Position in relation to overall portfolio

Portfolio management is about the management of a group of products and not just a single product. Therefore this technique must be capable of showing each product's strategic position relative to all other products in the firm.

Contribution to overall risk profile

A major issue in corporate strategy is the management of the firm's risk profile, ensuring that the balance of product markets served by the firm is such that it is not overexposed to a particular market or set of markets. The product market portfolio enables judgements about a firm's risk profile to be made quickly and accurately.

PRODUCT MARKET PORTFOLIO

In the 1970s the Boston Consulting Group (BCG) devised an approach known as the product market portfolio (2) which has become accepted by many[4] as providing the most suitable framework for accommodating the portfolio management issues raised above.

This technique starts with the assumption that there are just two fundamental determinants of a product's strategic position:

• the relative market share (RMS) of the product, i.e. the share of

the market which a product has relative to the other true competitors in its niche;
* the market growth rate of the product, i.e. the growth rate of a product's market niche.

These two co-ordinates determine the locus of a product's strategic position and the quality of this position is measured in cash flow. Each of these elements – relative market share, market growth rate and cash flow – is now considered in greater detail.

RELATIVE MARKET SHARE AS A DETERMINANT OF COMPETITIVE POSITION

When managers are asked to provide a single measure which will portray accurately the true strategic position of a product, or an SBU, they tend to give a great variety of answers: profits; cash flow; value of assets; return on capital employed; return on investment; return on shareholders' funds; dividends; market growth rate; market share; productivity.

Indeed given enough time managers will provide a list of measures which is almost endless and given more time they can provide almost endless arguments in favour of particular measures and against others. This variety of response begs the question: Is there any single measure which most managers would agree generally reflects the true strategic position of a product or an SBU? Fortunately there is. There would be widespread agreement among managers and researchers that the most important determinant of strategic success for a product, an SBU or a firm is success in the marketplace. In other words gaining a superior position in the market almost certainly guarantees superior returns.

The direction of this relationship is important as it implies that it is the strategies in the marketplace that drive the financials and not, as often happens in firms, the financials that drive the strategy. Examples of this were provided in Chapter 1 and there is rigorous empirical support from the PIMS studies (3).

BCG was among the first researchers in the area of strategy to highlight that it is not a product's actual market share of its niche that determines its strategic market position, but rather the product's market power within its niche, where this is determined by its actual market share relative to the market share enjoyed by rivals. BCG has called this relative market share and defined it is as:

The relative market share of a product is its market share of its niche market divided by the market share of its largest competitor in that niche.

The generic[5] importance of using relative market share rather than market share is illustrated in Table B2.2 by using two hypothetical firms in two hypothetical markets.

Table B2.2 Actual market share data for two hypothetical firms, A and Z

Small turboprop commuter aircraft		Pop music record production	
Competitors	Market share (%)	Competitors	Market share (%)
Firm A	40	Firm Z	20

In Table B2.2 there are two unrelated market niches, small turboprop commuter aircraft and pop music record production. Market share information about one player in each market niche is given:

- In the small turboprop commuter aircraft niche there is one firm called A which has a 40 per cent share of the market.
- In the pop music record production niche there is a firm called Z which has a 20 per cent share of its niche.

The strategic marketing question which arises is which is the more powerful firm in its market niche? Is it firm A which has a 40 per cent actual market share? Is it firm Z which has a 20 per cent actual market share? Is it impossible to say?

The only universally correct answer is that it is impossible to say because the strength of the other competitors in each niche are not known. Hence a judgement cannot be made about the relative power of firm A or firm Z. The additional information needed to make a judgement is now provided in Table B2.3.

As can be seen, the aircraft manufacturer firm A has just one rival – firm B – and so, by definition, firm B must have the remaining 60 per cent of the market. Similarly, in the record industry, firm Z has, as shown, 80 rivals all having just 1 per cent of the market. Therefore, it can now be seen that although firm A has an actual market share of 40 per cent it does not have the greatest power in its market

Table B2.3   Actual market share data for all firms in each market niche

Small turboprop commuter aircraft		Pop music record production	
Competitors	Market share (%)	Competitors	Market share (%)
Firm A	40	Firm Z	20
Firm B	60	Firm Z_1	1
		Firm Z_2	1
		etc. up to	
		Firm Z_{80}	1
Totals	100		100

niche – that accolade belongs to competitor B. Symmetrically, although firm Z has an actual market share of 20 per cent it is strategically much more powerful than firm A as it has a relative market share of 20 times that of any other rival.

BCG's definition of relative market share now enables Table B2.4 to show, more explicitly, the power of each firm in its market niche.

If just two figures are taken from Table B2.4, namely the relative market shares for firm A and firm Z, as shown in Table B2.5 below, then the true the power of the relative measure, as an indicator of strategic market power, is easily seen.

From the definition above and Table B2.5 it is now possible objectively to answer the answer the question: Which is the more powerful firm in its market niche? It is not firm A because it has a relative market share of 0.67. It is firm Z because it has a relative market share of 20.0.

It is possible to make a more detailed market analysis for each firm purely on the basis of this single figure.

Firm A is a follower in its niche. This is known because it has a relative market share of less than 1.0. To be even more precise it can be said that in market share terms firm B is 0.67 times the size of its largest rival and is therefore likely to have a higher unit cost structure and to be a price follower.

Firm Z is a leader in its niche. This is known because it has a relative market share of more than 1.0. To be even more precise it can be said that in market share terms firm Z is 20.0 times the size of its largest rival and is therefore likely to have the lowest units costs in the niche and to be a price setter. It is an extremely powerful firm.

Table B2.4 Actual and relative market share date for all competitors

Small turboprop commuter aircraft			Pop music record production		
Firms	Market share (%)	RMS	Firms	Market share (%)	RMS
Firm A	40	0.67	Firm Z	20	20.0
Firm B	60	1.5	Competitor Z_1	1	0.5
			Firm Z_2	1	0.5
			etc. up to		
			Firm Z_{80}	1	0.5
Totals	100			100	

Table B2.5 Relative market share data for firm A and firm Z

Small turboprop commuter aircraft		Pop music record production	
Competitors	Relative market share	Competitors	Relative market share
Firm A	0.67	Firm Z	20.0

Arithmetic examples to illustrate relative market share

Having illustrated the very real benefits of using relative market share as an indicator of strategic market power, some arithmetic examples to further develop readers' familiarity with the concept are now considered.

Table B2.6 shows the actual and relative market shares for four hypothetical firms in, say, a niche in the computer industry.

As can be seen in Table B2.6 the most powerful firm is Q which has a relative market share of 1.25, indicating that it is 1.25 times as large as its largest competitor P. Similarly, P is the second most powerful firm in its niche with a relative market share of 0.8, indicating that it is 0.8 times the size of the largest firm Q. Finally, R and S are the least powerful firms with relative market shares of 0.1 each, indicating that they are 0.1 times the size of the largest firm Q. Once again, Q is likely to be the price setter and also to enjoy the lowest unit costs.

From this it should be apparent that if a product is a clear market leader it must have a relative market share of greater than 1.0 and sim-

Table B2.6 Strategic market power of every firm within a niche

	Niche in the computer industry			
Firm	P	Q	R	S
Actual market share (%)	40	50	5	5
Relative market share (%)	0.8	1.25	0.1	0.1

ilarly if a product is a market follower it must have a relative market share of less than 1.0.

Table B2.7 shows a situation in the soap market niche and the oil distribution niche where there are a number of players that vie with each other for outright leadership. In the soap niche there are two firms, A and B. In the oil distribution niche there are three firms, Z, Y and X. All of these firms in both niches are joint market leaders which is reflected in their having relative market shares of exactly 1.0.

The relative market share figure of 1.0 is pivotal in understanding the power of the product market portfolio. Thus, when any product has a relative market share of exactly 1.0 this shows that it is a joint

Table B2.7 Actual and relative market share data for all competitors in the two niches

Soap Niche			Oil distribution niche		
Firms	Market share (%)	RMS	Firms	Market share (%)	RMS
Firm A	30	1.0	Firm Z	25	1.0
Firm B	30	1.0	Firm Y	25	1.0
Firm C	25	0.83	Firm X	25	1.0
Firm D	15	0.5	Firm W	15	0.6
			Firm V	10	0.4
			Firm U	10	0.4
Totals	100			100	

market leader. There is at least one other rival product in the niche which has an equal volume of sales. In this type of situation it is likely that there will be intense competitive pressure – often manifested in severe price erosion, quality enhancement and promotion battles – as joint leaders vie with each other in struggles to win outright leadership. Normally the competition will be extremely fierce as each joint leader will believe that with some additional effort and resources it could become the outright leader with all the benefits that this position will normally bring.

Plotting relative market share

In the product market portfolio matrix the relative market share of each product is plotted, as shown in Figure B2.2 on the horizontal axis using a log scale. Although there are no set values for the axis, it will often range from 0.1 to 10 with a score of 1.0 being at the centre of the axis.[6] This means that outright leaders are shown on the lefthand side of the matrix, followers on the righthand side and joint leaders will be located on the centre line of the matrix.

Market growth rate as determinant of competitive position

When asked about the major strategic marketing problems faced by their firms many managers will cite slow market growth. This reflects the prevailing managerial view that markets which have high growth rates tend to be good for firms while those which have low growth rates tend to be bad. This tends to be true, but not in all cases. The logic behind this viewpoint is clear. In high growth markets there is surging demand which makes sales relatively easy at premium prices and, additionally, most firms should be able to increase their sales without having to 'steal' sales from rival firms.

In low growth markets sales may be more difficult to generate and interfirm rivalry may lead to price or promotion battles, which tend to reduce profitability for all. In low market growth situations firms often overcome their dismal market circumstances and prospects through redefining their business (as shown in Chapter B1). Rather than addressing the poor market to which they have historically addressed, they focus more intensely upon one or more particular niches and serve them in a superior fashion.

Plotting market growth rate

As shown in Figure B2.2 the growth rate of the market is plotted on the vertical axis using a simple percentage scale. Once again the range on the axis will depend upon the analysis being undertaken. For example, in a high growth market such as information technology the range might extend from a low of 10 per cent, to an average of 30 per cent, to a high of 50 per cent. In a much lower growth market such as tobacco the range might extend from a low of -10, to an average of 0 per cent, to a high of 10 per cent. The scale chosen should be such that the average market growth rate is near the centre of the vertical axis. This enables markets to be divided into two types: high growth markets which will be in the top half of the matrix and low growth markets which will be in the lower half.

Thus the two measures relative market share market and market growth rate are the two co-ordinates that determine the strategic location of products in the matrix.

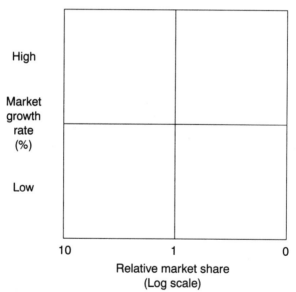

Figure B2.2   Constructing a product market portfolio

Value of annual sales

The final element in the construction of the matrix is showing value of annual sales of each product in the firm. This is done by plotting for each product, at the co-ordinates provided by the intersection of each product's relative market share and market growth rate, circles whose areas are proportional to each product's annual sales.

Illustration of a product market portfolio

The product market portfolio is illustrated by reference to Alban Chemicals whose data for its 1998 product market portfolio are reproduced in Table B2.8 and whose actual product market portfolio is shown in Figure B2.3.

Table B2.8   Data for Alban Chemicals product market portfolio, 1998

Products	Alban Chemicals sales volume (tonnes)	Largest rival sale volume (tonnes)	Alban Chemicals RMS	Alban Chemicals annual sales (£mn)
Chemical A	18,400	5,000	3.7	3.1
Chemical B	26,000	9,000	2.9	4.1
Chemical C	44,000	140,000	0.31	5.0
Chemical D	1,500	4,000	0.37	0.4
Chemical E	0	0	N/A	0
Total	89,900	158,000	N/A	12.6

Product Analysis

As can be seen in Table B2.8, Alban Chemicals enjoys dominance in the markets for Chemical A and Chemical B and although these products are cash cows[7] their markets have zero or negative growth. The main product in the Alban Chemicals portfolio, Chemical C, has an excellent growth rate of 10 per cent – and should continue to be a major contributor to the firm for many years. It should be noted that Chemical D has a low relative market share. Finally, the product Chemical E is currently not part of Alban Chemicals portfolio of products. Although the market growth rate for this product is low, Alban Chemicals believes that it can enter this market and enjoy substantial

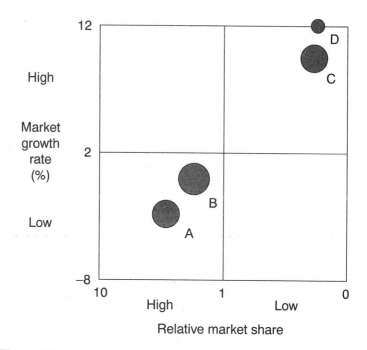

Figure B2.3   Alban Chemicals product market portfolio, 1998

strategic success because of the relative lack of competition and the
low barriers to entry.

Portfolio balance

Alban Chemicals believes that it needs a new major product to provide future growth: this will be Product E. The firm will continuously
strive to increase its relative market share. Currently it believes it has
competitive balance with market dominance in two products,
Chemicals A and B. It believes that the risk profile of the firm should
be reduced by reducing its dependence on Chemical C. This will be
achieved through the introduction of Chemical E.

CASH: THE NUMERAIRE OF PERFORMANCE

The product market portfolio of Alban Chemicals was considered
exclusively from a marketing perspective: relative market share, mar-

ket growth rate and value of annual sales. However, in addition to this perspective is the portfolio's financial dimension. Knowing the position of any product in the matrix ought to enable a prediction to be made about that product's likely cash characteristics. The likely cash characteristics of the various locations in the matrix are shown in Figure B2.4 and then considered in greater detail.

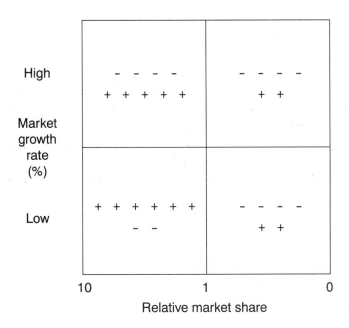

Figure B2.4 The cash characteristics of various locations in the product market portfolio

PROBLEM CHILDREN PRODUCTS

Products in this location tend to be major absorbers of cash because they have the following characteristics:

- *Low relative market share.* They are followers so they are likely to have relatively high unit cost positions, almost certainly higher unit costs than the market leader. Yet the products must be sold at the price set by the market leader, a price which is likely to be strategically acceptable to the leader but too low for higher unit cost followers.

- *Life cycle.* They are likely to be at the development/growth stage of their product life cycles. Such products require cash in order to build their positions and so cash flows are likely to be negative.
- *Market growth rate.* Market growth rate is high and product growth rate will require expenditure to keep up with the market. This will also tend to make cash flows negative. If anything this view actually understates the case because a firm with follower products is likely to wish to grow at a faster rate than the market so that it can improve its position relative to the leader.

This exclusively pessimistic view of problem children is balanced by a more optimistic one. All problem children have a major attribute – they are in fast growing markets which offer the best prospects for the future. Investment in such products is crucial because they are the products of the future that will build the firm's dynasty of products to provide continuing strategic stability.

Thus, the name problem children really is appropriate: for such products to become successful substantial investment in them must be undertaken. However, this investment does not guarantee future success because the current leaders are likely to fight fiercely to retain their leadership positions. Such investment is likely to be quick and large rather than incremental, say a doubling of investment rather than an annual increase of 10 per cent – a risky strategy. Investing in problem children will therefore tend to be hazardous, but failure to invest in them may be even more dangerous and could jeopardize the firm's long-term future if the current products decline and there are no replacements. In conclusion, problem children usually represent the riskiest of products in a firm's portfolio.

Strategies for problem children

Because of the costs of supporting, i.e. investing in, problem children firms can usually only support a limited number. Indeed supporting too many cash-absorbing problem children is a major, and potentially fatal, strategic error that many firms have committed. Irrespective of the attributes of each problem child, if their consolidated negative cash flows are such that they are causing the firm severe financial problems there must be disposals. In this type of situation selectivity becomes the issue. Selections must be made between the various cash-hungry candidates (each considering itself the most worthy). It is difficult to be prescriptive about which should be:

- *built*:[8] receive additional investment;
- *harvested*: retained but not receive additional investment;
- *divested*: sold.

Answers to the following questions can assist such decisions:

- What are the relative market shares of each candidate? Those which have relative market shares closest to 1.0 or that are moving westwards in the matrix will be in the strongest positions in their market niches and are likely to offer the best prospects.
- What is the ratio of cash flow to sales for each candidate? Those whose cash flow to sales is largest are likely to be the best candidates.
- Each year is cash flow to sales increasing, static or decreasing? If it is decreasing, this may indicate that the product is buying market position, i.e. it is draining cash to gain position and may never make a positive contribution. So increasing cash flow to sales candidates is more likely to be successful.

Finally, from a strategic marketing perspective it is worth remembering that it is generally better to have a small number of relatively strong positions than a larger number of weak or average positions.

If a firm has a small number of problem children relative to the other products in its portfolio, there are three clear strategies: build, harvest or divest.

Build

This strategy means that the product should be strongly supported with appropriate resources and pushed aggressively in its market niche. If successful, this will cause the product to move westwards in the matrix and may ultimately lead to leadership in the niche.

Harvest

This strategy reflects the view that the degree of competition in the market niche is so severe that the firm's problem child, even with the allocation of significant resources, is likely to fail. Consequently, the strategy is to maximize the cash flows from the product by investing as little as possible in it. This will cause the product to lose relative market share and drift eastward in the matrix with its eventual abandonment. However, its cash flow should have been maximized.

Divest

This strategy reflects the view that the degree of competition in the market niche is so severe that the firm's problem child, even with significant resources being allocated to it, is likely to fail. Consequently a more attractive option is to sell the product[9] to the leader in the niche and use the cash for other products. This type of action is often very attractive to the leader as it simultaneously removes a competitor and also increases the leader's relative market share.

STAR PRODUCTS

Products in this location tend to be either net cash contributors or else cash neutral for the following reasons:

High relative market share

The products have high relative market shares – they are leaders – so they are likely to have relatively low unit cost positions, almost certainly lower unit costs than the market followers (those competitors who have a relative market share of less than 1.0). In addition, the leader will be in a strong position to set price at a level that is most strategically acceptable. This price could be a skimming price and would be at a relatively high level so that the leader, who will have the largest volume of all the competitors, will make super profits.

While this strategy has the advantage of large profits it has the disadvantage that it creates a price umbrella (4) under which smaller, higher unit cost followers may shelter while the size of the profits will encourage new entrants. Alternatively, a penetration pricing strategy in which a lower price, say as a certain percent above unit costs, is set will have the strategic advantage that it will be much more difficult for followers to generate substantial profits. In addition it will lower the attractiveness of the market segment to new entrants. However, the strategy will have the disadvantage that profits will be lower, in the short term at least.

Life cycle

Star products are likely to be at the growth stages of their product life cycles. They enjoy strong strategic positions and they are strong in attractive high growth markets. However, because they will have problem children followers with ambitions to be leaders, they must continuously invest to defend and enhance their relative positions. Consequently, although the cash inflows are very large, because of the expenditures necessary to preserve leadership the cash outflows are also very large and the net cash flow is therefore likely to be neutral or mildly positive.

Market growth rate

Because of the high growth rate of the market and the necessity of defending leadership, the cash flow is likely to be neutral or mildly positive.

Once again the name of star really is appropriate. These are successful products which should bring greater and greater rewards, i.e. cash, to the firm.

Strategies for stars

Although it might appear that the more stars in a portfolio the better this may not necessarily be the case. Thus, as stars are at the growth stage of their product life cycles, having a portfolio comprised mainly or exclusively of stars will certainly bring great benefit, but such a portfolio is unbalanced. First, it does not have sufficient cash generators for today. Second, as the growth of the stars decays there will not be a sufficient number of products at the development stage to provide attractive cash flows in the future.

- *Build*. Under this strategy it is believed that the star can build even greater dominance in its market niche, i.e. a higher relative market share. Increased dominance ought to increase further the unit cost gap between the star and its followers, leading either to increased profits for the star or lower levels of profits for the followers. In order to do this significant resources must be invested.
- *Hold*. This strategy is based upon the view that sufficient dominance in the niche has been obtained and that rather than continue to devote resources to the already successful and established star, from a corporate perspective, these resources would be of greater benefit if provided to other products which do not have dominance, but have excellent future prospects, i.e. problem children.

CASH COW PRODUCTS

Products in this location tend to be major generators of cash for the following reasons:

- *High relative market share*. They have high relative market shares – i.e. they are leaders – in low growth markets so they are likely to have the lowest unit costs in the industry. Therefore the price can be set at an 'entry deterring' level. Because of the leader's low cost position it can set the price at a level which is attractive and profitable for the leader but unattractive for the followers and so low that new entrants are deterred from entering.
- *Life cycle*. Such products are likely to be in the mature or decline stage of their life cycles so the niche is likely to be less attractive to existing competitors and new entrants.
- *Market growth rate*. The market growth rate will be relatively low and this will have two major effects. First, the resources required to compete in this market are likely to be considerably less than for a fast-growing market. Second, the low growth rate will reinforce its unattractiveness to new entrants.

Strategies for cash cows

It could be argued that a firm could not have too many cash cows in its portfolio – after all each one will be a net contributor of cash. However, a portfolio comprised exclusively of cash cows would be unbalanced from a long-term perspective. As some cash cows died there would be no new products coming onstream to be the cash cows of tomorrow. Thus, in addition to its cash cows, a portfolio ought to have problem children and star products which will be the cash cows of the future. Thus the cash inflows from today's cash cows ought not to be returned to them but should be transferred to the developing products of the future.

- *Hold.* Dominance in the niche has been achieved and as the market is in decline the primary strategy ought to be to maintain position rather than build it more. There ought to be other products in the future which will, over their life, yield superior returns.
- *Harvest.* Such a strategy would be appropriate when the product appeared to be in terminal decline – the market will disappear entirely. In such a situation no resources should be allocated to the product, rather as much cash as possible should be harvested from it.

DOG PRODUCTS

Products in this location tend to be major absorbers of cash for the following reasons:

- *Low relative market share*: they have low relative market shares – i.e. they are followers – in low growth markets so they are likely to have relatively high unit costs and to be obliged to charge the price set by the industry leader. It is likely that the prevailing price will, because of their high unit costs, make such products loss makers or at best marginally profitable.
- *Life cycle*: such products are likely to be in the mature or decline stage of their life cycles and so if a strong position has not been developed at this stage it is unlikely to be developed in the future. Note that to develop a dominant position the problem child product must win market share from the leader – an unlikely situation.
- *Market growth rate*: the market growth rate will be relatively low

and this will have the effect of limiting the options of the dog products, i.e. the competitive rules of the game are well established,
brand loyalty is likely to be established and new ways of attract-
ing additional customers are unlikely to be available.

Strategies for dogs

It could be argued that a firm should have no dogs in its portfolio.
Each will be a net absorber of cash and so a firm would be better off
without them. However, there are two major arguments in favour of
having a limited number of dogs. First, not all dogs lose money. There
are examples of dog products which have been consistent earners of
cash. Second, there may be strategic reasons for having dog products,
for example, in order to have a complete product line. Thus it is not
unusual for carbonated drinks companies to derive most of their cash
from two or three star or cash cow products and also to have relatively small dog products. Although these absorb cash they do provide the
firm with a complete product range.

- *Hold*. Dogs may be held to provide a complete product range or
  for some other strategic reason.
- *Harvest*. Such a strategy would be appropriate when the product
  appeared to be in terminal decline, i.e. the market will disappear
  entirely. In such a situation no resources should be allocated to the
  product, rather as much cash as possible should be harvested from it.
- *Divest*. If a dog product is a genuine and major absorber of cash
  then, if possible, it should be sold. Although such a product may
  be very unattractive and prove impossible to sell, there are situations in which it can be an attractive buy, for example, to sell a
  dog product line to the largest rival. This situation is attractive to
  both parties for the following reasons:

  — the seller: a cash absorbing part of the portfolio has been sold.
  — the buyer: a competitor has been removed from the market and
    in addition the additional market share acquired will boost the
    buyer's relative market share.

- *Monitoring*. Although this is not a strategy it is vital that dog prod-

ucts are very closely monitored. Their strategic position is extremely weak and there is always a danger that managers will demand
more and more corporate cash in order to sustain them. This process
turns the dog product into a 'cash trap' (2) in which ever increasing
amounts of cash are injected into a doomed business that will never
yield any return and may ultimately bankrupt the entire firm.

In summary the 'cash aspect' of the product market portfolio makes a
dual contribution. First, it enables planners to see how well the actual
cash contributions from products accord with expected cash contributions as predicted by their positions in the product market portfolio. If
there is a significant discrepancy between the actual and the expected
this ought to be a cause for deeper investigations. Second, it enables
planners to perform an important central treasury function: namely to
examine the overall cash balance of the SBU. This process ensures
that the overall cash flow is in balance where it is such that the cash
generated by cash cow products, plus perhaps star products, is sufficient to ensure funding for dilemma products, dog products and to
meet overheads and dividend payments.

The product market portfolio is thus a beguilingly simple device
which integrates the market function and the finance function into a
unified strategic tool which can be used to:

- describe the strategic position of each individual product of a company and its overall portfolio of products;
- diagnose the strategic position of each individual product of a company and its overall portfolio of products;
- prescribe strategies for each individual product of a company and
  also its overall portfolio of products.

PRODUCT MOVEMENTS

When considering the movements of products they can be starkly categorized into 'ideal' and 'disaster' movements. Figure B2.5 shows the ideal
movements of products that reflect a well-managed portfolio in which the
products are moving in an 'ideal sequence' through their life cycles.

In contrast to the ideal sequence, there is a 'disaster sequence' as
shown in Figure B2.6. In this case all products are losing market share
to rivals and the portfolio is becoming progressively weaker.

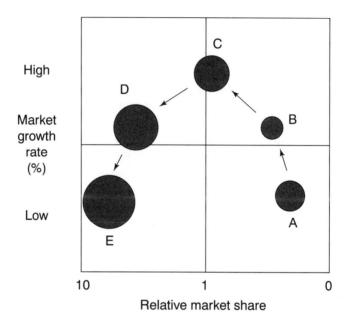

Figure B2.5   Ideal movements of products over time

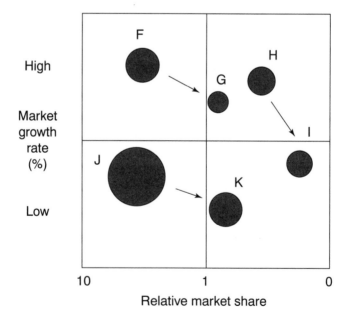

Figure B2.6   Disaster movements of products over time

CASH MOVEMENTS

Complementing product movements are cash movements and once again, as shown in Figures B2.7 and B2.8, there are 'ideal movements' and 'disaster movements'.

Figure B2.7 shows the ideal movement of cash: cash is withdrawn from today's cash cows to fund a limited number of problem children products and build a dynasty of products which will be the future stars and cash cows.

In contrast to the ideal use of cash, Figure B2.8 shows its disastrous deployment. The cash being generated by the cash cows is returned to them, a strategy which is likely to be a poor one because these cash cow products are in the declining stage of their life cycles. Their futures are likely to be at best limited and at worst none at all.

It should be noted that it is only in theory that this type of cross-subsidizing of problem children products can be conducted with ease. Normally managers who have products which are generating cash surpluses will fight tenaciously to have 'their' cash returned to 'their' products. They will argue in the following vein:

'This product of mine has for many years contributed cash to this division. Indeed if it wasn't for the contribution from this product the division's financial performance would be poor. Therefore for the good of the firm this product must receive continuous investment. Furthermore, the problem child product which it is intended to be funded has never ever made any money and furthermore there is no guarantee that it will.'

Although this type of argument may be correct from a single product perspective, when the overall portfolio is considered it can be seen to be flawed.

BALANCE IN PRODUCT MARKET PORTFOLIO

Balance is concerned with the overall composition of the portfolio in the following terms:

- *Risk balance*. Is the portfolio such that the firm's risk is spread or

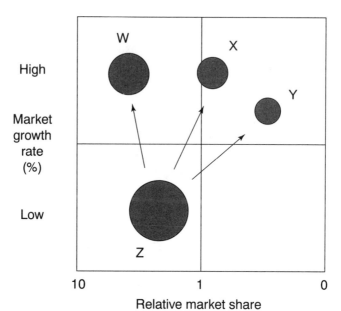

Figure B2.7   Ideal movements of cash over time

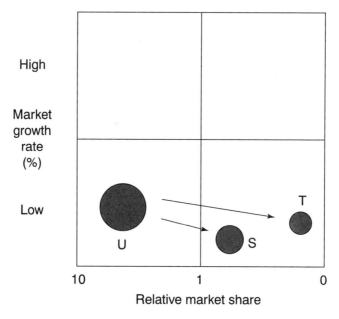

Figure B2.8   Disaster movements of cash over time

is the firm too dependent upon just one or two products?

- *Product balance.* Is the firm's product portfolio structured so that there is:

    — a limited number of problem children products which will be the firm's cash generators of the future?

    — a number of stars which are enjoying dominance in their markets and will be major cash generators in the future?

    — a number of cash cows which generate substantial cash today?

    — a limited number of dog products which are carefully monitored and controlled?

Finally Figure B2.9 shows a balanced product market portfolio.

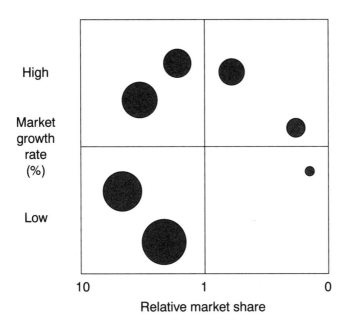

Figure B2.9   A balanced portfolio

Postscript

In the author's experience the achievement of a balanced portfolio is a most difficult task. Many firms have an unbalanced portfolio similar to that shown in Figure B2.10. In this type of portfolio there tends to be one absolutely dominant generator of cash which, although regarded by management as vital, nonetheless solicits the view that the firm's dependence on this single product must be reduced by 'bringing on stream' new products. Unfortunately in most cases this task proves impossible and the unbalanced portfolio becomes a permanent feature.

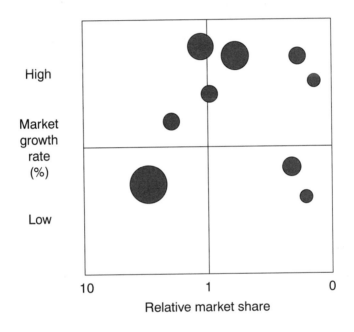

Figure B2.10 An unbalanced portfolio typical of many firms

LIMITATIONS OF THE PRODUCT MARKET PORTFOLIO

Although the product market portfolio is a most valuable technique for strategic planning, there are many criticisms of the approach, some of which are set out below.

Just two factors determine strategic position

The only determinants of strategic position and hence strategic direction are relative market share and market growth rate. It could be argued that this is too narrow a view as good strategic decisions often require a more comprehensive analysis of the factors which determine strategic position. The following factors may be influential in determining strategic position:

- technological lead, for example, Hewlett Packard has always sought to be a leader;
- favourable location, for example, being close to the City of London gives a competitive advantage to many financial institutions;
- political influence, for example, some oil companies will use political connections to help secure extraction rights and to help negotiate advantageous tax arrangements;
- style, for example, Levi 501 jeans command superior margins because of their accepted style;
- relative product quality, for example, Japanese car manufacturers enjoy premium prices because of their reputation for quality;
- reputation, for example, Waterford Crystal commands a premium price because of its reputation;
- low cost sources of supply, for example the low labour costs of emerging Asian countries have given many manufacturers located there considerable competitive advantage.

Only high relative market share positions are desirable

This assumption seems to imply that the only products of real strategic value are those which have the highest relative market shares in their served markets. It may be the case that products in such positions are likely to occupy the highest returns, but it is not an inexorable law that low relative market share products must earn inferior returns. There are many examples of low relative market share players earning superior returns. For example, premium priced 'designer beers' recently introduced into the UK markets have small relative market shares. Yet, because of superior promotion these beers tend to generate returns which are superior to those generated by high relative market share established beers.

Relationship between relative market share and profitability

The matrix suggests that the relationship between relative market share, and profitability is axiomatic, i.e. the higher the relative market share, the higher the profits. This may not always be the case:

The latest entrants into a market must by definition be the lowest relative market share competitors. However, they may enjoy the latest and widely available technology which gives them unit cost advantages in relation to larger share players. For example, in the personal computer industry the manufacturing process for many late entrants is one where components are manufactured in a low labour cost country, say, Malaysia. They are then assembled and branded in the higher cost target market region, say, Europe.

Low relative market share competitors may have an inbuilt advantage. For example, Norwegian aluminium smelters have the advantage of relatively cheap electricity.

Not all products have unit costs which are directly influenced by volumes. For example, it may not be in the best interests of high street banks continuously to enlarge their branch networks to increase their relative market share as the marginal costs of such a strategy may be greater than the marginal benefits.

Large share competitors may be subject to government control and regulation. Thus, in the recently privatized UK industries, because of the market power possessed by many of the players, government watchdogs have been established to monitor and prevent abuse of this power.

High growth markets are best

The matrix implies that high growth markets are the most fruitful ones in which to operate. This may not always be so. The entry barriers may be so high that the returns, even with high growth rates, are not deemed to be satisfactory. For example, the entry costs to the aero engines industry or the large aircraft manufacturing industry are now so high that major new entrants look unlikely.

The level of competition is so severe that it nullifies any advantage that the high market growth rate brings. For example, in the personal computer industry the severity of competition ensures that most manufacturers fail.

The competitive rules of the industry have not yet emerged and major strategic errors are likely to occur. This situation is likely to occur in high growth emerging industries. For example, in the rapidly growing information superhighway industry it is not yet clear who the winners are going to be and how they will win. Thus, the impact that telecommunications companies will have on retail banking and symmetrically the impact of retail banking on telecommunications is unclear.

Competitive equilibrium in modestly growing markets may be superior. For example, in industries where there is a small number of established competitors that abide by 'industry rules' a state of competitive equilibrium can develop which will often permit all the incumbents to enjoy acceptable returns. Thus, in spite of the often publicized rivalry between Coca-Cola and Pepsi Cola both companies are and have been for many years consistently profitable.

Dog products are worthless

The matrix suggests that dog products are worthless and should be sold. However, there are many examples of companies having dog products which, far from draining cash, make substantial cash contributions. For example, there are many small consulting firms whose scale is minute when compared to large well-known international firms and yet these apparently dog firms often enjoy remarkable success. They tend to achieve superiority by their flexibility and ability to tailor to local needs.

Definition of relative market share

The definition of relative market share is considered by many to be too narrow a view of power in the market. A false impression may be developed through comparing market share to just one rival. This is illustrated by a hypothetical example. In Table B2.9 it can be seen that firm A and firm Z both have a relative market share of 1.0 in their markets – they are both joint leaders. However, the competitive terrain in each market is distinctively different. In the automobile market there are five equally balanced competitors all having an actual market share of 20 per cent: a situation which may lead to intense competition if one of the competitors tries to establish outright leadership.

In the computer market there are two dominant players, Z and Z_1 and then 60 other players with a market share of just 1 per cent. In the computer market it is more likely that Z and Z_1 will reach some type of competitive agreement than the other competitors.

A definition that captures the nature of the competition is provided by the Strategic Planning Institute (3): Your market share divided by the sum of the market shares of your three largest competitors. Thus in the above case the PIMS market shares for A and Z are:

A has a relative market share of:

$$\frac{20}{20 + 20 + 20} = 0.3$$

While Z has a relative market share of:

$$\frac{20}{20 + 1 + 1} = 0.9$$

Thus the PIMS measure shows Z to have much more relative power, which indeed it does.

Table B2.9 Relative market share may not reveal competitive dynamics of market

Automobile market			Computer market		
Competitors	Market share (%)	RMS	Competitors	Market share (%)	RMS
Firm A	20	1.0	Firm Z	20	1.0
Firm B	20		Firm Z_1	20	
Firm C	20		Firm Z_2	1	
	20		etc up to		
	20		Firm Z_{60}	1	
Totals	100			100	

The served market

In comparing products it is essential that the comparisons are like with like. For example, to compare the relative market share of a small local consulting company with a major international consulting house may be inappropriate as they do not really compete in the same served markets. As shown in Chapter B1, great attention must be paid to defining the business in an appropriate manner as failure to do so will lead to mistaken assumptions on relative market share.

CONCLUSIONS

In spite of such criticisms the product market portfolio is still a strategic tool of immense usefulness. It is difficult to think of any other technique which so succinctly, comprehensively and effectively captures strategic position and suggests strategic direction. In short, for any firm, the technique can be used to:

- describe the strategic position of each individual product;
- portray the overall portfolio of products;
- diagnose the strategic position of each individual product;
- assess the overall balance of the portfolio;
- prescribe strategies for each individual product and the overall portfolio.

In addition the technique can be used at many levels:

- product level, where the portfolio of products is considered;
- SBU level, where the portfolio of business units is considered;
- industry level, where the relative positions of firms in the industry are considered.

  Irrespective of the level at which it is considered the product market portfolio can be considered to be the key to an appropriate strategic agenda.

NOTES

1. It is often the case that firms are highly dependent upon just one product area. For example, most major tobacco companies, in spite of attempting to diversify out of tobacco, are still highly dependent upon this market.
2. These are called dynamic because they change over time, i.e. the influence of life

cycle in 2000 will be somewhat different from its influence in 1995.

3. For further information on experience effects see (1).
4. There are of course many criticisms of this approach.
5. Generic importance means that the rules apply irrespective of the industry. In this example two obviously unconnected industries were used. In practice the industries chosen do not matter.
6. The scoring on the horizontal axis will be tailored to the particular circumstances which occur in any analysis. For example, the scoring could range from an RMS of 0.01 to an RMS of 100.
7. See page 138 for explanations of these terms.
8. See earlier for explanations of these terms.
9. This type of strategy is more often appropriate at the SBU level of portfolio analysis rather than the product level.

REFERENCES

(1) McNamee, P. B. (1985). *Tools and Techniques for Strategic Management.* Pergamon, Oxford.
(2) Henderson, B. (1970). The product portfolio, *Perspectives*, 66.
(3) Buzzell, R. D. and Gale, B T. (1990). *The PIMS Principles: Linking Strategy to Performance.* Free Press, New York.
(4) Hedley, B. (1976). A fundamental approach to strategy development, *Long Range Planning*, December 2–11.

B3
Analysing the Environment

In Chapter 1 the viewpoint was expressed that: The industry characteristics don't matter. It's the structural position that counts. It is now time to temper this observation with the caveat that, although a firm's structural position – its strategy – is a fundamental determinant of its success, a major influence upon its strategy ought to be the ability of the firm's managers to analyse and respond with appropriate strategies to its environment. Failure of senior managers to be responsive to the environment will often lead to corporate failure. Research studies (1,2) and casual observation show that sensitive and informed responses to environmental change are often a prerequisite to successful strategic market planning. For example, in the UK those city centre grocery retailers who failed to appreciate that grocery shopping would become a weekly event with the car playing central role and who did not move to out-of-town shopping centres with large car parks have generally failed or have not prospered. Similar examples of failure to adapt to changed environmental circumstances have occurred in almost all industries and these types of cases confirm the necessity of effective environmental analysis and response.

In the strategic market planning process there are two major axes on which the environment may be analysed, namely:

- analysing today's environment;
- analysing the future environment.

ANALYSING TODAY'S ENVIRONMENT

This analysis involves assessing which elements in the environment are currently impacting in some way upon the firm and assessing their effects. There is a natural inclination to assume that the significant changes which are taking place today must be obvious. This is not necessarily so. Only the more astute managers are able to discern truly critical environmental changes which are often hidden to others until the strategic opportunity has passed. For example, Microsoft's development and bundling of the initial standard operating systems for IBM-type personal computers has now provided it with global dominance, and commensurate profits, in the personal computer software market. Microsoft's deft development of this market niche was not universally perceived until the company had dominance.

ANALYSING THE FUTURE ENVIRONMENT

In many ways this is much more important as it involves forecasting the future in which the firm is likely to operate and assessing how it will be affected. There are some very real difficulties with this type of analysis.

Difficulty one

When considering the future environment in which the firm will operate, it is not certain that the firm will be in the same business or the same market niches in the future as it is today. For successful strategic market planning, it is essential that firms continuously question the assumption that those niches in which they currently concentrate are likely to be the best in the future. Hence forecasting the future for any firm on the basis that it will be the same environment as the current one may not be correct. For example, the nature of the environment for UK petrol retailing has changed dramatically in the 1990s. Because superstores had entered the petrol retailing market and were competing on the basis of very low price, many traditional petrol retailers came to the conclusion that selling petrol was less profitable than selling convenience goods. The reaction of many major petrol retailers was a massive transition of their traditional petrol stations into convenience stores. The extent of this transformation is shown in Table B3.1.

Table B3.1 Changes in the number of forecourt stores in the UK, 1989–93

Number of forecourt stores 1989	Number of company owned forecourt stores 1993	% change
637	4,363	585

Source: (3)

Difficulty two

Accurate forecasting for, say, even three years ahead is notoriously difficult and most precise mathematical forecasts tend to be fairly incorrect (4). One major reason for this is that unforeseen dramatic events occur which change utterly the assumptions upon which the original forecast was made. For example, in the 1990s one of the world's fastest growth regions was eastern Europe, a development not forecast even in the 1980s. Similarly, the future competitive consequences of the development of global digital superhighways cannot be confidently forecast, even though it is certain to have dramatic effects. Yet forecasts must be made. Senior managers have a major responsibility to forecast accurately the future environment in which their firm will operate. How can this difficulty be overcome? There are no easy answers but below is an approach in three stages which can be of help.

Stage 1

Qualitative rather than mathematical forecasts may be a more useful starting point in strategic market planning. As such planning is concerned with long-run strategic issues that fundamentally shape the ways in which business is conducted, being able to forecast 'sea change' events may be much more important than being able to give an accurate percentage change in market growth rate or currency rate. For example, to any firm which traded with eastern Europe in the 1980s a forecast of the break-up of the Soviet Union and the general disintegration of eastern Europe would have been much more important than, say, a forecast of percentage deviations in currency alignments or a forecast of changes in trade patterns. The political and economic upheaval in that region has been so profound that it swamps all other business issues. A splendid example of such a qualitative forecast was made in 1980 by Peter Drucker:

> As a result of demographics, the Soviet Union thus faces internal problems for which communism has no answers. It will have to retrench either industrially or militarily, or it will have to reform the collective farm, which can hardly be done without political convulsion. It cannot escape rising tensions between the population of a developed European Russia and the fast-growing populations of a developing Asian Russia. With the next twenty-five years the Soviet Union will be faced by the same kind of racial, ethnic, religious, and cultural tensions that have split asunder all other nineteenth-century empires since World War II (5).

It should be noted that this remarkable forecast contains no figures: it simply sets out the major structural/strategic changes which Drucker foresaw occurring in the Soviet Union. For managers to be able to make this type of qualitative forecast of the future 'ground rules' for their own firm and its industry can be invaluable. Such forecasts can be made by harnessing the opinion of managers and experts from outside the firm. Thus, a starting point for forecasting the future environment is to promote managerial discussion, without figures, of those major broad influences which are likely to have dramatic effects upon the firm. After this process, detailed marketing and other forecasts can be undertaken.

Stage 2

Managers should be wary of quantitative forecasts which claim to be highly accurate. For most business situations it is rare to find highly accurate forecasts. For example, in spite of enormous resources being devoted to forecasting future currency values such as the pound sterling's relationship with other world currencies, surprisingly such forecasts are quickly proved to be incorrect. This type of inaccuracy tends to prevail in almost all areas of business activity, including forecasts of future sales of products and market trends. For example, the received UK industry forecasts for such diverse products and services as: traffic growth through airports; sales of personal computers based upon specific chips; holiday travel; cinema attendance; numbers of students in higher education, all tend to be highly inaccurate. Although quantitative forecasts are necessary and must be made they should not become managerial acts of faith.

Stage 3

With the development of personal computers and their associated easy-to-use spreadsheet packages it is now possible for managers to build their own adjustable forecasting models. Initial models can be built and when events occur managers can change the original assumptions and develop new forecasts.

JUDGEMENT PLUS BETTING

No manager can forecast the future with certainty so forecasting the future business environment is always a risk – it is a bet. The odds of this bet will vary from industry to industry, from era to era, from country to country, and will usually be proportional to the time scale of the strategic market plan. Again it will always be a risk so what approach can be used to minimize it? Traditionally managers seek to do this by assuming, often incorrectly, that the future will be quite similar to the past. This leads to an assumption that the future will be a fairly modest extrapolation of the past. Although this conservative risk-averse approach may help a manager to avoid problems, it is unlikely to build strategic advantage. To build unique strategic advantage managers should forecast using the above three-stage methodology which is summarized as follows:

- Stage 1. Qualitative scenario setting of those truly major environmental changes which are likely to occur.
- Stage 2. Quantitative forecasts of the way these major environmental influences are likely to occur and how they are likely to affect the firm – in terms of sales and profitability.
- Stage 3. Build spreadsheet forecasting models in which the assumptions can be changed as conditions change.

This approach to environmental forecasting can be used to make forecasts about the key environmental influences on the firm. These are now discussed.

KEY ENVIRONMENTAL INFLUENCES

A fundamental and natural question when appraising the environment for any firm is this: Of all the environmental influences that impact upon a firm which are the key ones? Clearly the impact of specific elements in the environment has different effects on different industries. To illustrate, Table B3.2 shows what would often be agreed to be the most influential environmental influence in a selection of industries.

As can be seen from Table B3.2, a fundamental environmental determinant of success in the banking industry is the level of bad debt, i.e. banks which manage this most effectively are likely to be the most successful. In contrast in the personal computer industry those firms which are best able to integrate the latest technology into their operations are likely to be most successful.

Table B3.2   Key environmental influences on particular industries

Industry	Key environmental issues
Banking	Economy (i.e. level of bad debts)
Personal computers	Technology
Defence	Government
European agriculture	European Union policies
Luxury consumer goods	Disposable income
Oil industry	Political stability
Branded carbonated drinks	Advertising
Beer	Social norms
Paper and packaging	Location

However, irrespective of the industry in which a firm operates, the following environmental influences are likely to have some impact, although its intensity will be determined by the industry.

* The markets or niches – which are the best ones?
* The competition, is it benign or malignant?

- The economy, is it growing or declining?
- The technology, how important is it?
- The legal/political environment, is it likely to be conducive or not to success?
- The geographical location, is it an advantage or a disadvantage?
- The social environment, how are social changes affecting the firm?

Assessing the current state of these influences and forecasting their future evolution is the major task of environmental analysis. Managers who do this most effectively and then respond most appropriately are likely to build competitive advantage. Each of these key environmental influences is now considered.

KEY ENVIRONMENTAL INFLUENCE: THE MARKETS OR NICHES

One of the most important lessons for ambitious managers to learn is that today's industry leaders are not impregnable. Goliath firms are in perpetual danger from diminutive Davids. Indeed it is likely that many of today's giant corporations which occupy privileged and apparently unassailable market share positions will, over time, be replaced by other giants who, today, are just minor players. Like a great ferris wheel of business that is slowly rotating, those firms which occupy positions at the top of the wheel are descending (currently unnoticed) and being replaced by firms which are at the bottom of the wheel. This type of business evolution has always occurred and will always occur. It takes place in all industries and in all countries, as illustrated in Table B3.3 by the top twenty UK companies in 1995 ranked by market value.

Many of these companies did not exist or did not occupy such prominent positions even ten years earlier.

When a sufficiently long time span is taken it can be seen that dramatic changes, which are frequently obscured at the time, are taking place continuously. In the long run such evolutionary change is inevitable and inexorable. It cannot be stopped. The only variation is the speed at which the change occurs. In some industries, such as information technology, it is rapid, highly visible and often dramatic, while in others, such as the legal profession it is much slower, incremental and often difficult to chart. However, irrespective of the industry, evolution will always occur.

Table B3.3 Top twenty UK companies ranked by market value, 1995

Company	Market value US$mil
Shell Transport & Trading	40,648
Glaxo Wellcome	39,378
British Telecommunications	38,926
British Petroleum	38,880
HSBC Holding	33,996
BAT Industries	24,058
SmithKline Beecham	21,225
British Gas	20,847
BTR	19,707
Hanson	19,606
Marks & Spencer	18,309
Barclays Bank	17,528
Unilever plc	15,768
Guinness	15,278
Wellcome	14,788
National Westminster Bank	14,689
Cable & Wireless	14,666
Zeneca Group	14,058
General Electric	13,935
RTZ	13,621

Source: (6)

Exploiting change

The ability of a firm to exploit such change is a function of the quality of its senior managers. Generally, in successful firms senior managers are more sensitive to and react more appropriately to the messages from their markets and customers. Market niches and customer needs continuously mutate and whether or not a firm rises or descends in its industrial hierarchy it is profoundly influenced by the vigour and quality of managerial responses to these changes or, in other words, the quality of its strategic market planning. This chapter aims to make managers 'hair-trigger' sensitive to the changes in their markets and provide guidelines for selectivity when choosing which niches to exploit.

Analysing the markets or niches

Assuming that a firm has defined its business in the fashion of Chapter B1 and it clear about the markets or niches which it addresses or wishes to address, two question arise:

1. Which are the best niches on which to expend the greatest effort and make the biggest financial commitments? This will be discussed below.
2. Assuming that the 'best' niches have been selected, how should they be addressed, i.e. what marketing strategies will be employed to exploit them most successfully? This element will be considered in Chapter C2.

The best niches

Firms are required continuously to make judgements about the quality of the market niches which address and those on which they ought to concentrate in the future. This raises the question about the criterion that ought to be applied when appraising a niche. Here it is suggested that the criterion for the quality of a niche should be: The best niches are those which are most likely to provide sustained, superior returns.

The rationale behind the adoption of this criterion is that the effective exploitation of such niches will generate superior performance for the firm from all aspects. In addition, there is a number of other comments that can be made about the words used in this criterion.

*   *most likely*: in strategic market planning there are no certainties, only probabilities. For example, although a firm with the highest relative market share ought to have the highest returns, this is not certain, it is only likely to be true.
*   *sustained*: the concept of sustainability is crucial to strategic market planning, i.e. returns ought to last for many years and should not be ephemeral.
*   *superior*: the returns to which a firm aspires ought to be superior ones, i.e. superior to rivals.

Although it is impossible to give a universal list of yardsticks which would always determine the quality of a niche, it is often the case that superior niches have the following characteristics.

Materiality of the niche

A primary determinant of niche attractiveness is its materiality or absolute size. This raises the question whether the size of the niche is such that an acceptable return can be achieved from the investment necessary to exploit it. For example, irrespective of the attractiveness of some niches, there are some which are so small that the returns from serving them are not sufficient. Thus, although the niche for retailing high performance sportscars can be very lucrative, in a small market like Ireland this niche is so small that there are no agencies for certain highly specialised marques – the niche is not material.

In addition, large firms often choose not to address niches which are below a certain size or are structurally incapable of providing an acceptable size of return. For example, large steel companies tend not to address certain niches for steel – small-batch, labour-intensive, tailored products for small builders – as they regard the materiality of this market as insufficient.

Thus a key question in assessing the attractiveness of a niche is: Is it material, i.e. if this niche were to be exploited successfully would the returns be sufficient?

Niche trends: Life cycle

Niches are alive, they are always mutating. While commercially some are blooming, there are others which are withering. Some have great sustainability and will provide superior returns for many years while others are relatively transient. Therefore it is important to assess the sustainable profit potential of niches. A primary consideration is the life cycle stage of the niche. Generally those niches which are at the earlier stages of their life cycles (see Chapter B2) will tend to be the most attractive.

Key question: What are the trends of this niche in terms of its life cycle?

Niche trends: Growth rate

Linked to life cycle stage is the issue of the rate of growth of the niche.

Generally those niches which have the highest growth rates will tend to be the most attractive, although this is not always so. There may be other competitive pressures which can negate this. For example, in the personal computer industry technical obsolescence more than redresses the benefits of growth. In spite of this caveat most niches which have very low or negative growth rates tend to be unattractive.[1]

Key question: What is the growth trend of this niche and is it likely to be sustained?

Degree of competition

A fundamental determinant of niche attractiveness is the intensity of competition that prevails within it. For example, the carbonated drinks industry can be divided into two niches: drinks sold through large multiples and drinks sold through the licensed trade. It tends to be the case that the intensity of competition, reflected by prices and returns, for the large multiples niche is much greater than that in the licensed trade niche. Although the structural determinants of competitive intensity are discussed more comprehensively elsewhere in this book, Table B3.4 sets out some ready reckoners of competitive pressure.

Table B3.4 Simple indicators of competitive pressure

Number of competitors: are they increasing or decreasing? Generally growing numbers foment competitive pressure.

Basis of competition: is it price based or some other lever, e.g. quality? Price-based competition tends to be the worst.

Power of buyers: generally the more powerful they are, the greater will be the intensity of competition.

New entrant threat: is this a major threat and can barriers to new entrants be erected?

Price levels: are they being sustained or are they being forced downwards? Price erosion is a clear sign of competitive pressure.

Profit margins: are they being sustained or are they being forced downwards? Once again margin erosion is a clear sign of competitive pressure.

Finally, it is worth noting that those niches which are competitively the most benign and consequently the most remunerative will tend to be the most attractive for new entrants. For example, in the UK one of the fastest growing niches in the automobile market is the four-wheel drive, off-the-road vehicle. This growth has caused more and more firms with more and more models to enter the niche with a consequent increase in competitive intensity.

Key questions:

1. What is the degree of competitive pressure in terms of competitor numbers, price or non-price strategies, and gross margin pressures?
2. What is the greatest competitive threat, i.e. buyer power, threat of new entrants, supplier power?

Scope for strategic manoeuvre

Those niches which offer the greatest scope for innovative strategic manoeuvre will tend to be the most attractive. By strategic manoeuvre is meant a firm's ability to develop unique and difficult to replicate strategies. For example, in the licensed trade there are many niches and there is great scope for strategic manoeuvre: up-market pubs, sports pubs, old world pubs, music pubs, restaurant pubs. In the convenience store industry the scope for manoeuvre is much more limited.

Key question: What is the scope for non-price based strategies?

A firm's sales from the niche

The proportion of total sales that a firm receives from a particular niche is obviously of great importance when assessing the current and future contribution of a niche. In practice it is quite common for firms to be highly dependent – say more than 50 per cent of sales – upon a single niche. Any deterioration in the revenues from such a niche poses a severe threat. Indeed, extreme dependence upon a niche is often the trigger to diversification.

Key question: How dependent is the firm on that niche and what are the consequences of losing share in it?

Niche market share and relative market share

As shown in Chapter B2, when considering the product market portfolio the actual market share of a niche and the relative market share of a niche that a firm possesses is of immense importance in determining the profit contribution that the niche ought to make. Thus the current and future importance of a niche can be assessed in terms of whether a firm is a leader, a joint leader or a follower.

Key questions:

1. What are our current and future market shares?
2. What are our current and future relative market shares and what are the profit implications of these positions?

Per cent of profits from the niche

Bearing in mind that the profitability of a niche is a function of the firm's structural position within the niche, the profit contribution[2] is of fundamental importance to how it is assessed.

Key question: What percentage of our profits flow from this niche and what is its sustainable profit potential?

As set out in Chapter B1, from a strategic marketing perspective it is important to appraise not the overall market for a product, but rather the niche which it truly addresses. How niches can be appraised is set out in Table B3.5. This shows the characteristics which enable judgements to be made for four niches. Similar judgements can be made for the other niches which the firm addresses.

KEY ENVIRONMENTAL INFLUENCES: THE COMPETITION

Many managers often lament being in their particular industry and will, if encouraged, openly pine for industries that appear to be much better than their own. Such managers are really yearning for a less competitive industry. They feel that the competitive pressures which they must endure are uniquely high and some relief would be obtained elsewhere.

Although it is true that the degree of competition does vary from industry to industry with industries such as European shipbuilding and European steel having endured years of cutthroat competition while others, such as pharmaceuticals and the legal profession, having enjoyed a much more gentlemanly approach to competition plus higher returns, it is important to realize that the prevailing level of profitability in an industry is not a matter of luck or good fortune. Rather, it is determined by the competitive forces to which the industry is sub-

Table B3.5 How to appraise four niches

	Niche 1		Niche 2		Niche 3		Niche 4	
	Today	3 yrs ahead	Today	3 yrs ahead	Today	3 yrs ahead	Today	3 yrs ahead
Materiality, i.e. total sales value of niche								
Trends 1: life cycle								
Trends 2: growth rate								
Competition: number of compets								
Competition: greatest compet threat								
Scope for manoeuvre								
Ave gross margin (%)								
Firm's sales from niche								
Market share (%)								
Real mkt share								
Actual profits								
Percent of profits from niche								
Other comments								

ject. All industries are subject to competitive forces and the winning firms are those that best understand and then take action to minimize the buffeting they receive from these competitive forces.

Traditional economics and competitive forces

Traditional economists would tend to assert that, in conditions of perfect competition,[3] no single firm can influence the overall industry. The degree of competition prevailing in any industry is a function of supply and demand and the sole mechanism that can be used to achieve equilibrium between supply and demand is price. Expressed in even simpler terms, traditional economic theory asserts that from an industry point of view:

- If the demand for goods increases then price will increase.
- If the supply of goods increases then price will decrease.

When demand equals supply then there is equilibrium, a state to which all economic systems will tend in the long run.

From a firm point of view:

- If the firm lowers its price then demand for its goods will increase.
- If the firm raises its price then demand for its goods will decrease.

Once again, when demand miraculously equals supply then there will be equilibrium, the state to which all economic systems ultimately and inexorably tend.

While this approach has the commendable attribute of simplicity and may provide some explanation of how the competitive forces in industries operate, it does suffer from the major drawback that it does not reflect reality[4] and hence is of very limited value in strategic market planning.

The five competitive forces

The traditional view of the economics of competition was greatly expanded by Michael Porter (8), of Harvard Business School who asserted that the intensity of competition which prevails in an industry was more complex than simply the interaction of supply and demand.

He asserted that the degree of competitiveness in any industry was rooted both in its own underlying economic structure and of the other industries related to it. Competition in any industry depended not just on the two forces of demand and supply but on the following five forces.

Force number 1: Not just demand, but who makes the demand

It is not just the level of demand for a product that influences competition, rather it is the nature of who is making the demand. For example, in the aircraft components industry the two major buyers are Boeing and Airbus. These are very powerful buyers: first, because of their size; second, because they dominate the large commercial aircraft industry and there are no significant alternative buyers. Consequently a major competitive force which pushes down the levels of profits in the aircraft components industry is the *power of the buyers.*

In contrast to this industry, in most countries there is a very large number of buyers for the services offered by the legal profession. The power of the buyers of legal services tends to be extremely low and this lack of power is reflected in the steady and relatively high levels of profits enjoyed by that profession.

Thus, it is not just the level of demand that is fundamental in determining the competitive pressure faced by an industry, but also the nature of the demand. To use Porter's (8) expression, it is the power of the buyers. Generally the greater their power, the more they will squeeze their suppliers' profits, and the more they will restrict their strategic options. Porter asserts that buyer power tends to be most powerful when one or more of the following conditions applies:

- It is concentrated or purchases large volumes relative to seller sales, for example, large commercial aircraft manufacturers.
- The products it purchases are a significant fraction of the buyer's costs or purchases, i.e. buyers will 'shop around' when the value of the input is relatively high, for example, aircraft manufacturers tend to be very careful and powerful in selecting engine suppliers.
- The products purchased are standard, i.e. undifferentiated. This means that buyers have a wide choice in selecting their supplier. For example, petrol retailing suffers from being perceived as offering an undifferentiated or commodity product and this confers

power on petrol buyers.

- It faces few switching costs, i.e. the buyer can switch from one supplier to another with relatively little cost. For example, when a firm wishes to change its supplier of stationery, generally the costs of switching to an alternative supplier are low.
- It earns low profits, i.e. if the buyer is earning low profits it will not be in a position to be generous with its suppliers. For example, small businesses tend to generate lower returns than large ones and consequently the fees that consulting companies can command from small businesses tend to be lower than from large businesses.
- It poses a credible threat of backward integration. For example, in the automobile components industry the automobile manufacturers historically have used this threat, i.e. they will make their own components, as a competitive lever against their suppliers.
- The industry's product is unimportant to the quality of the buyers' products or services. Once again suppliers of stationery to large firms illustrate this pressure.
- The buyer has full information. When the buyer has full information on a supplier's costs and margins, the buyer's power is increased. Once again, major aircraft manufacturers often know the true costs of components (as the components will be made to the aircraft manufacturer's specifications). This enables such buyers to gauge and determine the margins which suppliers ought to make.

Force number 2: Not just supply, but who supplies

Symmetrically, with the comments made on demand, it is not just the level of supply of a product that influences competition, but also the nature of the supplier. For example, in the UK since the privatization of the electricity supply industry in the 1980s, many economic commentators have taken the view that although eleven regional electricity companies (RECs) were established to promote competition, because each REC has an exclusive regional territory they have been given excessive supplier power which has resulted in excessively high levels of profits and excessively high executive pay levels.

Thus, in assessing the competitive power of suppliers in any industry, it is not just the quantity supplied that is important, but also the *power of suppliers*. Generally, the greater the suppliers' power, the more they will squeeze buyers' profits, and the more they will restrict their strategic options. Porter asserts that suppliers tend to be most powerful when one or more of the following conditions apply:

- It is dominated by a few firms and is more concentrated than the industry or industries to which it sells. For example, there is just one REC for each region and each REC has a great variety of customers.
- No genuine substitutes exist. For example, the legal profession has great supplier power since in many transactions a lawyer must be used in order to comply with the law.
- It is not an important customer of the supplier group. Thus individually small independent petrol retailers are not important customers of the major oil companies. Consequently their suppliers are able to exercise great power over them.
- Its products are an important input to the buyer's business. For example, in the heavy earth-moving/construction equipment industry the speed and quality of service is so important (because down time is costly) that it confers power upon those companies that supply superior service.
- It has differentiated products. For example, Mercedes-Benz automobiles are able to command premium prices because of their degree of differentiation.
- Its products have major switching costs. For example, for many firms the costs of switching from Microsoft to another operating system are so high that they will never switch.
- It poses a credible threat of forward integration. For example, major oil companies always pose a threat to independent petrol retailers of integrating forward into retailing.

Force number 3: Not just the existing competitors, but new entrants

Traditionally competition is seen as a struggle among the competitors in an industry. This is reflected in the most common indices used to measure competition: market share, relative market share, number of competitors, growth rates of competitors. Although all these measures do indeed help to capture the competition in an industry, they are incomplete in that another and often more threatening source of competitive intensity is the entry of new players from outside the industry.

Porter has asserted that normally the easier it is for new firms to enter an industry, the greater will be the competitive pressures on existing competitors, i.e. the *threat of entry* is another major competitive force.

New entrants tend to intensify the competition for the following reasons:

- There are more competitors in the market. Axiomatically this increases competitive pressure.
- They increase overall industry capacity and this may lead to investment intensity, or surplus fixed assets, and so increase buyer power. For example, Korea's entry into the shipbuilding industry and its consequent resolute pursuit of growth has destroyed the profitability of the industry for most other nations.
- They alter the competitive rules of the game. This feature makes successful new entrants the most dangerous type of competitor. New entrants, especially if they have been successful in another unrelated industry, exacerbate and foment competition in new and unique ways and can wreak competitive havoc on the incumbents. They simply conduct business ignoring the established rules of the game and have quite different agendas and value systems from the incumbents. For example, for many years UK high street banks have enjoyed a type of competitive equilibrium. They compete in a relatively restrained fashion; competitive 'fights to the death' do not feature and market shares remain reasonably static over many years.
- However, a number of new and unpredictable players, for example, Microsoft, telecommunications companies, retailers, automobile manufacturers, entering through the Internet or other related medium such as cable, appear to be positioning themselves to join the banking industry. These new entrants are likely to create competitive chaos and perhaps the destruction of some established traditional banks by having value systems, goals, strategies and structures that are very different to the established industry norms. For example, an international telecommunications entrant will have as a major strategic issue and earner the maximizing of traffic through its network. In addition it may restrict access to or impose severe charges on banks and other financial institutions which use its network. Because such new entrants compete using rules which are so different from the traditional players, they pose a potentially greater threat than competition from a traditional

rival. (The issue of the havoc wrought by the entry of non-traditional players from outside the industry is discussed more fully below under 'Key environmental influences: technology'.

Two major factors determine the extent of the threat of entry:

- the height of the entry barriers;
- the anticipated reaction from existing competitors.

The height of the entry barriers

Generally, the higher the entry barriers, the smaller will be the threat of entry and hence the competitive pressure due to this force. Major barriers to entry include the following:

- *Economies of scale.* The largest competitors should have unit costs which are so low that new entrants are discouraged. For example, in the automobile industry the scale of the largest players is so great that new entrants are deterred.[5]
- *Product differentiation.* Products may have such a degree of distinctiveness that they preclude new entrants. For example, in the white rum market Bacardi has such a high degree of differentiation and such a high market share that this market segment is not besieged by new entrants.
- *Capital requirements.* Is the initial capital required to enter the industry so high that it will not offer an acceptable return to new entrants? This appears to be the case in the aero engines industry.
- *Switching costs.* A major barrier to entry in the software industry is the cost to users of switching from one system to another.
- *Access to distribution channels.* Existing competitors may be able to lock new entrants out of established distribution channels. This is a major fear of banks in relation to the electronic superhighways of the future.
- *Cost disadvantages independent of scale.* In some industries new entrants may have a cost disadvantage vis-à-vis incumbents for reasons other than scale. For example, existing players may have a low cost of supply, a government subsidy or proprietary technology.
- *Government policy.* Government may stop new entrants. For example, in the UK new entrants are prevented from entering the televi-

sion broadcasting industry through government control of licences.

Anticipated reaction from existing competitors

Generally, the greater the anticipated reaction from existing competitors, the less will be the threat of new entrants. Thus in the airline industry it is generally accepted that major carriers will react most strongly to new entrants, as was well documented by the reaction of British Airways to the entry of Virgin in the early 1990s.

Force number 4: Not just the product but substitutes

It was assumed above that competitive analysis is concerned with a single product or product grouping. This is too narrow a view. Products do not need to be direct competitors in order to have competitive impact. For example, fax transmission, verbal telephoning and letters are distinctively different products, yet they do compete with each other: they are substitutes. Thus, in considering competitive forces that prevail in any industry there must be a consideration of the influence of the *threat of substitutes*. Substitutes provide alternative methods of providing a product or a service.

Porter suggested that substitutes which present the greatest threat tend to have the following characteristics:

- They provide a better performance/price standard than the industry standard, for example, fax versus telex.
- When industries appear to earn high profits and to charge excessively, buyers may switch to substitute products. For example, the Channel Tunnel, the ferries, hovercraft and airlines all provide substitute means of travelling between the UK and continental Europe.

The existence of real substitutes therefore helps limit the price which can be charged for a good or service.

The degree of rivalry or competitive adversity varies greatly from industry to industry. Rivalry in the professions tends to be relatively gentlemanly, with price competition between the incumbents being rare, while in an industry such as personal computers the rivalry is much more intense, with product obsolescence and continuous price erosion being competitive features of the industry. Once again the degree of rivalry is not due to luck or lack of luck, rather, Porter suggests that rivalry is fostered when one of more of the following conditions obtains.

- *Many or equally balanced competitors.* In most industries, the greater the number of competitors, the more intense will be the rivalry as the spoils of the market must be divided among a greater number. Also if the competitors are fairly equally balanced, say in terms of market share, this will also tend to promote rivalry as the equally balanced competitors strive for outright leadership. These drivers of rivalry are clearly seen in the automobile industry.
- *Slow industry growth.* A consequence of this is that the only means of rapid organic growth is to take market share from rivals: a process which is likely to promote rivalry.
- *High fixed or storage costs.* These costs are likely to lead to investment intensity, or surplus fixed assets, which is likely to provoke intense rivalry. For example, the high fixed costs of IT have caused many firms with substantial IT investments to examine these costs and either to find additional products or services (to keep the IT network loaded) or else to outsource their IT in order to reduce these costs.
- *Lack of differentiation or switching costs.* This applies to products or service commodities which are purchased on the basis of price. For example, household soap manufacturers spend heavily on advertising and promotion to prevent erosion of their brands into commodities.
- *Diverse competitors.* When there is great variety among competitors in terms of their missions, goals, ambitions, scale, structures and strategies, this is likely to promote rivalry. For example, in Japan the sheer variety of electronics companies ensures intense

rivalry in this industry.

- *High strategic stakes.* When a firm considers that a particular part of a business is strategically important it may choose to stay in this part of the business even though it may be unprofitable. For example, drinks companies may choose to stay in unprofitable distribution businesses, not to make a profit from them but to guarantee 'a route to market'.

- High exit barriers. Exit barriers are structural impediments to leaving the business. The higher they are, the more difficult it is for a firm to leave and such firms may compete on commercially suicidal terms. For example, there are very high exit barriers in the shipbuilding industry – the plant and equipment cannot be used for other purposes. This is one of the forces that has led to intense rivalry in the industry, resulting in generally very low levels of profits or losses.

Porter's model of competitive strategy enables managers to ascertain the competitive terrain in which all firms operate. From this analysis managers ought to be able to decide upon which of the five competitive forces are likely to be the harshest and which are likely to be most benign and then develop appropriate strategies (see Chapter C3) that will enable their firm to gain true competitive advantage over rivals. The Porter approach is now generally accepted as being one of the leading methodologies for competitive analysis and the model is set out in diagrammatic form in Figure B3.1.

Problems in applying the Porter approach

There appear to be two major problems associated with the application of the Porter model to firms who are undertaking a strategic market planning analysis.

First, the very comprehensiveness of the model generates such an extremely large amount of data that it is difficult to isolate the small number of fundamental competitive forces which are key to gaining competitive advantage. It is therefore suggested that when conducting such an analysis managers should examine the competitive environment using a proforma similar to Table B3.6 which summarizes the forces and suggests responses. This table provides a summary of the results recorded by a group of managers in a DIY retailing chain. (Note

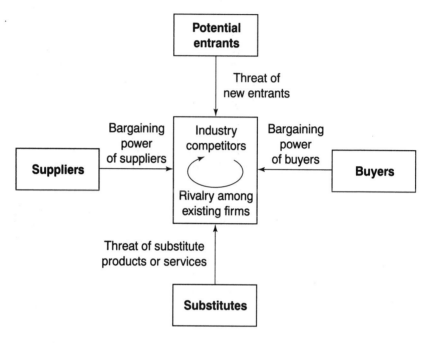

Figure B3.1   Porter's five competitive forces (8)

that the chain was number two in terms of annual sales.)

Second, the Porter approach is a competitive analysis very much at the industry rather than competitor level. It can be extremely useful to complement this with an analysis of the nature, extent and severity of threats from a firm's true competitors. Although many measures or yardsticks can be used to assess this, Table B3.7 presents a summary of those characteristics which tend to provide a comprehensive picture of any firm's main competitors. Each of the elements in Table B3.7 is now considered.

Scale and performance

This section gives an assessment of how well the firm is faring against its three major competitors. Most firms do not perceive competition coming from all firms in the industry, but rather principally from a small number of competitors – three or four – with whom they compete directly. The measures are as follows:

Table B3.6 How to summarize the competitive forces and firm responses

Competitive force	Threat	Opportunity	Action to be taken
Threat of entry	Expansion of no. 1 and no. 3 competitors. Saturation of the market. New large foreign entrants.	Consumer awareness of DIY increasing, leading to price and service competition. More competition pushing efficiency. Local knowledge.	Must expand more rapidly.
Buyer power	Low switching costs. Standard products. No customer loyalty.	Size and service.	Expand own brand. Seek USPs. Offer quality brands. Improve stock turn. Improve service.
Supplier power	Increasing.	Brand leaders must have shelf space.	Increase market share to give scale.
Substitute threat	Trend towards 'trade' which we do not supply.	Unique ranges of furniture.	Continuous promotions. Improve service. Increase loyalty – loyalty buyer card.
Rivalry	Intense with the no. 1 and no. 3. Market static: severe profit pressures. Difficult to maintain loyalty.	Use IT to: improve efficiency, stock control, margin performance, sales performance.	Lower cost purchasing. Review quality of sites, especially locations. Must become no. 1.

- Sales, market share and relative market share enable a judgement to be made about the firm's scale and changes of scale relative to its major rivals and to make judgements about whether it is a leader and increasing its leadership, or a follower and gaining or losing on the leader.
- Profits and profit growth rate give an indication of financial performance relative to true rivals.
- Scope: products, customers and territories provides an indication of the focus of the firm and its rivals. In practice scope will normally employ words such as full range or focused.

Goals and strategy

The purpose of this section is to stimulate managerial debate about the likely future direction of the firm and its three principal rivals. The issues include:

- Future goals. What does this firm have as its future goals and what are competitors likely to have? Normally goals will be expressed in terms such as: to be number one in sales in the industry; to be the low cost player; to be the premium priced player; to have the fastest growth rate in the industry; to be the most profitable in the industry.
- Fundamental strategy. What is the fundamental strategy of this firm and its competitors? Normally this will be expressed in terms such as: growth; regain leadership; improve margins; retrenchment; exiting certain segments of the business; adding new segments to the business.
- Generic strategy: scale, differentiation, focus. Which of Porter's generic strategies (see Chapter C3 for details) will be the desired route for achieving the goals? Although Porter (8) suggests that in order to earn superior returns firms must pick just one generic strategy and pursue it resolutely, in practice many firms will have more than one route. For example, a firm will often have the following characteristics:
  — a low margin commodity type product with a very large proportion of the sales for which a strategy of scale is clearly appropriate.
  — a number of much higher margin differentiated products with

a relatively low proportion of sales, but a disproportionately high proportion of profits, for which a strategy of differentiation is clearly essential.

- Route: acquisition or organic. Although firms pursuing a growth strategy will often do so through a combination of organic and acquisition, a firm will often be predisposed towards one route or the other with past behaviour often being a good guide to likely future behaviour.
- Structure. What is the structure of the firm and does it confer any advantage? For example, a firm which is part of a large and cash rich multinational may enjoy financing and other resource advantages over a smaller national rival.
- Particular strength. Most firms will have a particular strength which gives them their competitive advantage. It is important for managers to be aware of the particular strengths of rivals so that they use a different approach when competing against them. For example, if a major rival had as its particular strength 'scale – it was by far the largest in the industry with the consequent unit cost advantages – then it would probably be more appropriate to try to outcompete on the basis of an alternative strategy, for example, service or product range.
- Particular weakness. Most firms have weaknesses and it can be instructive to make judgements about the particular weaknesses of rivals and then move to exploit them. For example, if a rival did not carry a full range of products then emphasize the firm's own comprehensiveness of range.
- Comments. This is for any random comments which may occur. They could include elements such as myopic management, shareholder pressure, new team.

It should be noted that when managers are asked to undertake this type of exercise they will often make comments such as:

'Our industry does not have that type of information so this exercise cannot be carried out.'

'We know who our competitors are but we do not have the details being requested.'

'How could we possibly know what our competitors intend to do?'

This is a typical set of managerial responses which are both correct and incorrect. They are correct in that they do not have objective written data about competitors, but they are incorrect in that managers will often have a great deal of unwritten rumour and opinion about competitors. These data should be harnessed for strategic market planning purposes. In addition, it is a major responsibility of senior managers to think deeply and creatively about the future goals and strategies of their competitors and to build strategies, based upon some figures, some judgement and hunches which will advantage their own firm. Table B3.7 should foster this type of debate.

In order to build a strategically strong future it is essential that managers understand in depth the competitive terrain they inhabit today and will inhabit in the future. This understanding should take place at two levels: first, at the industry level where the five broad forces that affect all industries can be appraised; second, at the firm level where the specific strategies and actions that true competitors follow today and are likely to follow in the future can be appraised.

KEY ENVIRONMENTAL INFLUENCES: THE ECONOMY

All firms, irrespective of their size, are influenced by 'what is happening in the economy'. This phrase is continuously repeated in the media, often without any precision. In strategic market planning it is important to be able to winnow the mass of economic data with which managers are provided and then to concentrate on those, probably few, selected indicators that either present excellent opportunities or pose severe threats for the firm's performance.

So what are the key economic indicators upon which firms should concentrate? Although it could be argued that all firms are influenced by the economy, vital profit-determining economic influences are often industry and firm specific – for example, a firm that conducts the bulk of its business abroad will be much more influenced by exchange rate movements than one which operates exclusively in its domestic market. Similarly, in an industry with a high level of fixed assets funded by debt – for example, the property industry – a period of high inflation may suit it much more than an industry such as clothing, where the cost of stockholding in a period of high inflation may impose severe costs. In spite of how profits in different industries are affected by the economy, it is possible to disaggregate the economic

Table B3.7 Competitive characteristics of any firm and its three largest competitors

	My firm	Competitor 1	Competitor 2	Competitor 3
Scale and differentiation				
Sales (£)				
Sales growth rate (%)				
Market share (%)				
Relative market share				
Profits (£mn)				
Profits growth rate (%)				
Scope: products, customers, territories				
Goals and strategy				
Future goals				
Fundamental strategy				
Generic strategy: scale/differentiation/organic				
Route: acquisition/organic				
Structure				
Particular strength				
Particular weakness				
Comments				

environment into broad economic influences which will to a greater or lesser extent affect most firms. Individual firms can they select the influences which are of greatest importance.

The first level of aggregation is to subdivide the word economy into several constituent levels: the national, the greater regional and the world economy.

The national economy

A firm's national economy tends to have the greatest economic influence on its performance. For most western countries the major economic influences are the national economic goals and their constituent policies. These vary enormously from country to country and often from political party to political party. Thus countries such as Japan, Korea and Ireland articulate clear economic goals, often in the form of, say, a five-year plan, to which the major stakeholders, i.e. the unions, shareholders, managers and staff, subscribe. These policies can be one or more of the following types:

- *Fiscal policies.* What is the overall level of government spending and what are its policies on taxation? For example, is government, through public expenditure, attempting to raise the level of demand and hence reduce unemployment? Is the government's tax strategy designed to increase investment or increase public spending power?
- *Monetary policies.* How tightly are monetary measures such as money supply and public sector borrowing controlled? What is the government attitude towards using interest rates to stimulate or reduce economic activity?
- *Inflation policies.* What is the government's attitude towards inflation and what does it believe are its causes? What steps are being taken to influence the level of inflation?
- *Foreign exchange and balance of payments policies.* What is the government's attitude towards stability in the value of the national currency? How do changes in the value of the national currency affect the economy in general and the organization under analysis in particular?
- *Unemployment policies.* How committed is the government to having full employment and what policies does it use to achieve its employment goals?

- *Regional policy.* How committed is the government to strong regional policies to prevent the concentration of industry in favoured locations?

The operation of most of these economic indicators can be analysed and their influence on a particular firm assessed.

Greater regional economy

Most national economies are part of a greater regional economic or economic/political bloc which can have profound influences upon the performance of a particular industry or a particular firm. Currently the more important regional blocs include:

- European Union (EU);
- European Free Trade Area (EFTA);
- North American Free Trade Association (NAFTA);
- Association of South East Asian Nations (ASEAN).

All of these associations tend to have similar agendas:

- the promotion of free trade within the bloc through the removal of national impediments to trade;
- the promotion of competitiveness within the bloc;
- the promotion of a bloc-wide single market;
- the development of bloc-wide political, legal, administrative, business, scientific and social structures;
- the negotiation of links between the bloc, other blocs and individual countries.

At a more specific level typical developments are:

- protection of regional industries, for example, the European farming industry through the Common Agricultural Farm Policy (CAP);
- promotion of specific industrial sectors on an association-wide basis, for example the European space industry;
- promotion of competition within industries, for example, the restriction of national subsidies to the state-owned airline industries;

- economic regeneration in poorer countries within the bloc, for example, industrial grants and loans for such regions;
- trade facilitation through the pursuit of a single market;
- trade facilitation through currency alignment mechanisms, for example, the drive towards a common currency in the European Union.

All these measures in addition to the political decisions made by blocs, can have significant influences on the climate in which a firm operates.

The global economy

National economies and greater regional economies are increasingly linked throughout the world and the influence of this global economy rather than just a firm's national economy, is likely to continue to grow. Among the major global economic issues that are likely to affect most firms are the following:

1. The economic performance of the major industrial countries (usually known as the G7 group) as measured by:

   - rates of inflation;
   - real growth rates of GNP;
   - current account balances;
   - levels of employment;
   - interest rates.

The economic influence of these countries tends to have major effects upon other economies, and hence the prospects for firms.

2. The success of global economic regulatory bodies. As the global economy has developed, regulatory bodies which both stimulate and police international business can have great economic influence. Among the more important bodies are the following:

   - global efforts at monetary reform;
   - behaviour of the currency markets;
   - behaviour of international capital markets;
   - commodities;

- trade talks;
- activities of the International Monetary Fund;
- activities of the World Bank.

Any firm can select those elements in its national, larger regional and world economy which currently affect and in future are likely to affect it and make an assessment of their likely impact. In practice, it will usually be the case that national economic influences are the strongest. Once again, it is possible to summarize those economic influences that are considered to be the most important in the form of a table. See Table B3.8.

Table B3.8 How relevant future economic influences can be recorded and their impact ascertained

Element	Today	Three yrs from now	Comment
Inflation rate	4%	4%	No change
Interest rate	6%	6%	No change
Basic rate tax	25%	20%	Increase in disposable income
Unemployment	10%	12%	Increasing, less disposable income
Exchange rate	100	90	Devaluation: dearer imports

KEY ENVIRONMENTAL INFLUENCES: TECHNOLOGY

Rapid technological change is being experienced worldwide at a rate which is likely to accelerate even further. In most industries a major task of management is to keep abreast with the technological changes in their industry and an even greater task is to provide the resources to do so. However, in spite of the universal influence of technological change, its rate ranges from frighteningly rapid, in industries such as global news and financial services, to more understandable in industries such as the professions and education. However, technological change exists in all industries and often makes a major strategic impact.

Impact of technological change

This can be considered under two major headings: the magnitude of the technological change and the position of the firm in its industry.

Magnitude of technological change

Technological change can vary from the incremental, for example, an improvement in the performance of automobiles, to the dramatic, for example, the Internet. Such dramatic technological change is the most important from a strategic marketing perspective. Incremental change probably requires incremental strategic adjustment: the strategies which a firm has followed successfully in the past, with amendment, will probably be appropriate for the future. It contrast, dramatic change is likely to require the implementation of dramatic new strategies.

A traditional industry which is currently in the throes of major technological change is retail banking. Technology is transforming the competitive rules of the industry and the strategies and structures of retail banks. Technology is having two major strategic effects. First, retail banks are losing their monopoly as centres for the transmission of money. Entirely new entrants, such as Microsoft and cable companies, seem likely to enter the industry. Second, technology is providing a previously unavailable number of channels of distribution, for example, telephones, automatic teller machines (ATMs), mail and the information superhighway. An illustration of the likely magnitude of this change is indicated by the changes that have taken place already in terms of telephone banking. The success of the First Direct telephone banking system in the UK is well documented. Figure B3.2 shows that telephone banking can be up to 50 per cent cheaper than traditional retail banking for the same customer. This cost influence will cause banks increasingly to use this channel.

The position of the firm in its industry

The competitive rules for all firms in any industry can be defined as follows.[6] In all industries there are: the rule makers; the rule takers; the rule breakers.

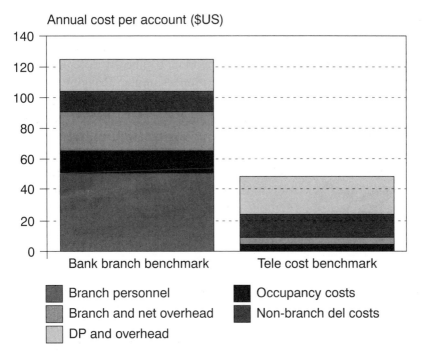

Figure B3.2 New channels are lower cost than retail branches (9)

The rule makers

The rule makers are the major competitors who have been in the industry for many years. These major incumbents are the barons of the industry that set the rules of success which must be obeyed as long as the industry remains stable.

The rule takers

These are the players who obey the barons. They could be called the serfs. They have no choice; the power of the ruler barons is so great that they must either obey or depart from the industry.

The rule breakers

These are usually small and dramatically different firms that set up new competitive rules and rupture the established norms for doing business. They could be called the revolutionaries because they destabilize the industry. There are two types:

- *Revolutionaries from within the industry.* These are players who have been in the industry and then adopt a radically different strategy from the accepted norms, for example, Royal Bank of Scotland's decision to set up the First Direct telephone bank.
- *Revolutionaries from outside the industry.* These are new entrants that are most likely to wreak havoc because they bring new strategies and agendas to the industry and destabilize or indeed destroy it. For example, satellite television has completely changed the nature of competition in the television industry with traditional national terrestrial stations generally being outmanoeuvred.

Process of dramatic technological change

When a major technological change occurs, the following stages in its adoption tend to take place.

- *Introduction.* The technology is not universally adopted and competitive battles with the incumbents and the existing technology occur.
- *Market niches.* The new technology focuses on specific market niches and does not compete head-to-head with existing technology.
- *New markets.* Previously unknown market niches develop for the technology.
- *Adoption.* The technology becomes more and more widely accepted and eventually replaces the existing technology.

In today's changing technological environment a continuous monitoring of relevant technological change is necessary for most industries. Finally, the likely impact of technological change can be analysed as shown in Table B3.9.

KEY ENVIRONMENTAL INFLUENCES: GOVERNMENT/LEGAL

Since the 1980s, most governments in the west have expressed the desire to be much less involved in business. The view that has largely prevailed since has been:

'The business of government is to govern while the business of business is to engage in business and therefore government ought not to become involved in business decision-making. It should be left to those who know best, i.e. managers.'

Table B3.9 Hypothetical example of how technological change may affect a retailing firm

Element	Today	Three yrs from now	Comment
Information technology	Electronic point of sale (EPOS)	Integrated EPOS, payments, warehousing, JIT, etc.	Major investment needed
Remote shopping	Infant industry	Substantial growth	Link with service provider
Giant hyper-markets	Very few	May be many	Cannot compete on price for many items

However, in spite of this aspiration most governments have found it extremely difficult to extricate themselves from business decision-making. With increasing government legislation and the economic difficulties facing the west, it often appears that government is becoming more rather than less involved in business. Consequently, all businesses, to a greater or lesser degree, must assess the influence that government has and is likely to have in the future. Government influence can be considered at three main levels: national, greater regional and global.

National government

This type of government influence will usually have the greatest impact on most firms: its influence is immense and so pervasive that it is difficult to catalogue. However, Table B3.10 divides this influence into two categories: aids to business and impediments to business.

In practice many managers, particularly of larger well-established firms, tend to take a doleful view of the influence of government:

'We [the large established company] cannot compete effectively with these smaller "fly by night" rivals. We have to abide by all sorts of government regulations – for example, health and safety, minimum wage, etc. while these smaller, less ethical rivals can avoid these costs.'

Table B3.10   How national governments can act both as an aid and an
                  impediment to industry

Aid to Business	Impediment to Business
A great buyer: large and will always pay	Excessive 'red tape'
Assisting research and development	Excessive tax
Provides protection from foreign goods	Imposes costs: health and safety, environmental legislation, consumer protection and equality of opportunity
Helps control wages	Can control prices
Assistance for training	Consumer rights
Assistance for start-up businesses	Prevents monopolies
Promotes deregulation	Promotes deregulation
Regional location assistance	Influences regional location
Develops quality standards, e.g. BS5750	Imposes quality standards, e.g. BS5750

Although superficially this may appear convincing, in practice larger firms tend to enjoy substantial advantages over smaller rivals. Indeed, firms that fail to meet government regulations may be precluded from certain areas of work – for example, firms failing to achieve BS5750 may not be eligible to tender for contracts. It could be argued that government regulations do, on occasions, act as a barrier to entry.

Greater regional

As in the case of the European Union,[7] the primary areas of legislation tend to be concerned with the establishment of pan-regional political, legal and economic structures that will facilitate the development of a single community. This overall policy thrust tends to result in an agenda which includes: the reduction in impediments to cross-border business; the protection and development of regional industry in the context of the global economy, plus supporting political, economic, social, environmental legislation designed to strengthen the overall regional grouping.

The main areas of concern to regional commissions and governments are:

• protection of regional industries, for example, the European farming industry;

- promotion of pan-European industrial sectors, for example, the European information technology industry;
- promotion of competition within industries, for example, the European anti-monopoly restrictions and restrictions on national government subsidies for particular industries such as shipbuilding;
- development of common industrial standards in terms of product specifications, environmental requirements and consumer rights;
- economic stimulation of poorer areas within the region, for example, EU grants and loans for least favoured regions;
- trade facilitation through relaxation of national customs and technical regulations, for example, the EU's drive towards a single market;

  trade facilitation through currency alignment mechanisms, for example, the EU's Monetary Exchange Union mechanisms;
- provision of regional infrastructures in areas such as transport, telecommunications, scientific databases.

Perhaps the most dramatic example of regional government influence was the EU's decision to ban the export of British beef in 1996.

Global/international

Although this influence appears to be rather remote, it can have material effects upon even the smallest business. Areas where international government is most clearly seen include:

- trading with particular nations, for example, Iraq, South Africa;
- international environmental regulations, for example, use of CFCs, marine pollution;
- trading in particular products, for example, arms, nuclear fuel, seal skin, whales;
- influence of tariffs and quotas upon sales, for example GATT tariffs and quotas;
- international currency facilitation, for example, agreements to smooth international payments;
- international property rights, for example, threat of nationalization of foreign assets by host governments.

In most societies the government exercises a major influence upon business operations which tends to be somewhat paradoxical in that it is often simultaneously a support and a handicap. In practice, it will usually be the case that national government influences are the strongest. These can be recorded and assessed as shown in Table B3.11.

Table B3.11   How future government actions can be recorded and their impact ascertained

Element	Today	Three yrs from now	Comment
Packaging	Disposable	Recyclable	Additional cost
Quality	Optional	Compulsory	Additional cost
Regulation	Regulated	Deregulated	New competitors

KEY ENVIRONMENTAL INFLUENCES: GEOGRAPHY

The strategic influence of geography is analysed under two main headings: the effects of globalization; the effects of actual location.

Strategic effects of globalization

Strategic market planning, for all but the very smallest firms, can no longer be considered in national terms. It must now be considered in regional (i.e. European, American, Asian) or global terms. We now live in an era of:

- global products, for example, Marlboro cigarettes, McDonald's hamburgers, Benetton clothes;
- global services, for example, Visa, American Express, Prudential Insurance, Century 21st Realtor Services;
- global markets, for example, the market for many electronic consumer products is predicated upon global sales;
- global brands, for example, Coca-Cola, Nestlé food products, Levi Strauss jeans;
- global production, for example, construction of Boeing 747s and Ford automobiles;
- global financing, for example, EuroDisney, the Eurotunnel.

The globalization of business has had and will continue to have profound effects upon the 'rules of the game' and, consequently, the way in which business is conducted in many industries. The major effects can be summarized under: marketing, production, finance, human resources, information technology.

Marketing and globalization.

The effects of globalization on the marketing function have been profound and pervasive. The four marketing levers have been affected in the following ways:

Product and service quality

Product and service quality is no longer benchmarked against locally produced competing products. Rather the benchmark is global quality. For example, it would be generally accepted that mass-produced electronics goods should be benchmarked against Japanese products.

Pricing

Pricing levels are increasingly affected by regional or global prices rather than local ones. For example, in the EU pricing differentials are being slowly eroded, as progress is made towards a single market. Another manifestation of the effects of global pricing is the undercutting of traditional prices for many goods by low-cost Asian producers, for example, Taiwanese pricing of bicycle parts.

Promotion

Promotion of many products is now conducted on a regional or global scale. For example, on European satellite television channels consumer products are promoted on a pan-European rather than a national basis.

Distribution

For competitive advantage in distribution many firms must adopt panregional or even global strategies. Thus there are many firms in many industries which have centralized their European distribution into a single central location.

Production and globalization

Production in many industries has been profoundly affected by globalization. The main effects are manifested in two ways. First, large production facilities are established to supply the world rather than a nation or region. For example, Honda's US plant provides specific models for the entire world including Japan. Second, globalization has permitted the decoupling of the production process so that the chain in the production process can include even geographically remote countries. For example, in the manufacture of personal computers one approach which many manufacturers take is to source the labour-intensive, commodity-type components from low-wage countries in Asia and tailor their products to specific markets in higher wage advanced economies.

Finance and globalization

The financial aspects of strategic market planning, whether internal to a firm or external, are increasingly global. Thus, the sources of finance whether debt or equity, the uses of funds, and the returns from operations and investments all have a global dimension.

Human resources and globalization

Human resources now have an unprecedented global dimension. The skills and costs of the employees of a firm are increasingly compared with those of international rather than national competitors.

Information technology and globalization

Perhaps the major stimulus to globalization has been the development of information technology. The facilitation of truly global operations, from car assembly to financial trading, have all required global information technology. As global networks develop further through information superhighways and services such as Internet it is likely that the process of globalization of business will accelerate.

Strategic effects of actual location

This can be considered under two headings: proximity to markets and national competitive advantages.

Proximity to markets

Firms which are located close to important markets often reap significant benefits. Those which are located in the geographical centre of the EU – between Brussels, Berlin and Paris – tend to have the major advantage of proximity to the richest and greatest concentration of consumers in the EU. Conversely, firms located in peripheral regions tend to suffer from remoteness from major markets. For many firms locating in a large or burgeoning market is often a crucial link in building a global presence, for example, foreign direct investment in Europe by American and Japanese firms and the symmetrical foreign direct investment in the USA and Japan by European firms.

National competitive advantages

In addition to market proximity, a firm may gain competitive advantage by being located in or transferring to a nation which enjoys a competitive advantage over other nations. In Porter's *The Competitive Advantage of Nations* (11), he asserts that the nations of the world can be divided into two broad types:

- 'winning nations' whose economic performance and hence the competitiveness of their constituent firms is superior to other nations;
- 'losing nations', i.e. nations whose economic performance and hence the competitiveness of their constituent firms is inferior to other nations.

A consequence of subscribing to this view is that the nation which is home base to a firm can have a major effect upon its competitiveness. In summary, Porter asserts that when assessing international competitiveness it is wrong to think of a particular nation as being particularly competitive. Rather, a more accurate observation is that in certain nations some industries happen to be particularly competitive as illustrated in Table B3.12.

Thus Porter's suggestion is that if, say, a pharmaceutical firm has as its home base the USA, then it is more likely to be successful than if it was in Italy. Similarly, if a shoe company has Italy as its home base, it is more likely to be successful than if it had, say, the USA. Porter asserts that the underlying causes for a nation to be particularly competitive in certain industries are revealed by the nation's 'diamond of competitive advantage', as shown in Figure B3.3. He claims that every nation has a unique set of:

- factor conditions;
- related and supplier industries;
- demand conditions;
- pattern of firm strategy, structure and rivalry.

As shown in Figure B3.3, in every nation these four major elements, plus the more random influences of chance and government, interact with each other to produce a unique set of circumstances which may or may not confer some unique advantages on particular industries in the nation. As illustrated in Table B3.12, Italy's diamond gives it advantage in shoes and tiles, while Denmark's is in brewing and furniture.

Table B3.12 Certain home nations are particularly competitive in certain industries

Nation	Competitive industries
Denmark	Brewing, furniture
Germany	Printing presses, vehicles
Holland	Cut flowers
Italy	Shoes, tiles
Japan	Electronics
Korea	Electronics
UK	Publishing and aircraft
USA	Pharmaceuticals and health care

Any firm can therefore assess the geographical implications of its location or locations in terms of:

- globalization and how it is affected by it;
- actual location and whether this augments or detracts from its competitive ability in terms of proximity to markets and national 'diamond of competitive advantage'.

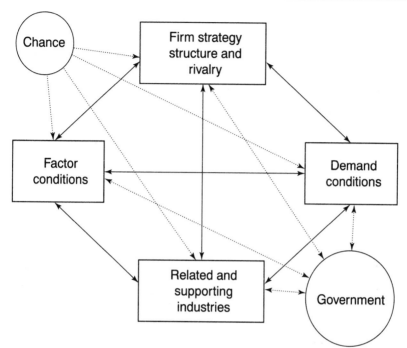

Figure B3.3 Porter's diamond of national competitive advantage (11)

KEY ENVIRONMENTAL INFLUENCES: SOCIETY

Introduction

In contrast to technological change, when social change is occurring it is often not apparent. Because of an inherent inability to recognize incremental social change, managers tend not to be take appropriate strategic action until the opportunity for gaining competitive advantage has passed. However, the fact that social changes may be difficult to see does not mean that they are not real and of strategic importance. For example, a major social change, permitted by technology, which took place in the early 1990s was remote or teleworking. In many industries staff no longer need an office in which to work. They can work at home or from their cars using personal computers and modems to headquarters. In the financial services industry, this development has permitted companies to remove completely office facilities for sales staff and to replace them with notebook personal computers and modems, with sales staff working from cars and home.

The cost benefits of this type of operation are very clear – the fixed assets associated with a salesperson are greatly reduced – but what is less clear are the social implications. What are the organizational implications of having sales staff who are remote from colleagues and are not part of a work community.

Although the changes in society that impact upon firms will vary from industry to industry, in most situations they can be categorized under the following headings: education; equal opportunity; religion, role of women; family and mobility.

Education

The influence of education upon social behaviour has been profound and is likely to be even more significant in the future. For example, in the UK between 1989 and 1995 the number of students in full-time higher education more than doubled. The effects of this are seen not just in the 'education industry', i.e. book publishers, providers of housing, but also in terms of the knowledge, skills and attitudes of this highly educated element of society.

Equal opportunity

Equal opportunity on the basis of sex, religion and race is now enshrined in the legislation of most western countries. The effects of this can be seen not just in terms of employment patterns but also in the lifestyles and hence the expenditure patterns of minorities. For example, equal opportunity for women has led to a great increase in the proportion of women having demanding careers with a consequent change in their buying behaviour.

Religion

Religion is a primary driver of many people's value systems and can have major effects upon the business environment. For example, the lessening of religious influence has led to relaxation in licensing laws and subsequent increased opportunities in the alcoholic drinks industry.

Role of women

The role expected of women in society has changed substantially since the 1980s. perhaps seen most clearly in the increase in their participation rate in the workforce. This has major strategic marketing effects, not just on employment patterns and personal expectations but also on their personal income. This great increase in spending power has obvious implications on the way in which many industries target their marketing, for example, the targeting of women buyers of cars, houses and holidays. Many other industries have also been affected:

- *Health.* Women's health is a growing and increasingly important industry. This growth is clearly due to the changing role of women, increase in personal income and promotion of the issue by many interest groups.
- *Retailing.* For women working outside the home shopping no longer has any real social connotation. The main issue is often speed and convenience. Consequently vast shopping centres with major carparking facilities have been developed with the chief attractions of speed of shopping and convenience.
- *Do-it-yourself (DIY) industry.* Historically, the DIY industry has been considered to be male orientated. However, women are becoming increasingly involved, as reflected in DIY store layout and display. Many stores are changing from a macho image with little product information to a more female image with attention to appearance and a great deal of product information.

Family

The nature of the family and its role in society is under continuous change. The previous norm of a stable, i.e. lifetime, family comprising mother, father and two children is in many regions no longer the case and has been replaced by: married couples who do not wish to have children; single parent families; divorced families; remarried families; childless couples living together; adults living alone; children who leave home in their teens.

These social changes can have profound strategic marketing implications, for example:

- *House and apartment size.* Smaller families tend to mean smaller house size, smaller rooms, smaller and less furniture.
- *Disposable income.* Smaller families tend to mean that more disposable income is available for non-essential purchases, for example, holidays, entertainment, non-essential consumer goods.
- *Food packaging.* For example, pack size, shelf life.
- *Marketing of consumer products.* The market for family purchased goods can no longer be regarded simply as 'the family unit', but must consider the many niches within this unit.

Mobility

Greater personal mobility for both work and leisure presents opportunities in many industries. For example, industrial estates do not need to be located close to the workforce. In the leisure industry this greater mobility has provided many opportunities for the development of out-of-town leisure facilities, golf courses and driving ranges. This increased mobility represents a major social change, the implications of which have not yet been fully ascertained.

Any firm can select those elements in its social environment which affect it now and are likely to affect it in the future. An assessment can be made of their likely impact, as shown in Table B3.13.

Table B3.13 Hypothetical example of the social elements which could affect a DIY retailer

Element	Today	Three yrs from now	Comment
Religion	Closed on Sunday	Open on Sunday	Increased trade
Role of women	Minority of purchasers but increasing	Increasing proportion	Change layout and displays: less 'macho'
Family	Two Adults plus two children	Smaller numbers and homes	Change ranges to suit smaller units

CONCLUSION

The firms whose managers are most adroit at dissecting their environment and responding imaginatively and often uniquely to significant
changes ought to be able to build true and sustained competitive
advantage. The strategic importance of this activity has been best
expressed perhaps by Levitt in his discussion of the demise of the
American railway companies:

> Even after the advent of automobiles, trucks and aeroplanes,
> the railroad tycoons remained imperturbably self-confident. If
> you had told them 50 years ago that in 30 years they would be
> flat on their backs, broke and pleading for government subsi-
> dies, they would have thought you totally demented. It was
> not even a discussable subject, or an askable question, or a
> matter which any sane person would consider worth speculat-
> ing about. The very thought was insane (12).

NOTES

1. Although such a situation could occur: for example, a dominant market share
   player could occupy the lowest cost position in a niche which was declining in
   size. If a number of its competitors left the market because of profit pressures,
   the dominant player might prosper due to increase in relative market share and
   decrease in number of competitors.
2. This could of course be cash contribution or some other measure.
3. See (7) for a definition of perfect competition.
4. For a detailed refutation of 'the case of economics', see Leontiades, M. (1989).
   *Myth Management: An Examination of Corporate Diversification as Fact and
   Theory*, Blackwell, Oxford.
5. Like all 'rules' in strategic market planning, this is only largely true: for example,
   Korea and Malaysia could be considered as new entrants in the automobile market.
6. The substance of this view of competition is taken from (10).
7. In this section reference will be made exclusively to the operations of the European
   Union although similar effects are seen in the influence of groupings such as
   NAFTA, ASEAN, EFTA.

REFERENCES

(1) Stoffels, J. D. (1994). *Strategic Issues in Management: A Comprehensive Guide to Environmental Scanning*. Pergamon, Oxford.
(2) Stewart, J. M. (1993). Future state visioning – a poweful leadership process. *Long Range Planning*, 26 (6), 89–98.
(3) Private management consultant's report by Management Horizons.
(4) Stekler, H. O. (1994). Are economic forecasts valuable? *Journal of Forecasting*, 13 (6) 495–505.
(5) Drucker, P. (1980). *Managing in Turbulent Times*, p. 90. Heinemann, London.
(6) The *Business Week* global 1000. *Business Week*, 10 July 1995, 63.
(7) Baumol, W. and Blinder A. (1982). *Economics: Principles and Policy*. Harcourt Brace Jovanovich, San Diego.
(8) Porter, M. E (1980). *Competitive Strategy: Techniques for Analyzing Industries and Competitors*. Free Press, New York.
(9) Deloitte and Touche (1995). *The Future of Retail Banking*. Deloitte and Touche, London.
(10) Hamel, G. and Prahalad, C. K. (1995). Competing for the future: the criticality of strategy. Paper presented to the Strategic Management Society Conference, Mexico City.
(11) Porter, M. E. (1990). *The Competitive Advantage of Nations*. Macmillan, London.
(12) Levitt, T. (1960). Marketing myopia. *Harvard Business Review*, July–August.

B4

Analysing the Firm

Firms are not inert structures, but complex living organisms which are really a coalition of people, both inside and outside the firm, who have agreed, for various reasons, not always financial, to cooperate with each other. When people form a coalition it is the behaviour of the people which determines what the coalition does. Thus it is behaviour which is the font from which spring all the firm's activities. The reality of this is illustrated in the starkly different behaviours or atmospheres that can be observed in similarly sized firms conducting similar businesses. Retailers of similar products in adjacent locations may have dramatically different levels of performance – one retailer is popular and thrives while the rival just survives. The difference in performance is often due to the different behavioural climates. Similarly, it is not unusual for poorly performing firms to be taken over and then energized into superior performance by the new managers. Often a major contributor to the change is the new behavioural climate.

Managers' comments, such those below, show just how important is a firm's behavioural climate.

> 'I wouldn't work for that firm even if I were to be paid double what I earn here. The atmosphere it terrible.'

> 'Morale in that firm is low.'

> 'I'd love to work there. I'd even work for less money. It's just the way they go about things.'

Ackoff (1) has expressed these types of sentiments more pithily: 'managers strive not just for results but also for life style'. Irrespective of the nature of the work being undertaken, all firms will receive much of their dynamic from their behavioural spring.

Behavioural

The behavioural spring of a firm is considered to be that unique set of attitudes, atmosphere and personality which gives it its particular behavioural climate. Just as in everyday life people are judged mainly on the basis of personality rather than say physique, by analogy if we wish to analyse the past performance and potential of any firm we must start not with its strategies, resources, operations and results but with the source of these activities: its behavioural spring.

Assessing behavioural climate

If firms do have distinct personalities and can be changed it is important to understand the source of these personalities and how they can be assessed or measured.

LEADERS: THE PERSONALITY SHAPERS AND DRIVERS

Within the home the fundamental determinants of the behavioural climate are the parents: these are the people who set the agenda for the family and determine the atmosphere in which it is pursued. By analogy, the leaders of a firm determine its agenda and the behavioural climate in which that agenda is pursued. Good leadership is obviously key to establishing a behavioural climate in which the firm will flourish.

There are many examples of exceptional leadership. The business autobiographies of recognized leaders are testimony to how strong is the interest in the issue of good leadership. While it is interesting to read such stories, from a strategic marketing perspective it is probably more instructive to try to divine generic rules for superior leadership.

GENERIC RULES FOR SUPERIOR LEADERSHIP

Just as there are generic rules for superior performance in the market, for example (as shown in Chapter B2), firms with a relative market share of more than 1.0 ought to have superior returns, so also there tend to be generic rules for superior leadership. Good leaders display certain characteristics irrespective of the industry and the actual firm. These characteristics can be considered as follows:

- *Public achievements*. What types of achievement publicly brand a leader as superior?
- *Characteristics*. What common characteristics do superior leaders tend to have?
- *Tasks*. What tasks do superior leaders tend to undertake?
- *Processes*. What are the typical processes which superior leaders tend to follow in order to achieve their objectives?

Public achievements of superior leaders

Business leaders often receive the greatest accolades for achievements such as the dramatic turnaround of a failing or poor performing firm and building shareholder value. A well-documented example is Waterford Crystal. In the late 1980s Waterford Crystal, the Irish prestige crystal glass manufacturer, was in deep crisis. It was sustaining enormous losses caused by:

- demand problems in its major market, the USA;
- severe competitive pressure;
- productivity and quality problems;
- unit cost problems: wage costs were viewed as 'out of control';
- major labour problems manifested in extreme militancy and a strike in 1990 that lasted 14 weeks.

In 1989 the company had a loss of £IR29.0mn and the problems looked so intractable that many feared that the company was doomed. However, that year Patrick Galvin was appointed as Chief Executive and under his leadership, after enormous strategic and operational analysis and effort, the company was transformed so that in 1995 it achieved profits of £IR28mn–30mn.

> The annual results, which are published today and which analysts expect to show an increase in pre-tax profits from

I£22.6m (£23m) to I£28m–I£30m, will effectively mark the end of the turnround phase (2).

This was a clear manifestation of outstanding leadership leading to major public achievement.

Characteristics of superior leaders

Although good leaders tend to have very strong and individualistic personalities, many tend to display the characteristics set out below.

Vision

Vision could be described as the ability to have unique, and long-run insights into business problems that are denied to the majority. For example, Richard Branson's vision in developing the Virgin chain of record stores and the Virgin airline provided excellent examples of vision of what could be achieved by the visionary altering of the rules of the game for these industries.

Effective and speedy implementation of change

It could be argued that this is the key senior managerial task. All industries are in a state of continuous change and those managers who are most effective at changing their firms' strategies and structures to accommodate, or pre-emptively implement strategies to deal with change will have the most successful firms. The most demanding leadership challenges are those in which major strategic change is required, for example, to turn around an ailing company. Clearly the ability to cause necessary change to be implemented with great speed and decisiveness is a hallmark of superior leadership. When a new leader is appointed it is quite often the case that progress will be judged by what has been achieved in the first one hundred days in office.

Power

Good leaders tend to be powerful people in that they are able to compel or persuade others to follow their agenda. The sources of this power usually include:

- *Personality.* Effective leaders tend to have strong personalities which may range from charismatic, i.e. persuade through charm and dialogue, to coercive, i.e. compel through threats.
- *Personal belief.* Related to personality is the issue of personal belief in oneself. Good leaders tend to have great belief in their own ability to solve the firm's problems, no matter how over-whelming the odds appear and irrespective of what the business pundits assert. Good leaders therefore tend to be courageous.

Verbal and communication skills

These are key attributes necessary for good leadership – the ability to articulate cogently and persuasively the messages about the future and in addition to communicate these messages to others, inside and out-side the firm, so that there is universal and agreed clarity on what the firm is hoping to achieve. Such leaders are often extremely focused. There is one major and usually simple message and they continuously return to it. This superior communication should to lead to the devel-opment of strong workforce 'buy in' and commitment.

Diagnostic skills

Good leaders tend to have rather good diagnostic skills, i.e. they can have unique insights and resolutions to the problems facing the firm and the industry. These diagnostic skills may take many forms. A good leader may have a unique knowledge of industry-specific key success factors, or non-industry specific generic key success factors which can be applied in any industry: for example, the steps to be taken to rescue any firm which is in a crisis.

Commitment, obsession and energy

A common characteristic of superior leaders is the relentless pursuit of their business agendas. Such leaders tend to spend enormous amounts of time and energy, often at great personal cost, in continous, dedicated pursuit of their strategies.

Tasks undertaken by superior leaders

The tasks which superior leaders undertake will vary according to the particular circumstances, but in the development of any new strategic agenda the following are likely to be included.

Future vision

The leader aims to provide everyone with a vision to follow of the future of the firm. This vision will often include issues such as:

- shareholder value, i.e. after implementation of the plan what will be the new market capitalization of the firm;
- future growth rate of the firm using various measures such as growth of sales and profits;
- risk profile, i.e. how vulnerable will the firm be during and after implementation of the strategy;
- market position, i.e. what will be the firm's market share in its chosen markets;
- competitive position, i.e. what will be the firm's position relative to its major competitors in terms of growth, markets, costs and returns.

Provide strategies

A vision provides the intention, while the strategies provide the routes to achieve those intentions. These high level strategies are likely to be market driven and will normally include phrases such as growth, turn-around and generic.

Develop change programmes

The development of programmes of organizational change which will implement the desired strategies is often required.

Measure performance

It will be necessary to develop and implement performance measures which will ascertain how well the new strategy is being implemented.

Incentives to achieve

The provision of a range of incentives is required, which may be negative as well as positive, that will cause all staff to strive towards the achievement of the firm's vision.

Communication

The continuous communication of the firm's vision must be made to all stakeholders. Normally this communication will focus upon a small number of key issues, perhaps only one, at any point in time.

The process of superior leadership

The process of superior leadership in the strategic development of a firm cannot be delegated or bought in. It must flow from and be seen to be owned by the leader of the firm and the senior management team. This can be achieved as follows:

Strategy ownership

The new strategy must be seen to be owned by the leader and the senior management team. This means that new strategies ought not to come from a strategic planning department or from outside consultants. New strategies must be seen to emanate from the team itself.

Strategy development and implementation

The senior management team alone cannot develop and implement the strategy. This can only be achieved through involvement of the staff of the firm. It can be facilitated by the development of project teams that undertake and implement specific projects within the new strategy. Typical examples of implementation projects could be:

• A team of four people to grow market share for a product by 10 per cent to 11 per cent within six months. This is to be achieved through a promotion campaign in local newspapers, starting in four weeks and being repeated on a weekly basis.
• An individual to monitor and report on response times by answer-

ing staff for a telephone sales office. Within four weeks all calls to be answered within three rings.

External benchmarking

For all firms their strategic position must be assessed relative to their existing and potential competitors. Consequently an additional task for the leaders in the strategic market planning process is to ensure that the practices pursued and the standards applied in their firms at least match rivals.

LEADERSHIP LIFE CYCLES

Many good leaders are really only good leaders once and for a limited period of time. They display the skills necessary for the achievement of some difficult goal and then stay on as leaders even though their contribution is of declining importance. Kets de Vries (3) has researched the issue of leadership contribution and has categorized it into three stages: entry and experimentation; consolidation; decline (see Table B4.1).

- Entry and experimentation stage. It is not unusual for good leaders, initially, to focus on a small number of key themes which will build or turnaround the business.
- Consolidation stage. When success has been achieved, to consolidate by following the original formula for success.
- Decline stage. When the original formula for success no longer works to cause decline by their ossification in a past that no longer exists.

Many good leaders will have just one pass of this three-stage process. Exceptional leaders will reinvent the entry and experimentation rules and have a second pass. Finally, truly great leaders will continuously appraise their skills and contribution in relation to the changing leadership needs and either reinvent themselves or leave the firm and repeat their original success in other similarly structured situations.

Table B4.1 Leadership life cycles

Stage	Entry and experimentation	Consolidation	Decline
Key activities	Focus on key themes	Follow the formula	Ossification

POWER AND HOW IT IS EXERCISED

Power and how it is exercised is a key element in leadership and behaviour within the firm. It is fundamental to the nature of the relationships that prevail in all firms. Power could be defined as the ability to cause people to behave in a way which, if left to their own devices, they would not. The sources of power and how it is exercised vary greatly from individual to individual and from firm to firm.

Powerful managers

For managers to be effective they must be powerful. They must be able to ensure that the strategies they wish to pursue are translated into reality and this requires power. Those managers who are most effective in terms of achieving the firm's goals will tend to be the most powerful. However, most powerful does not necessarily mean most aggressive: there are many routes to becoming powerful and some of the principal ones are discussed below.

Power through personality

Even though rarely mentioned in official corporate communications, the strength of personality of a manager is often a major source of power. Thus in many firms it is not unusual to hear the chief executive or some other senior manager being discussed as follows:

> 'He has great powers of persuasion and will be able to get everyone to agree to the proposal.'
>
> 'Everyone likes him: he is a breath of fresh air in the company.'
>
> 'He has such an eye for detail, he never misses any issue no matter how small.'
>
> 'He has such a network of contacts right throughout the industry.'

Pfeffer's (4) research into what makes an individual powerful suggests that there are four main sources of power:

• *Verbal skills and articulateness*. This is perhaps the most important skill for any manager to develop. As most business communications are verbal rather than written, it is vital that senior managers have the ability to talk cogently and persuasively.

- *Personal belief in oneself.* This is linked to articulateness and it implies that if managers do not have absolute and obvious conviction about themselves, then it is unlikely that others will.
- *Diagnostic skills.* This is the ability to diagnose any problem more speedily and more effectively than others. For example, in firms which are in need of rejuvenation those managers who are able to pinpoint the reasons for poor performance and then set out a strategy for robust improvement are likely to become powerful.
- *Understanding the rules of the firm.* In addition to the formal rules of any firm there will usually also exist unwritten and perhaps unspoken rules. (An example of an unwritten rule could be that there is a tradition that the chief executive must be informed when a customer is lost.) Individual managers may gain power through an intimate knowledge and use of all the rules of the firm.[1]

Power through knowledge

Managers who have proprietary or unique knowledge or skills tend to be sought after and hence are powerful. For example, in most large corporations there will be specialist tax managers whose major task is to reduce the tax liability of the firm. The financial contributions that really good tax advisers can make bestow upon them a power which is reflected in high salary levels.

Power through information

Managers who have superior information about their firm in terms of scope and detail tend to become powerful. Thus it is often the case that a firm's accountants tend, because of the nature of their function, to be in receipt of more information than other managers. The effect of this in western industry has been that traditionally accountants have been more powerful than other functions. The accounting function is often the fastest and most favoured route to senior management positions.

Power through resources

Those managers who have power over resources – financial, human, equipment – tend to accumulate power. This is another factor in making accounting the premiere route to senior management positions: the sanctioning of expenditure on resources will often need to be justified on the basis of an accounting rule.

Power through promotion

Managers who are in positions to determine who will be promoted (or demoted) tend to be powerful as those who are seeking promotion will naturally defer to them.

How power is exercised

How power is exercised will vary from firm to firm and there may even be variations between SBUs or even departments within firms. Table B4.2 shows a typical range of modes.

The appropriateness of a power regime

It is impossible to be prescriptive about which type of power regime is best for any firm – it is very much a function of the firm itself. However, the power regime can be influenced by key industry success factors. For example, in industries such as fashion, pop music or advertising where a key success factor is the creativity of the people, power regimes are likely to favour the consensus approach as the quality of the staff's creativity is key to success. In contrast in high volume commodity goods, for example cement, mass-produced food products, the power regime is more likely to be at the autocratic end of the scale as a key success factor in such industries is efficiency, i.e. low unit costs and speed.

CULTURE

Flowing from the leadership and power relationships that prevail in any firm is its culture, which could be considered to be the particular set of attitudes, behaviours and value systems that make the firm

Table B4.2 Various modes in which power is exercised

	Completely autocratic	Autocratic with team input	Trade-off	Team majority	Consensus
Features	All decisions taken by the leader. No questioning allowed.	Inner caucus work with leader to make decisions. Debate confined to the inner caucus.	Various contributors – different levels and functions – to tbe decision process with 'bartering' to reach decisions.	Larger teams with majority agreeing decisions. Debate encouraged.	No decisions without the agreement of all. Continuous debate by all.
Advantages	Speed and decisiveness. May yield uniquely successful strategy.	Speed and decisiveness. Benefit of more than one view. Builds top team.	Wider set of opinions. Likely to be more acceptable.	Wider set of opinions. Likely to be more acceptable.	Widest set of opinions. Will be acceptable. Agreed decisions so rapid implementation.
Disadvantages	May not be optimal. Is imposed. No correction possible.	Too small a group. Is imposed. Correction difficult.	Slower decision-making. May not be optimal – may be a compromise to reach agreement.	Slowness of decision-making.	Very slow. Individual creativity may be stifled.

unique. Although it is difficult to define a firm's culture, it is essential when appraising it to be well informed about its appropriateness. An appropriate culture will tend to have two dimensions: appropriate to the industry and appropriate to the firm's goals.

Certain industries demand certain cultures and if a constituent firm does not have that culture it will fail. For example, in the fashion industry firms tend to need a creative and open culture so that person- nel are attuned to and react quickly to nuances in consumer tastes. In contrast, in the heavy engineering industry a fairly conservative 'fig- ures driven' culture is likely to be more appropriate.

Irrespective of the industry, the goals followed by individual firms will demand certain cultures. Firms vary greatly in goals such as growth rate, product range, market scope, production depth, service strategy, pricing strategy, quality strategy and distribution strategy. These goals will only be realized if there is an appropriate culture. For example, firms which have as a core strategy 'superior personal cus- tomer service' are more likely to have a greater culture of individual flexibility about decision-making than firms which have a core strate- gy of selling commodity products at the lowest possible costs.

Archetypal cultures

Research (5) and casual observation show that firms' cultures can be categorized into two archetypes: the mechanistic Taylor (6) type and the behavioural Mayo (7) type.

The mechanistic Taylor type of culture is one in which it is assumed that the primary determinant of a firm's success is how efficiently the tasks are carried out. Thus when goals are being set or tasks being delin- eated it is important to break down the tasks into their constituent ele- ments and provide employees with detailed instructions from which there must be no deviation. Thus the people are 'human machines' pro- grammed to carry out the tasks in the most efficient manner possible.

The behavioural Mayo type of culture is one in which it is assumed that the primary determinant of a firm's success is the motivation, drive and knowledge of the people who comprise it. Consequently when goals or tasks are being set the best way to achieve them is not to give specific instructions but to empower people to work together using their own judgements and creativity.

The Taylor and the Mayo views have been stated very starkly above.

In most firms they tend not to be mutually exclusive and there will usually be a mixture of both approaches with a tendency towards one or other.

Common culture

Left to their own devices managers will often, perhaps unintentionally, seek to set up exclusive groups which have cultural values different from other groups. For example, it is not unusual for firms to classify their staff into the groupings of senior managers, middle managers, lower managers and operatives and for these groups to develop sets of rules which are exclusive to them. This could be manifested in, say, senior managers' dining room, car parking spaces, office locations. Similarly staff from different functions may develop separate cultures which promote the function. It is not unusual for the marketing function to have a spending and risk culture which is at variance with the finance function's culture. Additionally, in divisionalized firms different cultures may develop in different SBUs. This will almost certainly occur when there is great variation in the performance and potential of SBUs. For example, the culture prevailing in a mature, low profitability SBU will tend to be different from that prevailing in a high growth SBU.

Effecting a common culture – hierarchically, functionally and corporate wide – is a major task for senior managers. For firms to achieve superior performance not only must there be a clear sense of direction, but there must also be a common purpose. To have a common purpose there must be a common culture. Evidence of the benefits that accrue to firms which have a genuine single culture can be seen in the remarkable performance of so many Japanese firms: remarkable performances built on firms having remarkably common cultures.[2]

Changing culture

Adults find it extremely difficult, or often impossible, to change their own culture, personality, attitudes, behaviour patterns and tastes. Analogously, for firms, even when the managers know that it is in their own best interests to change the culture, it tends to be extremely difficult and often impossible. For example, in the late 1970s, even though senior executives at the US automobile manufacturer Chrysler knew they were incurring the greatest losses in the firm's history, they did not change their culture, structure or methods of working. Their behaviour, which had led to this failure, continued even though the figures showed that continuing to operate in the same way would lead to certain bankruptcy. The inappropriateness of the culture and structure was one of the first issues which Lee Iacocca observed and then acted upon when he was appointed to rescue the firm.

> It turned out that my worries were justified. I soon stumbled upon my first major revelation: Chrysler didn't really function like a company at all. Chrysler in 1978 was like Italy in the 1860s – the company consisted of a cluster of little duchies, each one run by a prima donna. It was a bunch of mini-empires, with nobody giving a damn about what anyone else was doing. What I found at Chrysler were thirty-five vice -presidents each with his own turf (8).

This inability to change is typical of most companies and often the only time it is possible to change a firm's culture is when it is threatened with bankruptcy. A typical sequence of culture change is as follows:

- *Stage 1*. The firm is in crisis and there is great fear for its future. The chief executive ineffectively strives for better performance amid extreme discontent and anxiety.
- *Stage 2*. Bankruptcy looms and the chief executive is sacked and a 'saviour' is brought in to rescue the firm.
- *Stage 3*. The saviour is given a honeymoon period by all stakeholders and in this period is given freedom of action to undertake strategies which could not even have been considered under the old regime.
- *Stage 4*. Two results are possible.

  —Through true strategic and operational redirection the saviour has indeed saved the firm which continues to build upon its success.
  — In spite of efforts to give the firm a new and successful strategy the results are disappointing, the sense of crisis returns and ultimately the saviour is sacked and a new saviour is brought in and the process returns to Stage 3.

ROLE OF STRUCTURE IN STRATEGIC MARKET PLANNING

For life to function effectively there must be effective structures. Structure is a key determinant of the quality of all aspects of life: it is all pervasive and always has the same function, namely to deliver. When structures fail to deliver they are either changed or abandoned. The universal nature of structures is illustrated in Table B4.3.

Each of the structures in Table B4.3 has a particular shape. For example, the 'armed services tends to be very hierarchical with a clear chain of command from the top of the structure to the bottom, whereas terrorist structures tend to be in small cells with little hierarchical reporting. Each structure is appropriate: the armed services structure reflects the fact that they are an official part of government and society and, in democracies, tend to operate with the support of society. The terrorist structure tends to represent a minority of people in society, operates in a clandestine manner and is structured so to avoid detection.

Table B4.3   Structures are needed to permit life to function

Structure	Purpose
Family unit	Provide future generations
Churches	Provide guidance, direction and support in pursuit of the afterlife
City	Provide a superior commercial and living environment
Government	Provide a means of ruling the city, council, nation, etc.
Professional bodies, e.g. medical professional body	Provide a means of regulating the profession in the interests of members and patients
Hospitals	Provide medical care for the community
Universities	Provide higher education and services to the community
Armed services	Provide the military means of achieving national goals
Terrorists	Provide political results through acts of terror

Returning to the purpose of a structure, it could be argued that its function is to permit the achievement of the organization's mission and that when it fails to do so it is changed or abandoned. For example, in the UK since the early 1980s there has been intense political debate concerning the Tory view of the failure to deliver the pre-1980 local government authority structures. This has led to numerous restructurings of the local authority tier of government in order to provide a better, as defined by Tories, delivery.

Similar debate has raged around the restructuring of the health service and indeed every other large organization which has engaged in major structural change. However, it should be noted that, irrespective of the organization, public or private, large or small, even when it is failing to deliver, it still tends to be very difficult and often impossible to change an established structure: there seems to be a universal inbuilt reluctance to change.

Just as appropriate structure is vital to all aspects of life, so the same arguments apply to business. The firms with the most appropriate structures, all other things being equal, will be the best at delivering their mission.

Relationship between structure and strategy

The issue of the relationship between a firm's structure and its strategy has been a major topic of debate in strategic market planning since the publication of Chandler's seminal work *Strategy and Structure* (9), which showed rigorously that for most firms the following relationship between strategy and structure obtains. Firms first set their mission, strategies and goals and therefore the logical conclusion is that the organizational structure is developed in response to these primary determinants – structure follows strategy. However, subsequent research (10) has shown that this is not universally true. There are many organizations, or rather many organizational structures, which develop a 'life of their own' so that strategies and operations pursued are a result of the existing structure rather than the strategy. For example, it is not unusual for traditional UK parliamentarians to argue that the most important thing that parliament can do is to preserve its structures without any change, with performance, efficiency or delivery being secondary matters. Although this is an extreme example of total resistance to structural change, in most firms there tends to be an inherent opposition towards structural change for the following reasons:

• People have grown accustomed to the traditional way of doing things and regard new structures as unlikely to be any better.

People are 'held by history'.
- Reporting relationships and evaluation procedures are likely to be altered and there will normally be resistance to this. A frequent managerial comment after restructuring is: 'To whom will I be reporting?'
- Any structural change tends to replace past certainty – perhaps a mediocre performance – with new uncertainty. There is no guarantee that the new structure will deliver any better than the past one.
- The implementation of major structural change tends to be expensive.

Development of an appropriate structure

There are no guidelines on the development of an organizational structure but usually it will be a function of the following:

- *The firm's mission and goals.* The structure ought to be able to deliver these in the best possible manner. For example, if a firm wished to be the low cost producer its structure ought to facilitate this.
- *How the firm has defined its business.* When the firm has defined its business in terms of products, markets, customers and technologies (see Chapter B1) its structure should reflect this definition. For example, if a firm had defined its business in terms of six major product areas in three territorial regions then its structure ought to reflect this.
- *Key success factors in the industry.* In most industries there are some key success factors or rules for success by which firms must abide if they are to be successful. Firms must structure themselves in such a way that those key success factors are harnessed. For example, in many industries buying power is a key success factor. For firms in such industries the maximization of their buying power, through centralized buying, is clearly essential. In other industries where superior marketing is a key success factor, firms must have structures which permit marketing managers to address their markets.

Typical key success factors and their influences on structure is shown in Table B4.4.

Table B4.4   Influence of key industry success upon organizational structure

Key industry success factors leading to	
Centralized structures	Decentralized structures
Large economies of scale	Low economies of scale
Low unit costs	Superior quality
Commodity type products	Differentiated products
Typical industries: tyres, automobile engines, consumer electronics	Typical industries: hotels, management consultancy, building

Evaluation of strategy and performance

In addition to the above considerations, any structure ought to permit the evaluation of the strategy being pursued. This performance evaluation should take place at the levels of: the individual manager; the product; the market; the department; the SBU; the overall firm.

TYPES OF ORGANIZATIONAL STRUCTURE

Typical organizational structures, the rationale behind them, the arguments for and against each type and finally the likely type of decision-making – centralized versus decentralized – are shown in Figures B4.1 to B4.5.

Small business structure

- *Comment*: This is the simplest type of structure and it often evolves, as the firm grows, into a functional business structure (see Figure B4.1).
- *For*: Simple and clear.
- *Against*: As the business grows too many diverse tasks for the owner manager.
- *Decisions*: Centralized.

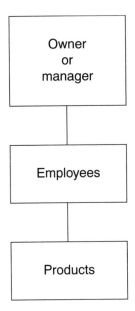

Figure B4.1   Small business structure

Functional business structure

*   *Comment*: This type of structure divides the management tasks according to disciplines, i.e. marketing, finance, production, personnel and IT (see Figure B4.2).
*   *For*: Clear delineation of tasks.
*   *Against*: Management compartmentalized and lack of multidisciplinary approaches.
*   *Decisions*: Centralized.

SBU or divisional business structure

*   *Comment*: The organization is broken up according to its constituent SBUs (see Figure B4.3).
*   *For*: Product markets clearly addressed.
*   *Against*: It is likely to be increase costs to have such a break-up.
*   *Decisions*: Decentralized.

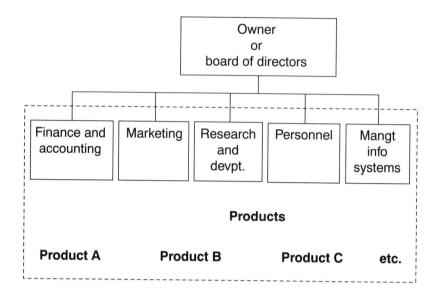

Figure B4.2   Functional business structure

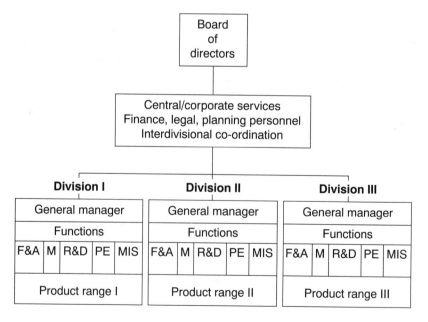

Figure B4.3   SBU or divisional business structure

Holding company structure

- *Comment*: Headquarters tends to act as a 'bank' which judges each division's performances largely on the basis of financial results and tends not to be involved in internal SBU decisions (see Figure B4.4).
- *For*: Allows each SBU to clearly address its product market segments.
- *Against*: Lack of direction, in terms of product market scope, from the centre.
- *Decisions*: Decentralized.

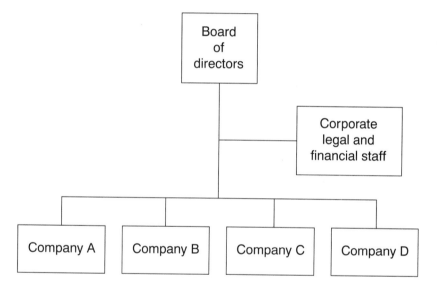

Figure B4.4   Holding company structure

Matrix structure

- *Comment*: This type of structure is often found in large multinational corporations where, for example, strategies for specific regions or territories (say, Europe) are regarded as of equal importance with strategies for specific products (see Figure B4.5).
- *For*: Gives equal weight to crucial success factors, for example, product management and territory management.
- *Against*: Confusion over where the true power lies, often on element will come to be dominant.
- *Decisions*: Decentralized.

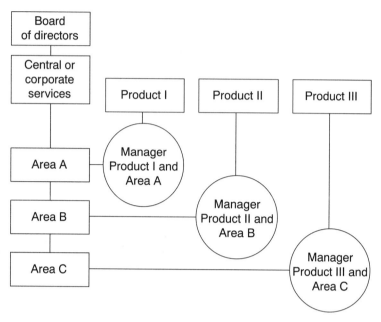

Figure B4.5   Matrix structure

CHANGES IN ORGANIZATIONAL STRUCTURE

Industries, markets, market niches, customer needs and attitudes, technologies, competitors and competitive behaviour are all in a constant
state of flux and change over time. A major responsibility of senior
management is to be sensitive to these changes, especially those that
are key industry success factors, and to adjust their organizational
structures to gain competitive advantage over slower reacting rivals.

An example of structures responding to this type of change is provided by the financial services industry. The rise in power, decrease in price
and portability of personal computers has been a major technological
change that has had profound effects upon this industry. Thus, historically financial services firms were structured as shown in Figure B4.6.

As shown in Figure B4.7 the headquarters contained an IT department with a mainframe and associated expert staff which had, as a
major task, to computerize sales data. The advent of powerful personal computers has enabled more astute firms to restructure as shown in
Figure B4.7. Under this new structure the very expensive mainframe
and its associated staff have been replaced by mobile sales people who

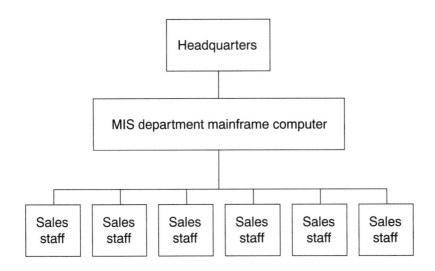

Figure B4.6 Typical financial services firm structure prior to computerization

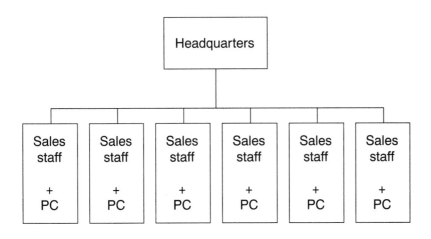

Figure B4.7 Typical financial services firm structure post-computerization

do not have an office but record their data on portable personal computers and send these to headquarters via a modem. The advantages are clear. The sales people have control of their own data and are likely to be better able to interact with customers. The new structure is likely to lead to considerable savings. The headquarters' IT budget will be significantly reduced and the office accommodation costs for sales people will be lower.

In practice, firms' structures usually lag behind industry changes and significant structural change often occurs only when there is severe profit decline or loss. A consequence of this lag is that when structures are finally changed it can both be quite traumatic and extremely costly.

When a long-term perspective is taken on most firms major structural change is an infrequent, but periodic, event. Over time key success factors in industries alter, or perhaps a new entrant joins the industry and the incumbent players find, as manifested in their results, that their structures have become inappropriate. It is not unusual to read in the business press comments from the chief executive on the annual report such as:

> 'In spite of real sales growth of 15 per cent net profit is down by 10 per cent due to a one-off charge of £10 million for restructuring.'

A good example of this type of restructuring is provided the Canadian aluminium producer Alcan.

> Canadian aluminium producer is in the final stages of a rigorous restructuring process . . . Since 1991, the group has cut annual costs by US$600m, mainly by direct management action, and has driven down debt by selling non-core assets worth about $1bn . . . Alcan has emerged as a streamlined organization, concentrating on three main areas: raw material; and chemical; power and smelting; and rolling . . . By the middle of 1996, each Aolcan business will have finished an analysis to determine its full potential and will have a clear set of objectives and trgets to meet. 'And business unit managers will be held accountable for their achievements,' says Mr Bougie. But Mr Bougie (President) points out that stream-

lined does not necessarily mean smaller.

In passing it should be noted that the primary factor in causing this massive restructuring was the entry of a 'rogue' player into the industry:

> Alcan was almost brought to its knees in the early 1990s by the sudden jump from less than 500,000 tonnes to more than 2m tonnes a year in aluminium exports from Russia that pushed prices down to record lows (11).

From the above it should be clear that the design and development of an organizational structure is not scientific. There are certain principles to be employed, but equally important is the art of managerial judgement. Managers who are particularly astute will be able to see and implement original and new structures which ought to confer benefit denied to rivals. Additionally, organizational structures are inherently messy and imprecise. Irrespective of the logic behind any structure there will always be elements which do not fit neatly into the structure. For example, it is not unusual for a firm which is structured on a product-based SBU system to have, say, one SBU which is based on a region: it could be that the individual product sales from the region are so small and the region is so different that it merits a unique stand-alone structure.

Finally, it is difficult to overstate the importance of structure as the means of delivering the firm's mission. Indeed, Doz (12) in his research into appropriate structures in multinational corporations, has shown robustly that for multinational corporations superior performance simply cannot be achieved if they do not have structures appropriate to their industries, the countries in which they operate and their goals. He has called those firms which have inappropriate structures 'misfits' and found that such firms always have a worse performance than their appropriately structured rivals. Thus, sensitivity to the appropriateness of existing structures and, when required, the speedy implementation of structural change are major responsibilities of senior management.

PERFORMANCE MEASUREMENT AND KEY PERFORMANCE MEASURES

Although qualitative judgements about the behaviour, culture and structure are vital – they are the spring from which all the firm's activities flow – a comprehensive strategic analysis also needs quantitative measures of performance. These measures are necessary as they provide answers to questions such as:

- *How good is the firm?* Quantitative measures enable this to be answered by comparing the firm's performance with:

  — its historical performance, i.e. is it improving or becoming worse?
  — its true competitors, i.e. in relation to them is its performance superior, equal or worse?
  — similar firms, i.e. in relation to similar firms, perhaps in different regions, is its performance superior, equal or worse?

- *Which parts of the firm are performing well and which are not?* Quantitative measures should pinpoint those areas which are performing well and those which are performing poorly and need to be strengthened.

In assessing performance, once again a generic approach can be used. Thus the firm's performance can be analysed at the following levels:

- Functional performance, i.e. how well is the firm performing in terms of: marketing; production; human relations; finance.
- Overall SBU performance.
- Corporate or group performance.

Each of these levels is now discussed.[3]

Performance measures at the functional level

Marketing function performance

The quality of a firm's marketing performance can be analysed by making judgements about:

- the resources available, i.e. staff (quality and numbers) and expenditures on marketing;
- employing some or all of the measures of marketing performance shown in Table B4.5.

Table B4.5   Measures of marketing performance

	Two years ago	One year ago	This year	% change	Comments
Sales volume					
Sales (£)					
Market share (£)					
Relative market share					
Sales per employee (£)					
Sales per employee (real £)*					
Marketing expenditure (£)					
Marketing staff					
Gross profit (£)					
Gross profit/ sales (%)					

* Real £ means adjusted for the rate of inflation.

In Table B4.5 the real £ is calculated as this tends to give a better measure of productivity and is illustrated in Table B4.6 by means of a hypothetical example. In this case it is assumed that a firm has had annual sales per employee of £100 for the past three years and that the rate of inflation has been running at 5 per cent per annum. To determine the value of sales per employee in real terms, actual sales per employee must be deflated as follows. Taking two years ago as the base year:

Sales per employee (real £) two years ago = £100

Sales per employee (real £) one year ago = £100 x 0.95 = £95

Sales per employee (real £) this year = £100 x 0.95 x 0.95 = £90.25

Table B4.6 Hypothetical illustration of the concept of of sales per employee (real £)

	Two years ago	One year ago	This year	Change %	Comment
Sales per employee (£)	100	100	100	0	Sales static
Sales per employee (Real £)	100	95	92.5	(10)	Sales in decline

Thus the sales per employee (real £) shows that there has indeed been a real decline in sales per employee of 10 per cent.

Production function performance

The quality of a firm's production performance can be analysed by making judgements about:

- the resources available, i.e. staff (quality and numbers) and expenditures on production;
- the age of the facilities;
- employing some or all of the measures of production performance shown in Table B4.7.

Human relations function performance

The quality of a firm's human relations performance can be analysed by making judgements about:

- resources available, i.e. staff (quality and numbers) and expenditures on human relations;
- training and development programme
- employing some or all of the measures of production performance shown in Table B4.8.

Table B4.7   Measures of production performance

	Two years ago	One year ago	This year	% change	Comments
Sales (£)					
Sales volume					
Total investment					
Sales/total investment					
Unit costs (£)					
Unit costs (real £)					
Stock turnover (times)					

Table B4.8   Measures of human relations performance

	Two years ago	One year ago	This year	% change	Comments
Payroll (£)					
Number of employees					
Unit labour costs (£)					
Unit labour costs (real £)					
Training expenditure (£)					
Training expend per employee (real £)					
Absenteeism: total no. of days					
Staff turnover rate (%)					

Finance function performance

The quality of a firm's financial performance can be analysed by making judgements about:

- resources available, i.e. staff (quality and numbers) and expenditures on the finance function;
- employing some or all of the standard measures of financial performance shown in Tables B4.9 to B4.12.

Performance measures at SBU level

The overall quality of an SBU's performance can be analysed by using key strategic ratios such as those in Table B4.13. These ratios help to provide an overall strategic view of the firm:

- *Competitive position* ratios[4] show how well the firm is faring in relation to its main competitors. Firms that are succeeding would expect these measures to grow.
- *Market characteristics* ratios show the quality of the markets which the firm addresses. Generally the higher the growth rates and the greater the degree of concentration, the better the prospects for the firm.
- *Cost and investment structure* ratios show how well investment in the firm is being used. Generally the better investment is controlled in relation to sales, the better the prospects for the firm.
- *Productivity* ratios show the effects of the firm's strategies and are key measures of performance. Generally all these measures should be increasing continuously.
- *Profitability* ratios show how the profitability of the firm is changing.

Performance measures at corporate level

Although this book is concerned primarily with strategic market planning at the SBU level, SBU activities are usually determined by corporate attitudes, parameters, guidelines and resources. When assessing SBU performance it is important to place it in a corporate context. Corporate performance may be assessed using financial measures

Table B4.9 Profit and loss statements

	Two years ago	One year ago	This year	% change	Comments
Sales (£)					
Purchases (£)					
Value added (£k)					
Manufacturing and distribution (£)					
Depreciation (£)					
Gross profit (£)					
Other expenses (£)					
PBIT (£)					

Table B4.10 Percentage profit and loss statements

	Two years ago	One year ago	This year	% change	Comments
Sales (%)					
Purchases (%)					
Value added (%)					
Manufacturing and distribution (%)					
Depreciation (%)					
Gross profit (£)					
Other expenses (%)					
PBIT (%)					

Table B4.11   Balance sheet

	Two years ago	One year ago	This year	% change	Comments
Current assets (£)					
Fixed assets (£)					
Goodwill (£)					
Stocks (£)					
Debtors (£)					
Creditors (£)					
Total investment (£)					

Table B4.12   Cash flow statements

	Two years ago	One year ago	This year	% change	Comments
Net income (£)					
Depreciation (£)					
Sources (£)					
Fixed assets and goodwill (£)					
Working capital (£)					
Uses (£)					
Net cash flow (£)					
Cumulative (£)					

Table B4.13 Key strategic ratios

Year	Two years ago	One year ago	This year	% change	Comments
Competitive position					
Sales					
Market share (%)					
Rel mkt share					
Market characteristics					
Market growth rate (%)					
Cost and investment structure					
Total invest					
ROI (PBIT/total inv (%)					
Invest/gross profit					
Invest/sales					
Productivity ratios					
Number of employees					
Sales/emp curr (£)					
Sale/emp real (£)					
Invt/emp curr (£)					
Invt/emp real (£)					
Profitability measures					
Gross profit (£)					
Gross profit/sales(%)					
PBIT (£)					
PBIT/sales (%)					
Cash flow (£)					

which tend to have the following dual orientation:

* *inwards*. To measure performance and provide overall strategic direction.
* *outwards*. To send signals to the stock market, other financial institutions and other external stakeholders.

The principal measures of corporate performance are set out in Tables B4.14 to B4.21.

Table B4.14   Consolidated profit and loss statements

	Two years ago	One year ago	This year	% change	Comments
Sales					
Gross profit (£)					
Gross profit (%)					
Payroll					
Overheads (£)					
Exceptional (£)					
Total costs (£)					
Profit before tax (£)					
Tax (£)					
Profit after tax (£)					
Ordinary dividend (£)					
Preference dividend (£)					
Retained for year (£)					

Table B4.15 Consolidated key profit and loss ratios

	Two years ago	One year ago	This year	% change	Comments
EPS* before exceptionals (pence)					
OP Margin (PBIT/ sales) (%)					
Net profit/sales (%)					
Interest cover (PBIT/interest)					
Dividend per share (pence)					
Dividend cover (EPS/dividend)					
Share price+ (£)					
Market capitalization (£)					

* EPS is earnings per share and is calculated by dividing profit after tax by the number of shares.

+ This will be based upon the historic price to earnings (P:E) ratio. For example, if the firm historically had a P:E ratio of 11:1, then its share price would be calculated using the equation: share price = 11 x earnings per share.

Measures of sales performance and profitability

Sales and profitability can be appraised using first the consolidated profit and loss statements from the SBUs and second profit ratios derived from them. These are shown in Tables B4.14 and B4.15.

Measures showing how well assets have been used

Sales and profitability can be assessed using consolidated balance sheets from the SBUs and also performance ratios derived from them. These are shown in Tables B4.16 and B4.17.

Table B4.16   Consolidated balance sheet

	Two years ago	One year ago	This year	% change	Comments
Stocks (£)					
Debtors (£) (%)					
Creditors (£)					
Dividend (£)					
Loan notes (£)					
Bank (£)					
Investment (£)					
Fixed assets (£)					
Net worth (£)					
Shareholders funds (£)					

Table B4.17   Consolidated balance sheet ratios

	Two years ago	One year ago	This year	% change	Comments
Ave net worth (£)					
Ret on inv (PAT/ANW) (£)					
Gearing including loan notes (%)					
Gearing excluding loan notes (%)					
Net asset value per share (£)					
Share price (£)					
Share price premium on NAV					
Market capitalization (£)					
Net worth (£)					
Shareholders funds (£)					

Measures to show the firm's cash position

The consolidated corporate cash position is derived from the consolidated SBU cash flows and is shown in Table B4.18.

Table B4.18   Consolidated cash flows

	Two years ago	One year ago	This year	% change	Comments
Profit before tax (£)					
Depreciation (£)					
PBT + depreciation (£)					
(Increase)/decrease in stocks (£)					
(Increase)/decrease in debtors (£)					
(Increase)/decrease in creditors (£)					
Movement in working cap (£)					
Total funds gen from trading (£)					
Dividend paid (£)					
Loan notes repaid (£)					
STC loans repaid (£)					
Asset disposals (£)					
Fixed assets purchased (£)					
Finance lease repayments (£)					
Application of funds (£)					
Net cash inflow/outflow					
Opening bank position (£)					
Closing bank position (£)					
Net cash inflow/outflow (£)					
Cash gen before capital expenditure (£)					

Key strategic ratios

Corporate key strategic ratios are the consolidated SBU key strategic ratios and are shown in Table B4.19.

Table B4.19　Consolidated key strategic ratios

Year	Two years ago	One year ago	This year	% change	Comments
Competitive position					
Sales (£)					
Market share (%)					
Rel mkt share					
Market characteristics					
Market growth rate (%)					
Cost and investment structure					
Total invest (£000)					
ROI (PBIT/total inv (%)					
Invest/gross profit					
Invest/sales					
Productivity ratios					
Number of employees					
Sales/emp curr (£000)					
Sale/emp real (£000)					
Invt/emp curr (£000)					
Invt/emp real (£000)					
Profitability measures					
Gross profit (£000)					
Gross pro/sales(%)					
PBIT(£000)					
PBIT/sales (%)					
Cash flow (£000)					

Exceptional capital expenditures

At the corporate level it is important to monitor overall capital expen-

diture, especially on major capital projects. Table B4.20 itemizes the
exceptional capital expenditures which have occurred in the past three
years. There have been three such projects: one 'This year', one 'One
year ago ' and one 'Two years ago'.

Table B4.20   Consolidated exceptional capital expenditures

	Two years ago	One year ago	This year	% change	Comments
Capital expenditure item 1 (£)	XXX				
Capital expenditure item 2 (£)		XXX			
Capital expenditure item 3 (£)			XXX		
Total capital expenditure (£)	XXX	XXX	XXX		

Bank borrowings and banking facilities

Corporate banking facilities need to be monitored to ensure that the
firm's bank continues to have confidence in its financial prudence.
Accordingly, Table B4.21 shows how the overall company has arranged

Table B4.21   Actual bank borrowings and facilities

	Two years ago	One year ago	This year	% change	Comments
Target bank borrowing levels (£)					
Total borrowings available (£) (40% of net worth)					
Year end bank borrowings (£)					
Bank facilities (£)					
Ongoing working capital facilities (£)					
Total facilities (£)					

its banking facilities during the past three years:

1. It has been agreed that the firm's banks are happy to provide borrowings up to a total of 40 per cent of its net worth.
2. Year end bank borrowings show the levels of borrowings at each year end.

CONCLUSION

Firms tend to drift. Over time deviation from previous standards of practice occurs. Perhaps they become less competitive through failing to stay in sync with their markets or perhaps their internal operations become less efficient. The major problem for most managers is that although they may be 'mildly aware' of the process of deterioration they are usually so close to the day-to-day operations that they do not address such drift until a crisis occurs.

This chapter sets out a framework which will enable managers to carry out a comprehensive audit of their firm's operations from the following perspectives:

*   leadership;
*   behaviour;
*   structure;
*   functional;
*   SBU level;
*   corporate level.

This type of analysis should allow managers to isolate those areas which for the future success of the firm will need to be strengthened and those which are functioning well.

NOTES

1. This is particularly true in periods of poor performance where the emphasis may shift from building the firm to preserving one's position.
2. See the Dunlop case in Chapter 1.
3. In the following pages there is a large number of tables and it is difficult and often too time consuming to obtain all these data. In practice not all these tables would be completed. They have been provided here for reasons of comprehensiveness.
4. Although a number of these ratios occurs in previous tables, it is nonetheless use-

ful to bring them together in a single table so that a comprehensive view of the SBU may be obtained.

REFERENCES

(1) Ackoff, R. (1970). *Concept of Corporate Planning*. Wiley, Chichester.

(2) Dyer, G. (1996). Ambitious goals in the crystal ball. *Financial Times*, 30 March 1996, 11.

(3) Kets de Vries, M. (1994) CEOs also have the blue. *European Management Journal*, September.

(4) Pfeffer, J. (1981). *Power in Organizations*. Pitman, London.

(5) Van der Erve, Marc. L. B. (1995) Evolution management: planning for corporate development. *Long Range Planning*, 28, (5)101–108.

(6) Taylor, F. W. (1911). *The Principles of Scientific Management*. Harper Brothers, New York.

(7) Mayo, E. (1945) *The Social Problems of an Industrial Civilization*. Harvard Business School, Boston.

(8) Iacocca, L.with Novak, William (1984). *Iacocca*, p.161. Bantam Books, New York.

(9) Chandler, A. D. (1992). Strategy and structure. In Strage, H. M. (ed.), *Milestones in Management: An Essential Reader*. Blackwell, Oxford.

(10) Greiner, L. (1992). Evolution and revolution as organizations grow. *Harvard Business Review*, July–August, 55–64.

(11) Gooding, K. (1996). Alcan moves to consolidate its revolution. *Financial Times*, 11 May, 30.

(12) Doz, Y. (1986). *Strategic Management in Multinational Corporations*. Pergamon, Oxford.

B5
Key Strategic Issues

This section summarizes all the key issues which have been raised in the analyses carried out in Chapters B1, B2, B3 and B4. The issues can be considered under: external issues, those outside the control of the firm; internal issues, those within the control of the firm. It is not possible to categorize all the issues that will be raised in every strategic market plan but a structured checklist relevant to most situations is provided.

EXTERNAL ISSUES

External issues can be summarized using the headings in Chapter B3:

- *Markets*

  — Overall.
  — Product market niches.
  — Customers.
  — Territories.

- *Competition*

  — Nature.
  — Major threats.

- *Economy*

  — What are the likely major changes if any?

- *Technology*

  — How will it change and what will be the impact?

- *Legal/political*

  — What, if any, will be the major changes and what will be their impact?

- *Geographical*

  —What, if any, will be the major changes and what will be the impact?

- *Social*

  — What, if any, will be the major changes and what will be the impact?

INTERNAL ISSUES

Internal issues can be summarized using the headings in Chapter B1, B2 and B4:

- *Business definition*

  — Will it change, should it change?

- *Portfolio balance*

  — Should the overall balance by changed?

- *Leadership*

  — At every level, is the firm providing appropriate leadership?

- *Behavioural climate*

  — Is appropriate or should it be changed?

- *Functional performance*

    — Which functional areas need to be strengthened?

- *Overall SBU strategic performance*

    — On the basis of the key strategic ratios, which aspects of firm performance need strengthening?

- *Corporate performance*

    — On the basis of the consolidated SBU performance measures, how is the overall company performing?

C1

Future Mission, Goals, Targets and Portfolios

This chapter is the first step in formulating the future strategy of the firm. So far a strategic review of the firm has been undertaken. Using this review as a base, the future strategy of the firm will now be built. This process involves the following linked steps:

- *Vision, mission and strategic intent of the firm.* This sets the broad long-run agenda.
- *Future goals.* These add precision to the mission.
- *Future business definition.* This defines the future business in terms of products, market niches and territories.
- *Future product market portfolio.* This shows the balance of the firm's products at the end of the planning period and its relative competitive position.

The firm and its planning horizon

Although there will be some consideration of corporate issues, the focus of the exposition will be a three-year strategic market plan – 'This year', 'One year ahead' and 'Two years ahead' – for a manufacturing SBU within a divisionalized corporation.

VISION, MISSION AND STRATEGIC INTENT

Good leaders have good vision about the future of their firms. Superior leaders are able to weave this vision into the fabric of management practice within their firms. They transmit and implement their vision and make it the mission of the firm. The word mission is appropriate for describing the long-term overall agenda and value system of the firm. If the word mission is considered in its more traditional religious context then it becomes clear why the word is so appropriate. It is associated mainly with the Christian church and, typically, a mission is a religious service whose aim is the spiritual rejuvenation of the people attending.

By analogy, the mission or the mission statement of a firm ought to set out the overall agenda and value system of the firm in such a way that it is seen to be the primary driver and all the firm's activities and operations must comply with it.

MISSION STATEMENTS

Mission statements come in many forms: precise versus broad; long versus short; financial and non-financial. A number of examples to illustrate this variety is set out below:

> Guinness plc is one of the leading alcoholic drinks companies in the world. Our strategy is to focus all our resources on the two core businesses of spirits and beers. Our aim is to build the strength of an outstanding portfolio of brands with consumers around the world, and thereby provide superior long-term financial returns for our shareholders. We provide opportunities and support to our people to help them perform to their fullest potential as the way to achieve our business goals (1).

> Bombardier is a Canadian-owned company engaged in design, development, manufacturing and marketing activities in the fields of transportation equipment, civil and military aerospace and motorized consumer products.
>
> Bombardier's growth strategy is based on the following fundamental principles: control over the technologies related to its manufactured products, through research and develop-

ment, technology transfers and the acquisition of companies with complementary expertise; the identification of niche markets offering a relatively high potential in terms of overall sales, and in which Bombardier can play a leading role; industrial involvement in countries and regions where Bombardier wishes to establish a strategic national presence in major markets; and decentralized management that promotes an entrepreneurial attitude and a sense of commitment in all employees and which is concerned with satisfying the needs and requirements of customers while achieving a level of profitability that is attractive to shareholders and investors (2).

To provide core banking and selected financial services professionally, efficiently and competitively to achieve a pre-eminent position in chosen markets (3).

There is considerable variety in the degree of precision which firms give their mission statements: at one extreme there is very short National Australia Bank mission statement while at the other extreme there is the much more comprehensive Guinness mission. The question arises as to the appropriate structure for a mission statement. There are no guidelines but it is likely to be influenced by factors such as the following.

Target audience

The content and style of a mission statement is likely to be influenced by the target audience at which it is aimed. The principal audiences for mission statements and their primary interests are set out in Table C1.1.

In some firms more than one mission statement may be developed. For example, there may be a statement for external consumption which is much broader and more externally focused than the statement for 'other employees'.

How much detail?

The dilemma of detail versus breadth has been well considered by Campbell and Yeung (4). Their research suggests that an effective mission statement can be derived using The Ashridge mission model, as shown in Figure C1.1.

Table C1.1 Target audiences for mission statements and their typical primary interests

Target group	Typical primary interests
Shareholders	Share price, market capitalization, profits, growth rate, risk, major areas of activity, strategic position.
Senior managers	Share price, growth rate, risk, markets, generic strategies, competitive position
Other employees	Growth rates, markets, strategies, products, markets, customers, employment conditions
Outside stakeholders, for example, customers, suppliers, government and society	Stability, reliability, integrity, environmental and societal consciousness
Competitors	Future intentions, arenas of primary activity, key areas of unique expertise and relative competitive position

In summary Campbell and Yeung suggest that a mission can be created from four elements: purpose; strategy; behaviour standards; values.

Purpose

What is the overall purpose of the firm and for whose benefit is it being run. Generally they have found that when there is agreement about this it falls into three categories:

•   For the benefit of shareholders.
•   For the benefit of all stakeholders.
•   For a higher ideal than either of these, for example improving some aspect of life.

Strategy

To achieve its purpose the firm must have a strategy and this will often delineate the product market segments in which it will compete and how it will compete.

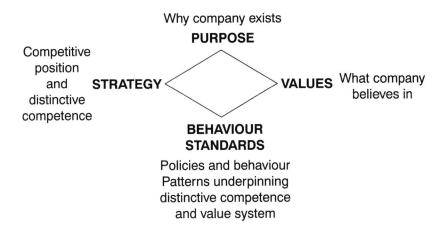

Figure C1.1 The Ashridge mission model

Behaviour standards

These are the actions and activities undertaken by people in the firm to ensure that the purpose and strategy are translated into daily behaviours and standards.

Values

These are the corporate beliefs that support the firm's behaviour and attitudes which provide a particular way of operating. For example, in the case of Waterford Crystal (Chapter B3) it has a core value that its Waterford Crystal range will always be the premium crystal glassware available. Hence, no seconds are ever available, the product is never discounted and it is only ever sold through approved distribution outlets.

Unwritten mission statements

Some firms, particularly smaller ones, never write out a mission statement. However, this does not mean that they do not have a mission, they do. All firms do. Even if the managers in such firms say they do not, they do. It is just that it is not explicitly written. The true mission for firms which do not have written mission statements can be inferred from their actions and how they deploy their resources. For example, in small family firms a frequently found mission is that the firm should be a source of employment for immediate members of the family. Even if this is never stated, the firm's actions will over time illustrate the veracity or otherwise of this. Similarly, the resources which firms devote to various activities are clear indicators of their missions. For example, firms which devote considerable resources to research and development clearly have technology leadership as a mission whereas those which devoted minimal amounts to this and are content to follow others with copycat often cheaper products have a mission of being a low cost follower.

Mission and strategic intent

The mission of a firm will be influenced by its strategic intent (5) and its strategic intent will be influenced by its mission. Strategic intent is usually taken to mean that often illogical intention to become dominant in a market niche or industry when most indicators show that:

- the firm does not have the resources to become dominant;
- the current dominant player is so powerful and entrenched that it appears to be impregnable;
- the risks in challenging the dominant player are so great (there may be crippling retaliatory reaction) that they outweigh any benefits;
- the logical strategy may be to accept a non-dominant position and enjoy the returns which it provides.

Yet in many industries, in spite of the logic demonstrated above, a non-dominant player will often have a strategic intention to oust the dominant player. For example, in the world construction machinery industry, for many years the Japanese manufacturer Komatsu, although much smaller in every respect than the American world leader Caterpillar, has had the strategic intention of becoming the dominant player. Similarly, Pepsi Cola has always had the strategic intent of ousting Coca-Cola as the world's largest supplier of carbonated drinks.

The vision, mission and strategic intent are the three, often insepara-
ble, elements that are fundamental to the delineation of the ambitions,
activities and value systems for all firms: the 'soul' of the firm which
is crafted by its leaders.

GOALS

When considering the goals of a firm it can be useful to think of the
analogy of individuals and families. All individuals and all families
have goals. In most cases the goals pursued are not in written form
but they are nonetheless real. For example, individuals tend to have
career, social and professional goals and families tend to have goals
for their children, for example, educational, recreational and social.
These goals are primary influences on the behaviours and actions of
individuals or families. Indeed, it is impossible to understand the
actions of individuals and families without understanding their goals.

All firms have goals and even if not written out they do exist and it
is impossible really to understand a firm's activities without understanding its goals. Although the actual goals followed by a particular
firm are unique to it, just as the actual goals pursued by individuals
and families are unique, it is still possible to consider any firm's goals
from a generic perspective and develop a framework for analysing
them.

Relationship between goals and mission statement

The mission statement of a firm is its unequivocal overall long-run
agenda. The goals of a firm should be the refinement of its mission
statement, the addition of substance to its strategic intent. They give
the necessary precision to, what is essentially, a set of aspirations.
Consequently, a firm's goals ought to flow from and be consistent with
its mission. If they are not they should be changed to achieve such
consistency.

Sources of goals

Striving superior firms tend not to be the supine recipients of agendas
set by others. They set and pursue their own unique and ambitious

agendas which other firms follow. They do this through goal setting. Consequently knowing the sources of a firm's goals and the various influences that come to bear in goal setting is key to understanding the strategic development of a firm. Figure C1.2 shows the major influences that tend to determine the goals which firms follow. Each of these influences is now considered.

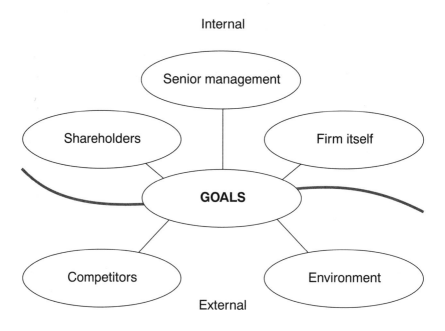

Figure C1.2   Sources of firm's goals

Source 1: Senior managers

Senior managers are usually and, indeed, ought to be the main seed from which a firm's goals grow. They are the creators and key decision-makers who have overall and final responsibility for the firm's strategic direction and performance. Therefore they must provide the goals towards which the firm should strive. Consequently any firm's goals will have a very human dimension. They will tend to reflect the natures, attitudes, value systems and obsessions of the firm's senior managers. When considering the goals that any firm will follow in the future, an analysis of the nature, attitudes, value systems and obsessions of the senior managers generally provides good insights. In addition, their future behaviour will tend to be similar to their past behaviour. Senior managers who have developed a reputation for being growth crazy will continue to be growth crazy. Cost cutters will continue to be cost cutters. The ruthlessly efficient will continue to be ruthlessly efficient. The downsizers will continue to be downsizers.

The characteristic of managers behaving in the future as they have behaved in the past is clearly seen when a poorly performing firm is taken over and a new proven senior management team is installed. The new team will tend to apply the strategies, actions and behavioural style that have been applied previously in similar situations. Thus, if the new team has turned around a poorly performing firm mainly through downsizing or cost reduction strategies (for example, redundancies and selling off non-core assets) it will be likely to repeat this strategy. The value systems and culture will also tend to be those used in previous situations. For example, if the new team had fostered cultures such as low cost, superior engineering, rapid growth, autocratic style or consensual style, then it is likely to develop a similar culture in any firm in which it operates.

Finally, for most firms the term senior management is too broad to describe the people who are key in setting the firm's goals. It is more likely that the key goals and thinking of the firm are set by a single-minded and often very dominant chief executive who follows his own unshared agenda or, as is often the case, they are set by the chief executive plus a few trusted senior managers – an inner caucus or kitchen cabinet. To understand the future direction and goals of a firm it is essential to know who is party to this inner caucus and what are their histories, natures, attitudes, value systems and obsessions.

Source 2: Shareholders

Large shareholders, especially when they are represented by non-executive directors, can have profound effects upon a firm's goals. Ambitious and aggressive shareholders will often buy substantial shareholdings in firms that they believe are currently underperforming because of poor management but which will, through pressure from them, become excellent performers with a consequent increase in the value of the shareholding. Typically after such a purchase, the new shareholder will demand and obtain a position as a non-executive director on the board and will then push the firm into setting goals greatly in excess of its historical achievements. The goals often include:

- removal of senior managers whose performance is considered unsatisfactory;
- dramatic increase in revenues through focused aggressive sales;
- dramatic decreases in unit costs often through redundancies and exiting non-performing businesses;
- significant increases in efficiency through the implementation of strong control systems.

All these measures lead to dramatic increases in profits[1] or earnings with a consequent rise in the value of the shares and hence the market capitalization of the firm.

Just how this process operates can be illustrated by means of a simple hypothetical example.

Company X is regarded as an underperformer and has annual net earnings of £100, a price to earnings (P:E) ratio of 10 giving it a stock market capitalization of £100 x 10 = £1,000.

A significant shareholding is bought by an aggressive shareholder who demands and is given a seat on the board. Subsequently action is taken to boost the profitability which builds net earnings to £150 per annum. The change in strategy causes the stock market to raise its expectations of Company X's potential and its P:E ratio is upgraded to 15. Thus the final result is that Company X has a stock market valuation of £150 x 15 = £2,250,[2] an increase of 225 per cent. This is summarized in Table C1.2.

It should be noted that firms which have low P:E ratios with a consequent low market capitalization tend to feel very vulnerable to unwelcome takeovers[3] and will often make significant strategic moves and increase their performance goals to prevent such action.

Table C1.2 Hypothetical example of the effects on shareholder value

Annual net earnings (£)	Price: earnings ratio (P:E)	Value of shareholding £
Prior to a major stake being taken		
100	10	1,000
After the major stake is taken		
150	15	2,250

Source 3: Competitors

Competitors can have three major effects upon a firm's goals. They can act as constraints, stimulants or benchmarks.

Competitors as constraints

By definition competitors vie for market shares of product lines, customers and territories. However, it is not unusual, particularly in mature industries which have a small number of well-established major players, for a type of competitive equilibrium to occur. Instead of outright competitive warfare among the major players, the competition is much more benign with the unwritten and unspoken code being: as long as no one rocks the boat there will be enough margin here for all of us. In such a situation the goals of the incumbents will be constrained to 'avoid rocking the boat' as any dramatic increase in competitive pressure, for example, a truly aggressive marketing campaign to grab market share, is likely to provoke retaliation with a consequent spiralling downwards of profits for all players.

Even in a less cosy competitive situation the threat of retaliatory reaction by rivals can often act as a constraint on goals. For example, it is not unusual for major players in an industry to tolerate some degree of competition from a relatively minor player. It may suit the majors to have a number of minor players which help to give the impression of true competition. However, should such a minor player start to strive for significant increases in its market share, this will often provoke severe retaliatory reaction from the major, say, pricing below cost, which will inflict great damage on the minor. In such a situation the goals are clearly constrained by competitors.

Competitors as stimulants

Paradoxically, competitors may also act as a stimulant to a firm to set more ambitious goals. For example, in most industries there tend to be leading competitors who set the pace through:

- growth rate;
- quality improvement;
- product development;
- service quality;
- technology development;
- productivity;
- cost position;
- geographical scope.

These pace setters may stimulate following players into more ambitious goals through the realization that if they lose touch with the leaders they may lose key industry success factors and hence their ability to compete. For example, in the information technology industry those competitors who do not keep up with technological development will lose their ability to compete and ultimately have to exit the industry.

Competitors as benchmarks

Firms often wish to know the answers to questions such as: How good are we? What would be acceptable/sensible targets for us in the future? One means of answering such questions is for a firm to examine the goals and performance of its true competitors and use this information as benchmarks for itself. In the UK, for example, it is relatively easy to determine the goals and performance levels for many in many industries using electronic databases and reports from firms such as ICC[4] Data Stream and Excel. These types of data enable individual firms to set their goals in relation to the performances achieved by true competitors.

Source 4: The firm itself

All firms are alive, they have their own life and vitality. They have agendas for continuously recreating themselves as new generations of managers succeed each other. A consequence of having a life of their own is that firms have goals which exist almost independently of the managers. It is true that managers will often make major changes to goals in times of great crisis or great opportunity. However, established firms tend to have goals which, over time, have become part of the culture and all managers will tend to conform to them. For example, the firms in Table C1.3 are well known for their goals.

Table C1.3 Firm-specific goals

Firm	Public goal
Daimler-Benz	The world's leading luxury car manufacturer
Sony	One of the world's most innovative electronics firms
Benetton	High-quality youth fashion
Sainsbury	High-volume, quality food at reasonable prices

Managers joining any of the firms in Table C1.3 must subscribe to the corporate goals: they lie at the heart of the life of the firm.

Source 5: The environment

A firm's degree of success is determined by how well it adapts to its environment: the more effectively it does this the more successful it is likely to be. Consequently, the goals that a firm follows will often reflect those elements in its environment which are likely to have an impact upon it. In addition to the normal register of business goals, firms will often include environmental goals:

* ecology, recycling, conservation, environmentally friendly;
* energy conservation and wastage;
* equal opportunity;
* political considerations;
* animal rights;
* ethical considerations.

Levels of goals

In most firms goals can be classified according to where they occur in the organizational structure. Typical goals in an SBU-structured organization and their associated characteristics are shown in Table C1.4.

Setting goals

In most firms the relationship between the setting of the goals is an interative process, as shown in Figure C1.3. First, corporate goals are set. Second, these corporate goals are refined into more specific goals for the SBUs. Finally, the SBU goals are further refined into specific departmental targets.

Table C1.4 Typical goals at different levels in an SBU-structured firm

Level	Typical goals	Time scale	Degree of risk
Corporate goals	Growth of revenues, market capitalization, share price and risk reduction.	Many years	High
SBU goals	SBU sales and profits growth, market position, competitive position; performance goals in terms of finance, marketing, productivity, human relations and risk reduction.	Many years	Relatively high
Departmental targets	Sales and profit growth by product, customer and territory; performance goals in terms of finance, productivity, IT human relations.	Up to one year	Low

Thus the goal setting can be considered as a hierarchical process in which the broad, often financial, corporate goals are given progressively more precision and their time span is shortened as they percolate downwards through the firm.

It should be noted that in practice, although strategic direction is given from the corporate level, the process does not proceed in this orderly hierarchical manner. It will tend to be the case that the SBUs are given a general and perhaps informal 'sense of corporate direction' which they interpret and develop as a 'tentative strategic plan'.

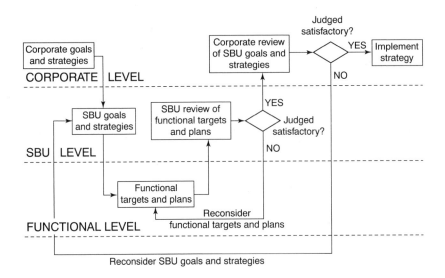

Figure C1.3 How goals are set throughout the firm

After discussion and guidance from the corporate level this is eventually fashioned into the agreed SBU plan. The final corporate plan is usually the consolidation of the completed SBU plans.

Actual goals

When asked what goals their firm follows many managers will answer: 'Survival'. Although this response has the beauty of succinctness and surely reflects a sense of exasperation, it provides little practical guidance from a strategic marketing perspective. What are needed are more concrete goals to give strategic direction. Once again, although every firm has its own unique set of goals, it is still possible to place them in the following generic categories: Growing/improving in value and risk. This will be achieved by a combination of: Building and controlling.

These generic goals apply at the corporate, SBU and functional levels and are now discussed.

Corporate goals

Typical corporate goals are illustrated in Figure C1.4.

These corporate goals can be divided into two sections, the profit-building goals and the risk-controlling goals, each of which is now considered.

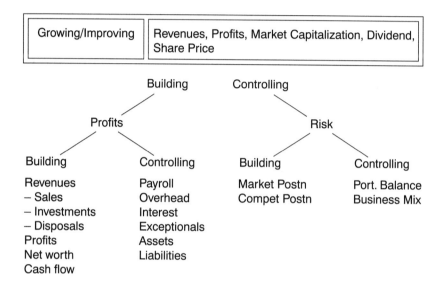

Figure C1.4   Generic goals at corporate level

Profit-building goals

Goals can be summarized in consolidated standard statements that show: profit and loss; balance sheet; balance sheet ratios; cash flows; key strategic ratios; exceptional capital expenditure; project bank borrowings and expenditure. (Tables B4.14 to B4.21 in Chapter B4). These tables cover the time period: Two years ago, One year ago, This year, Percentage change. These measures are now concerned with projections so the time period is changed to: This year, One year ahead, Two years ahead, Three years ahead, and Percentage change. A the tables are largely identical they will not be repeated.

Risk-controlling goals

The risk-controlling goals can be summarized in statements or tables showing how they risk profile and balance of the portfolio of businesses in which the firm engages will be controlled or managed.

For example, if a fiprm which had a portfolio of three SBUs, X, Y and Z, and 60 per cent of its revenues and 70 per cent of its profits were coming from X, it could have a goal of building the other two SBUs or entering new businesses to reduce dependency on its main activity. This strategy is illustrated in Table C1.5.

Table C1.5 Risk reduction through reducing dependency on SBU X

	This year		One year ahead		Two years ahead	
	% Revenues	% Profits	% Revenues	% Profits	% Revenues	% Profits
SBU X	60	70	55	61	50	56
SBU Y	30	20	33	24	35	27
SBU Z	10	10	12	15	15	17
Total	100	100	100	100	100	100

SBU goals

Typical SBU goals are illustrated in Figure C1.5.

These SBU goals can be divided into two sections: the profit-building goals and the risk-controlling goals, each of which is now considered.

Profit-building goals

As this book is concerned mainly with strategic market planning, it is assumed that the primary determinant of superior performance will be success in addressing the firm's markets. Consequently it is the marketing goals or targets which are key.

As shown in Chapter 5 in the Alban Chemicals strategic market plan, three separate tables can be drawn up to illustrate sales targets for: Products (Table 5.13), Customer Group (Table 5.14); Territories (Table 5.15). These projections measures: This year, One year ahead, Two years ahead and Percentage change.

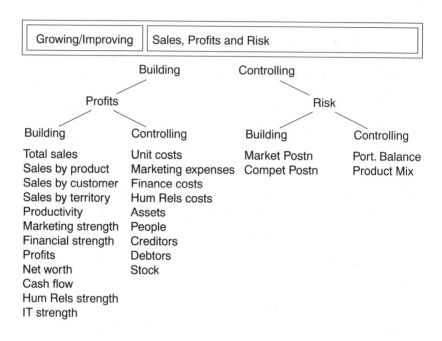

Growing/Improving	Sales, Profits and Risk

Building   Controlling

Profits   Risk

Building	Controlling	Building	Controlling
Total sales	Unit costs	Market Postn	Port. Balance
Sales by product	Marketing expenses	Compet Postn	Product Mix
Sales by customer	Finance costs		
Sales by territory	Hum Rels costs		
Productivity	Assets		
Marketing strength	People		
Financial strength	Creditors		
Profits	Debtors		
Net worth	Stock		
Cash flow			
Hum Rels strength			
IT strength			

Figure C1.5   Generic goals at SBU level

Risk-controlling goals

A product market portfolio for two years ahead can be drawn up and superimposed upon the current one, using the techniques provided in Chapter B2.

Other goals

These can be summarized in the standard statements shown in Chapter B4: marketing performance; human relations performance; profit and loss; balance sheet; cash flow; key strategic ratios. These projections cover the time period: This year, One year ahead, Two years ahead, and Percentage change.

CONCLUSION

This is the most creative stage of the strategic market planning process – the setting of the long-run strategic marketing agenda, or blueprint for the future, into which the firm will lock for many years. This agenda will either:

- transform the firm into an admired superior performer;
- permit the firm to muddle through;
- destroy it.

The blueprint for the future, especially if it is a major break with the past, will usually require immense dedication and effort by the senior management team to translate their aspirations into operating realities. More specifically, this chapter set out a framework which enables managers to carry set out a comprehensive strategic agenda at the corporate, SBU and functional levels. How realistic these agendas are will be considered in Chapter C2.

NOTES

1. This process is often described as 'making the assets sweat'.
2. For further information on this topic see (6).
3. For good insights into the corporate insecurity caused by having a relatively low stock market valuation see (7).
4. ICC stands for Inter Company Comparisons and these reports provide performance comparisons, using standard financial data, of firms by industry sector.

REFERENCES

(1) Guinness plc Report and Accounts 1992.
(2) Bombardier Inc. Annual Report 1990.
(3) National Australia Bank Ltd Annual Report 1993.
(4) Campbell, A. and Yeung, S. (1991) Creating a sense of mission. *Long Range Planning*, 24 (4), 10–20.
(5) Hamel, G. and Prahalad, C. K. (1989). Strategic intent. *Harvard Business Review*, 67, May–June 63-76.
(6) Clarke, C. (ed.) (1993). *Shareholder Value: Key to Corporate Development. The Best of Long Range Planning*. Pergamon, Oxford.
(7) Burrow, R. (1991). *Barbarians at the Gate: Fall of RJR Nabisco*. Arrow Books, New York.

C2
Gap Analysis

Chapter C1 provided a structure for setting out the future strategic agenda for a firm in terms of its:

- mission;
- goals;
- targets;
- portfolios.

In practice when managers are setting these targets they often do so in a bullish and over-optimistic atmosphere. They set goals that are significantly higher than anything achieved in the past which in reality may prove impossible to realize. The results of this process are typically:

- initial enthusiasm for the ambitious targets;
- major efforts to achieve the targets;
- little or no success in achieving them;
- a return to the previous levels of growth and performance.

The above result is often caused by:

- a failure to recognize that meeting the ambitious targets will require strategies and actions which are very different from the past – the past will not do.
- lack of commitment to buy in and subsequent lack of drive on the part of managers.

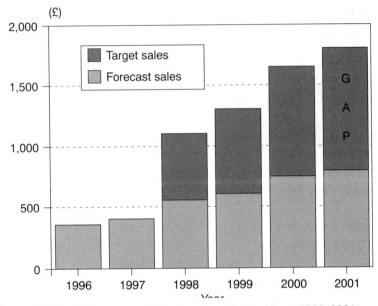

Figure C2.1   Sales gap analysis for a hypothetical firm, 1996–2001

For example,in the UK in the 1990s many retain banks saw the household mortgage market as one in which they could achieve dramatic growth and consequently set ambitious market share targets. To achieve these targets they made major marketing efforts. For many banks, however, the results were disappointing in that their assaults on the market were made mainly on the basis of price, for example, a reduced mortgage rate. The consequence was a lowering of the margins for all competitors with the subsequent market share gains being relatively profitless.

One approach for highlighting how new ambitious strategies ought to be pursued is gap analysis.

GAP ANALYSIS

Gap analysis is what its name implies – the gap between the aspiration and what will be achieved if there is no change. For example, Figure C2.1 shows a sales gap for a hypothetical firm. In 1998 the firm has the goal of having sales of £1,000 in 2001. However, if its past performance is extrapolated it will only have sales of £800 in

2001. Thus, it is likely that there will be gap of £200 if the firm's future operations are conducted in the same manner as the past.

A gap analysis for Alban Chemicals

To illustrate gap analysis more precisely, in the case of Alban Chemicals its actual sales for 1996 to 1998, its forecast sales for 1999 to 2001, its target sales for 1999 to 2001 and the gap between forecast and target are shown in Table C2.1 and Figure C2.2.

Table C2.1 The gap between Alban Chemicals forecast and target sales

	1996	1997	1998	1999	2000	2001
Actual sales (£k)	10,000	11,040	12,650			
Forecast sales (£k)				12,750	12,425	12,480
Target sales (£k)				14,950	17,250	19,230
Sales gap (£k)				2,200	4,825	6,750

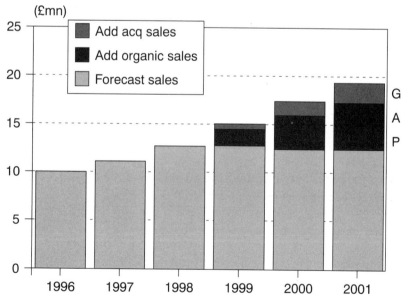

Figure C2.2 Sales gap analysis for Alban Chemicals, 1996–2001

If Alban Chemicals were to continue its past strategy a sales gap of £2.7mn would have developed in 2001. The process of gap analysis is now considered in greater detail.

The process of gap analysis

Gap analysis can be carried out in the following four steps.

Step 1: Goals or targets are set

These are set in section C1 of the strategic market plan. The sales targets for Alban Chemicals for 1999 to 2001 are shown in Table C2.1.

Step 2: Current performance is extrapolated

The firm's historical performance is examined and a forecast for the planning period is made. This forecast assumes that there will be no change from the previous strategy – the future future will be a continuation of the past. There are many ways in which this forecast can be made. For example:

- the experience of the managers, i.e. their subjective views on the future;
- graphing the past and then extending the graph up to the end of the planning horizon;
- a mathematical forecast of the future.

In Figure C2.2 Alban Chemicals forecast was made on the basis of a graph.

Step 3: Forecast gap is measured

The differences between the forecast sales and the targets are measured. As can be seen on this occasion it is £6,750k.

Step 4: Strategies are developed to close the gap

Clearly major change must occur in order to close this gap. In the case of Alban Chemicals there are two major strategic initiatives which will be undertaken:

- Additional annual sales of £4,725k by 2001 to be provided by organic growth.
- Additional annual sales of £2,025k by 2001 to be provided by acquisition.

Finally, a more comprehensive gap analysis for Alban Chemicals is provided in section C2 of Chapter 5.

The scope of gap analysis

In the previous example a sales gap analysis – the most commonly used one – has been conducted. However, the process of gap analysis is generic and a similar approach can be used on almost any target. Gap analysis could be conducted for the following:

- *Share price*. Target share price, the gap and strategies to close the gap.
- *Profitability*. Target profits, the gap and strategies to close the gap.
- *Return on investment*. Target return on investment, the gap and strategies to close the gap.
- *Productivity*. Target productivity, the gap and strategies to close the gap.
- *Numbers of products*. Target number of products, the gap and strategies to close the gap.
- *Geographical spread of sales*. Target spread, the gap and strategies to close the gap.

CONCLUSION

Although gap analysis is an extremely simple process, it helps managers to focus in detail on the necessity of developing new strategies which may be a major break with past traditions if ambitions, goals and targets are to be achieved. The strategies available to close such gaps are considered in Chapter C3.

C3

The Strategies

Retrospective experts abound. A retrospectively expert manager is one who is able to give prescriptions for difficult problems after the problem has disappeared. For example, retrospective experts would generally agree that the decisions in the late 1980s to lend money to the Maxwell Communications Corporation was for many banks a profound mistake.

Retrospective experts would probably agree that organizations which lodged funds in the 1980s with the failed Bank of Credit and Commerce International (BCCI) also made a grave error.

Similarly, retrospective experts would probably agree that Daimler-Benz's disastrous decision to diversify out of automobiles and trucks into domestic appliances and aircraft in the 1980s was indeed an incorrect strategic decision.

No one can really disagree with such retrospective expertise: it is 100 per cent correct. What managers require when they are building winning strategies is advice on how to develop new and effective strategies for an uncertain and difficult future. In other words: What are we going to do in the future?

The difficulty of developing and implementing such strategies is immense and well documented. For example, many leading firms in the tobacco industry have been concerned to reduce their dependence on tobacco. They have proclaimed publicly that the long-term future of tobacco is at best precarious and at worst unsustainable, and have consequently made considerable efforts and committed commensurate resources to diversify out of tobacco. However, when the recent accounts of leading tobacco companies are examined they reveal a continued heavy dependence on sales from tobacco.

Although this difficulty of developing a new and different strategic agenda has been illustrated with reference to the tobacco industry, it applies to almost all industries and almost all sizes of firms. In practice it is possible to observe the following sequence of events:

- *The trigger*

  'Our firm is highly dependent upon one product line or market segment. This market is static or in decline so we must diversify into other, faster growing, more competitively benign areas, in order to secure our future growth.'

- *The strategy*

  'We will acquire businesses which have better prospects than our core business and use our managerial skills to enhance their performance and so build a growing and more diversified corporation.'

- *The initial disappointing results*

  'Although the recent moves to diversify out of our core business have not yet had the anticipated commercial results, we are confident that with the continued application of our management techniques and rigour, particularly in the areas of cost reduction and performance measurement, that the new acquisitions will provide both the returns and the reduction in risk that we anticipated when we purchased them.'

- *The final even more disappointing results*

  'The results are poor and unacceptable and we would have been better sticking to the business we know.'

- *The new strategy*

  'The new strategy is back to basics through the disposal of non-core businesses.'

This process, which is repeated in many industries, is shown schematically in Figure C3.1.

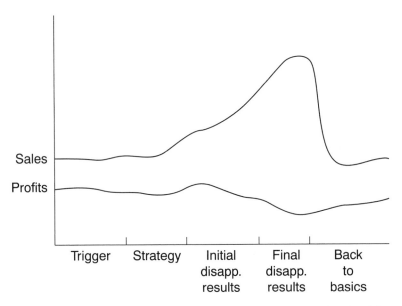

Figure C3.1 A commonly observed sequence when diversification fails

This type of inability to diversify into new areas is typical of many industries: knowing just what to do in the future is often alarmingly difficult. However, because developing new and original future strategies is difficult, this does not relieve senior management of the necessity for doing so: it is a major senior management task. There follows a generic approach that should enable managers at least to have a systematic approach to the developing of future strategies.

A SYSTEMATIC APPROACH TO PLANNING FOR THE FUTURE

Irrespective of the firm, its industry or geographical location, future strategic market plan will involve one or more of the following 'rough possibilities'. The firm will either:

- become larger – grow;[1]
- become different – refocus;
- stay the same – neutral;
- become smaller,[2] – reduction.

How each of these 'rough possibilities' can be carried out is shown in Table C3.1.

BECOMING LARGER: THE STRATEGY OF GROWTH

The importance of growth or, perhaps more accurately, growth relative to competitors, is difficult to overstate. For many firms growth is absolutely essential for survival: if they do not grow they perish. Two brief case studies to illustrate this view are given below.

Case 1: Industries where costs are strongly influenced by volume

There are many industries in which unit costs are very largely determined by volume.[3] Those firms which have the largest volumes will tend, all other things being equal, to have the lowest unit costs and hence, if there is a prevailing price, the greatest margins. In addition those firms which do not have sufficient volume may not be able to make money at the prevailing price.

Case 2: Industries where market position is more important than profits

In many industries a firm can distance itself from rivals by concentrating on fast growth at the expense of profits. Such a strategy may, ultimately, give the firm such dominance in the market, in terms of large market share and hence low unit costs, so that its profits are significantly larger and more sustainable than rivals who had previously chased profits rather than growth. For example, in the zip industry the world's leading player is YKK which has consistently since its foundation resolutely pursued a core strategy of high growth rather than profits. The founder of the company, Mr Yoshida, has stated this explicitly:

Table C3.1 How rough possibilities can be executed

Rough possibility	Become larger		Become different	Stay the same	Become smaller
Strategy effected	Growth		Refocus	Neutral	Reduction
Markets	Increase spread	Concentrate	Change focus	Same	Fewer
Products	Increase range	Concentrate	Change focus	Same	Fewer
Technologies	Increase range	Concentrate	Change focus	Same	Fewer
Production depth	Deeper	Shallower	Change balance	Same	Shallower

Now suppose that we succeed in reducing the cost of a certain product to Y50 while other companies make the same product for Y100. Then, we will pass on two-thirds of the balance of the cost saved to consumers and related industries, and we will retain the remaining one-third ourselves, which we will use, as much as possible for future investments (2).

The substance of Mr Yoshida's strategy is reflected in the company's growth and the extremely low level of dividends paid (see Table C3.2.)

Because growth is clearly so important, this book will concentrate on the strategy of growth although, of course, the other strategies will also be considered.

Table C3.2   Recent performance of YKK

	3/3/89	31/3/90	31/3/91
Sales	2,073*	2,216	2,483
Profit after tax	108	128	138
Net worth	1,151	1,312	1,454
Dividends	N/A	N/A	7

* In US$mn converted at a rate of 1$=Y133.5
Source: Dun and Bradstreet

Why growth is sought

There can be a large number of reasons for firms seeking growth. Among the more common ones are the following:

1. Growth may be a strategic imperative. If a certain threshold level of growth is not achieved then the firm will fail because it will be unable to match the unit costs of faster growing rivals.
2. Growth may be an imperative for stock market/ownership reasons. Thus it is not unusual for publicly quoted firms to have a threshold level of growth of earnings. Otherwise they become targets for unsolicited takeovers as they will be attractive to more aggressive growth-orientated firms which will purchase them because of their relatively low market capitalisation, caused by having a relatively low share price and PE ratio.
3. Growth is attractive to the managers who cause it, as the growth of a firm is frequently reflected in the parallel growth of their compensation and status. Indeed quite a large proportion of managers

could be described as 'pathological growers', i.e. they have no sense of achievement and fulfilment if they are not growing their firm at a faster rate than in the past and also faster than their rivals.

4. The consequences of not having growth greatly complicate the management task and reduce the rewards. Firms which do not grow continuously cannot provide security of employment and continuous promotion. When these features are lacking, the creative energies of managers tend to become directed towards political positioning to try and gain promotion through the displacement of other rival managers rather than through building the firm. In other words the enterprising energies of the managers are directed against their internal rivals rather than being channelled into growing the firm. In such circumstances it is not unusual for morale to become low and the culture one of resigned acceptance of, at best, mediocrity and, at worst, terminal fatigue and failure.

Having illustrated the importance of growth, a number of fundamental questions arises:

- What does growth mean?
- What is an appropriate rate of growth for a firm?
- How can growth be achieved?
- In what circumstances should particular strategies for growth be pursued?

What does growth mean?

Growth means different things to different people; to different industries; to different countries; to different firms. Even within firms, different units are used to measure growth as shown in Table C3.3.

Table C3.3 shows that there is no single measure for growth. In most firms which are structured as in the table many of the measures listed will be used, but they will have different emphases at different levels of the firm.

Thus growth will have different meanings to different groupings. As this book is about strategic market planning the measures of growth which are considered to be most appropriate are those at the higher levels within the firm. Consequently the measures used will be mainly marketing, financial and production. Table C3.4 lists the principal measures, the ultimate being growth of turnover.

Table C3.3 Different measures of growth used by different levels within the firm

Level	Typical measures of growth
Corporate Directors and top management	Turnover, profitability, cash flow, assets, dividends, return on investment, return on equity, earnings per share, number of new businesses, corporate position relative to rivals
Business unit Directors and top management	Turnover, sales volume, cash flow, assets, profitability, return on investment, number of products, number of markets, market positions relative to rivals, number of customers, productivity, portfolio position, business unit, position relative to rivals, unit costs, productivity
Business unit Senior managers	Turnover, sales volume, number of products, number of markets, number of customers, customer satisfaction, unit costs, productivity, number of staff, product, market and cost positions relative to rivals

What is an appropriate rate of turnover growth for a firm?

Conventionally appropriate growth rates are often considered in terms such as:

• At least as good as last year (always safe).
• At least as good as the industry average (again, always safe).
• The fastest in the industry (only achievable by one firm).

So just what is an appropriate growth rate? An appropriate growth rate is one in which a firm's strategic position relative to its direct rivals is enhanced. The most observable way in which this can be achieved is through a firm profitably increasing its market share relative to its direct rivals. The phrase direct rivals is of great importance as it is a firm's strategic market position relative to its rivals that counts rather than relative to its industry or in relation to its historical performance.

Table C3.4   Principal measures of growth

	Growth
Marketing	Turnover, market share, relative market share, relative product quality
Financial	Turnover, profitability, gross margin, cash flow, assets, investment intensity, value added, productivity
Production	Value added, productivity, degree of innovation, degree of vertical integration

How growth can be achieved: the tree of growth

The 'tree of growth' is set out in Figure C3.2. As can be seen, it bifurcates into two main branches: organic growth and growth through acquisition.[4] Each of these major routes is now discussed in greater detail.

Branch 1: Organic growth

This occurs when a firm grows through using its own resources rather than acquiring another firm. For example, a company which has achieved outstanding results for many years through following this strategy is the famous Japanese manufacturer of bicycle parts and fishing tackle Shimano. This company has enjoyed sustained high growth through adhering to a strategy of organic growth within its core businesses only. In passing, it is interesting to note that Shimano asserts that it will never make a bicycle, it will only make specific parts for bicycles. Some brief details on Shimano are given in Table C3.5.

This type of growth shown in Table C3.5 could be described as *internal concentric diversification* for the following reasons:

- *Internal.* The growth has taken place through internal development and not acquisition.
- *Concentric.* Because all the products of the firm, the new ones and the initial ones, are centred on a core product or service. They have a common centre as shown in Figure C3.3.

Table C3.5 Recent performance and history of Shimano Industrial Company Ltd

	1992	1993	1994
Sales (£mn)	735	867	672
Profit after tax (£mn)	51.7	73.4	44.2
Profit margin (%)	11.6	14.2	10.7

Brief history

New cold forging technology developed inhouse 1960.
Shimano American Corporation established in New York, 1965.
Announcement of Dura Ace racing component series, 1972.
Development of Positron, the world's first click-stop derailleur shifting system.
Motorized fishing reel introduced, 1987.
Dura Ace integrated 8-speed SIS and Nexus components introduced, 1988.
Titanos Digital motorized boat reel introduced, 1989.

Source: (3)

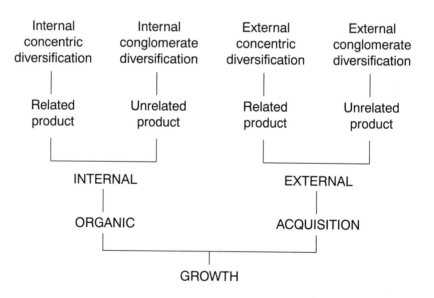

Figure C3.2 The tree of growth

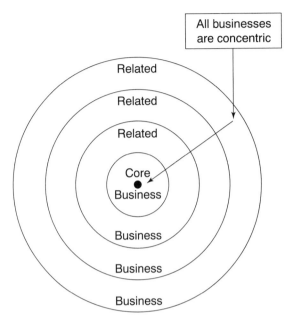

Figure C3.3   The concept of concentric organic growth

- *Diversification.* Because the range of products and/or markets has been extended.

This rather broad categorisation is now refined into more operational substrategies which show how growth through internal concentric diversification can be achieved.

Greater internal efficiency

This can be achieved through one or more of the following:

- reduction of costs;
- improvement of relative quality;
- better human relations;
- rationalization of production methods, products and markets.

Deeper penetration of existing markets with existing products

Here growth is achieved through growing the sales of existing products in existing markets. This is the least risky strategy in that it represents the smallest amount of change. Such penetration is likely to involve more effective marketing and could include activities such as:

- promotion campaigns;
- enhancement of product quality;
- new price strategies;
- new distribution strategies.

Selling new related products in existing markets

Here growth is achieved through developing new products which can be sold in existing market segments. For example, in the yoghurt business many manufacturers are continuously seeking to expand their product ranges of yoghurt-related products. There tends to be more risk associated with this strategy as there is no guarantee that the products will be successful.

Selling existing or related products in new markets

Here growth is achieved by entering markets which the firm did not previously serve. This could take the form of:

- entering new geographical markets;
- servicing or developing new market segments;
- servicing new customer groups.

This strategy is somewhat more risky in that the firm is entering markets of which it has no previous experience.

Selling unrelated products in new markets

Finally, a firm may grow organically through developing product/market areas which are new to it. For example, it is not unusual for large companies which have developed significant inhouse training or consulting skills to set up a separate training or consulting unit and offer these services to a wider set of clients. The training skills are generic and have wide applicability. For example, one of the world's leading steel wire companies is the Belgian firm Bekaert. While having a mission of engaging only in activities related to its core business of the manufacture of steel wire, it has nonetheless developed a consulting company called Bekaert-Stanwick which specializes in total quality control, production and technology management, human resources management and marketing. This company has evolved out of internal development.

This type of growth could be described as *internal conglomerate diversification* for the following reasons:

- *Internal.* The growth has taken place through internal development and not acquisition.
- *Conglomerate.* Because the products bear little relationship to the firm's initial products.
- *Diversification.* Because the range of products and/or markets has been extended.

This is shown schematically in Figure C3.4.

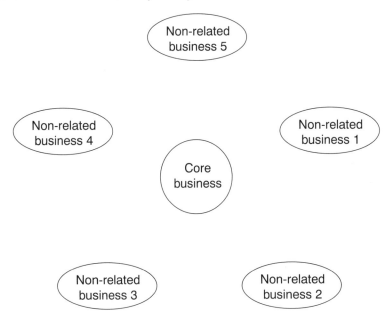

Figure C3.4   The concept of conglomerate organic growth

Branch 2: Growth through acquisition

This process takes place when a firm grows through acquiring another company. A company which has practised this strategy since 1927 and in the process has built up a strong global presence is the Dutch brewing and beverage company Heineken (4).

> In recent years Heineken continued its expansion into new and existing markets. A licensing agreement in 1968 with the United Kingdom's Whitbread proved to be a very successful operation. In 1972, Heineken acquired a financial participation in a French group of breweries which later led to a fully owned subsidiary in this large market. Two years later, Heineken entered into a joint venture in Italy with its British partner, Whitbread. Further expansion in South America and the Caribbean opened new geographical areas to Heineken. Since 1975 Norway, Sweden, and Ireland were added to the European countries where the Heineken or Amstel brands were produced under license(4).

This type of growth could be described as *external concentric diversification* for the following reasons:

- *External.* Because the growth is achieved through external means, acquisition.
- *Concentric.* Because all the products of the firm, the new ones and the initial ones, are centred on a core product or service. They have a common centre (as shown in Figure C3.3).
- *Diversification.* Because the range of products and or markets has been extended.

An alternative way of pursuing a strategy of growth through acquisition is to acquire companies which are not connected to any core business: to acquire other firms whose product/market areas are not in any way related to existing operations. An example of the successful adoption of such a strategy is provided by the UK conglomerate, Hanson Trust. Hanson Trust is continuously acquiring firms which are purchased not for their product market configurations but because the Hanson team believes that it can 'squeeze' higher returns from the assets than the existing management. Consequently the range of products in the Hanson portfolio is extremely diverse, for example, from bricks to typewriters.

This type of growth could be described as *external conglomerate diversification* for the following reasons:

- *External*. Because the growth is achieved through external means, acquisition.
- *Conglomerate*. Because the products bear no relationship to the firm's initial products.
- *Diversification*. Because the range of products and/or markets has been extended.

The final and complementary means of achieving growth concerns deepening or widening the firm's production process. This is usually referred to as integration. The various types of integration are set out in Figure C3.5 and described below.

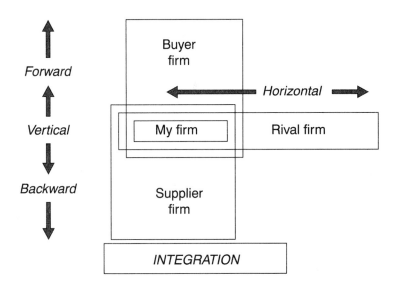

Figure C3.5   How integration may occur

Vertical integration can occur in two ways:

• Backward integration which occurs when the firm grows, either organically or by acquisition, through taking on the tasks previously carried out by a supplier. For example, in the car components industry major manufacturers use the threat of backward integration to apply competitive pressure to their parts suppliers.

• Forward integration occurs when the firm grows, either organically or by acquiring a firm, through taking on the tasks previously carried out by a buyer. For example, the decision of Sony to buy CBS could be regarded as growth through forward integration. A major motive behind the acquisition was to ensure that Sony had greater control over the final element in the purchasing decisions of consumers, i.e. the artistes etc.

Horizontal integration occurs when a firm extends, through acquisition, the range of its existing activities, for example when a firm acquires a direct competitor. The acquisition of Zanussi by Electrolux was an example of horizontal integration in the domestic appliances industry.

Finally Table C3.6 shows the various means by which growth can be achieved and also indicates the circumstances most appropriate for each type.

MERGER AND ACQUISITION STRATEGIES

Because of the controversy that merger and acquisition frequently incur, a short section is included to discuss some the features of this growth strategy which are often ignored in the debate.

Mergers and acquisitions, like integration, can take place in two ways:

• Concentric acquisition which can be achieved by forward, backward and horizontal means.
• Conglomerate acquisition in which there are no product, market or technological relationships.

Table C3.6 Means of achieving growth and the appropriate circumstances

Circumstances: type of growth	Core market growth rate	Level of competition in core business	Riskiness	Payoff period	Managerial skills required	Environmental conditions
Organic growth: concentric	Good/high	Relatively low	Low	Long run	Core business	Good
Organic growth: conglomerate	Poor	Relatively high	High	Long run	Core business plus	Good
Acquisition: concentric	Good/high	Relatively low	Medium	Short run	Core business plus financial	Less good
Acquisition: conglomerate	Poor	Relatively high	Very high	Short run	Financial	Poor
Integration: backward	Average	Relatively high	Medium/ high	Intermediate	Core business	Good/fair
Integration: forward	Average	Relatively high	Medium/ high	Intermediate	Core business	Good/fair

Concentric acquisition

In concentric acquisitions managers will usually seek to wring two types of benefit from the exercise. The internal benefit will be achieved through rationalization, leading to savings and unit cost reductions. The external benefit will normally be achieved through reducing the number of competitors, having a greater degree of control over the environment and risk reduction. It is instructive to note the dramatic effect which a large acquisition can have on relative market share.[5] This is illustrated hypothetically in Table C3.7 where it is assumed that there is an industry in which the three leading market share firms are A, B and C. Firm A acquires Firm C and forms New Firm A. As can be seen in Table C3.7 the acquisition has altered dramatically Firm A's strategic position relative to Firm B.

Table C3.7   How acquisitions can boost strategic position

	Pre-acquisition			Post-acquisition	
	Firm A	Firm B	Firm C	New Firm A	Firm B
Market share (%)	25	20	15	45	20
Relative market share	1.25	0.8	0.6	2.2	0.44

There are many examples of firms which have successfully used this route for development. One well-known firm which has this method as a core part of its strategy is the Canadian company Bombardier;

> Bombardier is a Canadian-owned company engaged in design, development, manufacturing and marketing activities in the fields of transportation equipment, civil and military aerospace and motorized consumer products.
>
> Growth strategy is based on the following fundamental principles: control over the technologies related to its manufactured products, through research and development, technology transfers and the acquisition of companies with complementary expertise (5).

Bombardier's success can be seen via the following summary figures shown in Table C3.8.

Table C3.8 Summary financial performance of Bombardier Inc.

	1983	1984	1985	1986	1987	1988	1989	1990
Sales ($mn)	412.8	394.4	400.7	548.7	989.5	1389.1	1396.2	2093.8
Net income ($mn)	6.1	6.3	10.1	16.2	46.1	66.8	68.3	91.5
Net income per share ($)	0.14	0.14	0.22	0.33	0.82	1.00	1.03	1.36

Source: (5)

Conglomerate acquisition

In conglomerate acquisitions managers will usually seek to wring benefit from the merger chiefly through rationalization, superior management skills, cost reductions and the benefits of a higher PE ratio. Companies such as Hanson and BTR exemplify this strategy.

Why do acquisitions occur?

There are two main catalysts for acquisition: managers and the competitive environment.

Managers and their motives for acquisition

The principal managerial motives for acquisition are as follows:

- *High growth.* Most successful managers continuously strive for high growth. This is perfectly logical. High growth solves so many difficult managerial problems, for example, promotion. For many growth is also a surrogate for success and is recognized as such. Most managers would assume that the larger the firm, the greater should be the rewards for managing it.
- *Speculative gain.* Managers may promote acquisitions for speculative reasons. Newbould and Luffman (6), in a major study of UK acquisitions, found this to be a primary motivator.
- *Entrepreneurial versus professional management skills.* The entrepreneurial skills needed to start and run a small business are often different from those needed in larger and more established businesses. As small businesses mature they may be acquired by professional managers.

- *Grow to sell.* It is not unusual for managers of small businesses to build them up with the hope that at some stage they will be acquired by a larger rival.
- *Surplus cash.* Cash-rich firms need projects for their cash.
- *Displace existing managers.* When there is a desire within a significant faction of management to displace the top managers acquisition may be used as a route.

Competitive environment motives

- *Market power.* The larger the market share the more powerful the firm.
- *Insufficient market demand.* When there is insufficient demand to sustain all the players there may be no alternative to acquisition. For example, in the European truck industry the consortium Iveco, comprising Fiat, Magirus, Unic and Ford, reflect the situation where there is insufficient demand to sustain these players independently.
- *Critical mass.* In many industries success demands that the firm be of a certain critical mass. For example, because of its lack of scale the UK car manufacturer Rover became a 'small league player' and was eventually bought by BMW.
- *Risk reduction.* This is the reason often put forward as part of the rationale behind conglomerate acquisition. By diversifying the business into a variety of markets, products, technologies and customers, downswings in one area of the business will be counterbalanced by upswings in another. This was a major motivation behind Harold Geneen's strategy of acquisition pursued by ITT in the 1960s and 1970s.
- *Synergy.* Advocates of acquisition will often argue that it makes commercial sense to bring together businesses in which the whole will be greater than the sum of the parts. The argument is often couched in terms such as: 'Why should we pay a firm to undertake work, for example, transportation of our products, which we could profitably undertake ourselves?'
- *Gaining expertise.* Acquiring companies may gain access, for example, to a technology which it does not possess.

Conclusions on acquisitions

The question of the appropriateness of an acquisition versus an organic growth strategy is a complex one to which no clear answers are available. Commentators tend to polarize into pro and anti. However, it is interesting to note the authoritative view of Leontiades, who believes that US industry has tended to overspecialize.

> In fact none of the major industrialized countries believes in a theory of specialization to the extreme that it is espoused in the United States. Japan, for example, is only one competitor nation that practices nonspecialized diversification. British, Italian, French, German and Dutch corporations are busily diversifying – in scope as well as in size.
> In referring once more to the success of Japanese competition, one is struck less by its strategic vision than by an unrelenting emphasis on the execution of relatively simple strategies. Having no biases against nonspecialized diversification, Japanese companies have followed what they see as a natural progression from declining to growing industries (7).

BECOMING DIFFERENT: THE STRATEGY OF REFOCUS

All industries are in a continuous process of evolution. The speed and nature of this evolution varies from industry to industry. It is normally manifested in areas such as products, product characteristics, markets, customer behaviour, distribution channels, promotion methods, production processes, technology, industry fragmentation and industry consolidation. However, because of closeness to their day-to-day work many managers do not observe the sea changes that are taking place in industries until the such changes have, often to their surprise, conferred competitive advantage upon a rival company. A clear example of this type of evolution is provided by the aircraft industry.

In the 1970s, with the advent of the jumbo jet it was assumed by many that the cost savings afforded by such a large aircraft meant that the jumbos would be the main carriers of the future and that smaller jet aircraft, with less than 200 seats, would become a minor market segment. However with the deregulation of the industry in the USA (and currently in Europe) there developed a large number of hub and spoke systems with a major airport (the hub) at the centre supporting a large number of minor airports (the spokes). The aircraft requirement for this transport configuration was: jumbos to fly between hubs and also large fleets of small jets (70 to 130 seats) and modern turbo-props to service the spokes.

The effect of this can be seen in the traffic flows in one typical hub and spoke system in the USA, Buffalo – Fort Meyers as shown in Table C3.9.

Table C3.9   Traffic flows, hub and spoke system, Buffalo, Fort Myers

	1971	1991
Flights/day	3	18
Ave. trip time	6 hr 32 min	4 hr 44 min
Airlines	2	6
Hubs	2	9
Stops	2	1

Source: Fokker Aircraft Company

The figures in Table C3.9 show clearly the trend away from large air-craft towards smaller aircraft flying shorter distances more frequently and thereby providing greater passenger choice.

This 'unexpected' development in the aircraft industry is, in practice, actually a characteristic of most industries. The conventional wisdom of future developments by industry experts frequently turns out to be at variance with what actually occurs.

What is it that causes industries to evolve? Are there searching questions that managers should be asking in an effort to divine what major changes are likely to occur in the future? How can planners sensitize their strategic antennae so that they are aware of these sea changes before rival firms?

Catalysts of industry evolution

Although the catalysts for industry evolution will vary from industry to industry there is a small number of forces which time after time appear to be most influential:

* Technological change.
* The entry of a rogue player.

- The influence of government.
- The economics of production.
- The economics of servicing the market.

Technological change

This is perhaps the easiest influence to observe. Technology is continuously evolving and having effects upon industries depending upon the degree of change. For example, the technological change wrought by the personal computer has utterly altered almost every aspect of the established computer industry and many other industries as well (for example, publishing, information services, architecture, engineering.)

A further example of the profound strategic influence of major technological change is provided by the record/tape industry. The changes in technology have greatly altered entry costs, breakeven costs and industry structure. During the late 1980s compact disks (CDs) became a major recording medium. The capital cost of setting up CD manufacturing facilities was extremely high, leading to a relatively small number of manufacturers seeking to achieve volume through established major record labels and by encouraging independent producers. Tape cassettes, a rival to CDs, became the primary release medium for many independent record companies as the product cost and the equipment needed for duplication were both relatively cheap.[6] These twin developments facilitated the development of an increasingly fragmented market for recorded music.

Entry of a rogue player

A rogue player, as considered in Chapter B2, is one that does not play by the established 'rules of the game' by which existing industry players abide. Successful rogue players develop unique ways of defining their business which shatters the prevailing competitive harmony.

For example, Seiko (K. Hattori Company) and other Japanese manufacturers began marketing an electronic quartz watch in 1969. Within ten years Seiko became the volume leader in the global watch market. This company was a rogue player which did not play by the existing rules of the game which had been established largely by Swiss manufacturers. Seiko dramatically changed the rules through:

- employing assembly line production;
- using the USA as an entry point on to the global market;
- developing vast ranges;
- developing global distribution and service;
- spending enormous sums on advertising.

The effect of Seiko and later entrants on the global watch industry is illustrated in Table C3.10.

Table C3.10   Percentage of worldwide watch production by Switzerland, Japan and Hong Kong, 1960–83

	1960	1970	1975	1980	1982	1983
Switzerland	43.0	42.0	32.0	18.4	10.8	9.3
Japan	7.2	13.7	14.0	22.5	24.7	26.1
Hong Kong	—	—	—	18.5	30.0	35.0

Source: (4)

When successful these types of rogue player have the unique ability to exploit opportunities in the industry that have developed through some aspect of industry evolution which has not been observed or at least acted upon by incumbents.

Influence of government

Government can have a fundamental effect upon how companies structure their operations, particularly their international operations, especially when two conditions apply: first, government is a large purchaser of the firm's products; second, government controls a large market.

The influence is well illustrated by the activities of the highly successful Swedish firm, Asea Brown Boveri (ABB). ABB is one of the world's leading producers of electrical engineering products and systems. The business segments which ABB serves include (8): power plants, power transmission, power distribution, industry, transportation, environmental control, financial services. The first six activities usually involve government purchases, i.e. in most countries decisions about each of these activities will be strongly influenced by the national governments. Most governments have a strong interest in promoting employment in their own countries and consequently will seek to influence multinationals to set up local manufacturing operations. This influence is reflected in the very large number of joint ventures in which ABB participates. These joint ventures show that it is likely that local contracts would be more difficult, or impossible, to obtain without local manufacture and influence.

Another particularly clear influence of the role of government in influencing industry evolution has been the rise in the number of Japanese manufacturing plants in the USA and Europe. If left to their own devices there is little doubt that many of the Japanese firms which currently manufacture in Europe and the USA would not do so; they would supply these markets from Japanese plants. The threat of government restrictions on their sales is a major stimulant to local manufacture.

When managers consider refocusing their company they should at an early stage of the analysis research which of these generic forces appears to be dominant in forcing change and evaluate the costs and benefits of refocus.

Economics of production

Production methods change continuously and these changes may greatly affect the economics of how the production process is managed. Two contrasting examples – where economics has forced production depth to be made shallower and where it has increased production depth – illustrate this influence.

Production depth made shallower

In the aircraft manufacturing industry in general the development of new aircraft is now so expensive that few manufacturers are able to carry the development and production costs alone. This situation has created alliances among manufacturers in which the development and production process is split up, with the alliance partners specializing in particular parts of the process.

> Worldwide, a large future market is expected for jet airliners
> in the broad 100-seater category for short-to-medium haul
> regional flights. Various estimates have set it at around 2,000
> aircraft by 2010, but the competition to win shares of it is so

intense that it has already forced a restructuring of the manufacturing industry involved.

This restructuring, which is set to continue, is dominated by
the emergence of international consortia as a means of reducing development costs and strengthening competitive market
power. The widely publicized collapse of Fokker of The
Netherlands earlier this year was the most visible indication of
the difficulties facing the manufacturers. Fokker's conundrum
was how to reconcile high development costs, including those
incurred in applying advanced technology to improve the performance of new designs, with a highly competitive market's
demands for lower operating costs (9).

Production depth made deeper

Historically in the tobacco industry major companies have acquired
'Confectionery, Tobacco and News' (CTN) retail shops as a means of
guaranteeing their products a route to market. This has been a strategy
of 'deepening' the production depth of such firms.[7]

The economics of servicing the market

The costs of servicing markets may change over time. For example,
even in the relatively slow moving food industry there has been dramatic change. Until quite recently, because of transport and freshness
considerations, the food industry needed to be located close to its final
customers. However, with the increase in the technical ability of firms
to prolong freshness – through refrigeration, irradiation – and via
declining unit transport costs, there has been an increase in the international trading of finished food products. In Europe examples include
dairy products, meat products, beers and bottled waters. The economics of servicing the market will often be reflected in two contrasting
refocusing strategies: reducing the range of products and/or markets
or increasing the range of products and services.

Reducing the range of products and/or markets

It is not unusual for firms to lose focus on their core business or market and, with little success, to allow an unrelated portfolio of prod-

ucts, businesses or market positions to develop. For example, prior to its turnaround, Guinness had diversified into a range of product, for example, leisure and publications, which had little in common with the core businesses of brewing and distilling. Refocusing on global brewing and distilling was crucial for the firm's resurrection.

Extending the range of products and/or markets.

When firms believe that they are over-dependent on a particular product line, market segment, customer group, geographical market or when they see attractive opportunities they will often seek to redress this through extending their ranges of products, customers and geographical markets. For example, when Japanese car manufacturers initially penetrated the European car market most did so by concentrating on the lower priced utilitarian small family car. Since the initial success they have proliferated their product lines to become true full range competitors.

How to refocus

The options for refocusing are set out in Table C3.11.

Table C3.11   Options for refocusing

	Market served	
Production depth	Reduce	Increase
Shallower	Concentrate on core	Concentrate on core and extend to new markets
Deeper	Extend core and reduce markets	Extend core and extend markets

BECOMING SMALLER: THE STRATEGY OF REDUCTION

Generally managers do not welcome a reduction strategy. Most managers do not wish to be a member of a smaller firm. They will tend to want to grow with their firms. So the question must be asked, when might it be logical for a firm to adopt a reduction strategy? This could occur when one or more of the following situations obtains:

- A decline in the absolute value or volume of sales.
- A reduction in the range of products.
- A reduction in the range of markets served.
- A reduction in its total assets.
- Making the production process shallower or narrower – deintegration vertically or horizontally.

The conditions are rather similar to those which trigger the adoption of a recovery strategy as described in Slatter (10), which provides many of the ideas set out. These are briefly considered under the same headings, namely internal causes and external causes.

Internal causes

- *Poor senior management.* The senior management have not had the skills, drive and vision to build the firm.
- *Major strategic errors.* Major strategic errors have 'bled' the firm of resources and now it is not sufficiently strong to support its existing range of activities.
- *Poor functional performance.* Performance in the areas of finance, marketing and production has failed to build the company.
- *Portfolio incompatibility.* When the activities of a firm or unit within a corporation, or indeed part of a firm, become incompatible with the firm's other activities this may lead to reduction.
- *Strategic importance.* If the activities of a firm or unit within a firm are seen as strategically unimportant and it is feasible to divest then reduction may be undertaken.
- *Inadequate resources.*When the firm's resources are not sufficient to sustain its current level of activities, for example, the investment needed for new process technology, then a reduction strategy may be appropriate.

External causes

If the firm cannot cope with its changing environment there may not be any alternative to reduction. Examples of such change could include the following:

- *Severe competition.* The indigenous European consumer electronics industry has retreated to smaller and smaller specialist market niches as it has been largely unable to meet the severe competition from Asian manufacturers.

- *Market structure and marketing method changes.* For example, the development of large out-of-town stores and hypermarkets has often led to more traditional downtown retailers engaging in reduction strategies.

- *Economic depression.* For example, in the UK the rather negative economic conditions that prevailed in the 1980s caused a reduction in scale of many industries.

- *Legal/government.* National, or supranational governments (for example, the European Community) will, as part of anti-monopoly legislation, break up companies into smaller units with the aim of encouraging competition. In the USA the federal government legislated in 1983 that AT&T, the world's largest firm, and almost monopoly supplier of US telephone services, be broken into seven local telephone companies.

- *Social/cultural attitudes.* Social attitudes can cause reductions in the sizes of firms, for example, the demise in western Europe of large numbers of fur retailers.

- *Technological change.* The influence of technological change in the traditional Swiss watch industry has already been considered.

It should be noted that the external causes of decline are usually more serious than internal causes. External causes are often largely outside the control of the firm and all that can be done is to attempt to develop an effective response to pressures.

HOW TO ACHIEVE REDUCTION

Reduction, which tends to mean reduction in scale (e.g. numbers employed and plant), is usually manifested in a reduction of products provided and market niches served. This strategy may be achieved through two main methods: divestment and liquidation.

Divestment

Divestment is a generic term which usually means the sale of part of a firm to another party.

Spin-off

This occurs when a part of the firm is severed and made operationally independent via the following methods:

- *Managed as an independent firm.* In this situation there may or may not be an ownership interest by the parent in the newly spun-off firm.
- *Sold to an independent buyer.*
- *Management buy out.* Here, the severed unit is sold to the existing management which then become the owners and managers.
- *Franchise.* This occurs when a complete business package or system is licensed to a number of independent users.

Liquidation

Liquidation occurs when the firm ceases trading, its assets are sold and the proceeds, if any, are divided among those who have first claim on the assets. There are two situations when this type of strategy is appropriate. First, when the break-up of value of the assets exceeds any returns which the firm's operations are likely to generate, then the financial interests of shareholders are best served through liquidation. Second, there may be no choice about liquidation. If the firm is heading towards bankruptcy and will soon be, or indeed is, trading illegally, then liquidation may be inevitable.

GENERIC STRATEGIES

A range of strategies from growth to reduction has been considered. Irrespective of which of these is being followed, most successful firms will have a particular approach to how they follow any strategy. They will either have an approach which emphasizes low prices, value for money, superior quality, superior warranties, or perhaps superior service. The particular approach that any firm adopts is known as its generic strategy. Porter (11) has written extensively on this topic and asserts that all firms can group their strategies into the following broad generics: overall cost leadership, or high volume low cost; differentiation; focus. Each is now discussed.

Overall cost leadership

This type of strategy has been most clearly seen in the high volume low cost strategies of the Japanese, and more recently Korean electronics manufacturers. Its logic is inescapable: a firm which has the largest volume of production ought to have the lowest unit costs and should therefore earn superior returns (the gap between its unit costs and the industry unit prices ought to be the highest in its industry). It should also enjoy a strong and defensible competitive position as its low unit cost position ought to provide superior margins which can be reinvested in new equipment and modern facilities in order to maintain or extend its leadership.

Although overall cost leadership has been the basis of many companies' success, it is risky and there are many examples of failure. Such a strategy requires very heavy capital investment with no guarantee of a static environment which will yield the substantial fruits necessary to justify such heavy investment. The principal risks of adopting this strategy include:

- Technological change that nullifies past investments.
- Low cost learning by followers. Although the leader or pioneer in the industry will have to bear the heavy development costs of a low cost strategy (R&D, building production facilities, setting up channels of distribution and mounting effective marketing campaigns) following firms may be able to achieve similar positions at a much cheaper cost. For example, the technology needed to manufacture electronic watches and calculators is now widely available and cheap.
- The strategy may cause too strong a focus on cost reduction with a consequent lack of weight given to responding to changes in the environment. This was one of the reasons for the demise of the Model T Ford.[8]
- The difference in costs between the leaders and the followers may

be narrowed because of inflation and changes in costs of production factors. For example, Japanese shipyards now find it extremely difficult to compete against South Korean shipyards on the basis of unit costs.

Differentiation

This has been the strategy employed by firms such as Leica, leading business schools, Gucci goods, Rolex watches, Scottish whisky distillers. The objective of the strategy is to make consumers believe that the firm's products and services are unique and worth the premium prices charged for them. Usually such differentiated products and their associated services are perceived to be of higher quality than rival products. This cachet of quality enables them to command a premium price. The consumer is prepared to pay more than the 'normal' or average price because the items are regarded as relatively high quality.

Once again the logic of this strategy is inescapable. A firm with this reputation of distinctiveness can charge premium prices and therefore should earn superior returns (the gap between its unit prices and unit costs ought to be the highest in its industry). It should enjoy a strong and defensible competitive position as its reputation will be difficult and arduous for rivals to match. The resulting high margins can be reinvested in further enhancing the distinctiveness of the firm's products.

The most common ways in which differentiation can be achieved include: relative quality; value for money; reliability; chicness; customer service. It should be noted that achieving differentiation may sometimes preclude gaining high market share as it often requires a perception of exclusivity which is incompatible with high market share. Thus mass-produced large volume fashion clothes, no matter how well they are made, cannot normally be sold on a differentiated strategy as their numbers negate such a connotation.[9]

Japanese automobile manufacturers such as Honda appear to be moving to a strategy where they will combine low cost plus differentiation (on the basis of quality).

Just as a low cost strategy has its attendant risks, so also does a strategy of differentiation:

- The cost differential between the low cost and the differentiated competitor may become too great and consumers may not be prepared to pay the differential. Leica cameras suffer from this.

- The consumers of the product may no longer feel that differentiation is so important. Many businesses now buy IBM 'look-alike' personal computers because they believe that the difference between the machines is not important.
- Imitators may erode the perceived difference between the differentiated and the low cost product. This is a major problem that affects IBM's personal computers. There are now so many IBM clones which claim to be better than the genuine IBM that the perceived difference has really been eroded.

Focus

A strategy of focus involves targetting a particular buyer group, segment of the product line, or geographic market. A focused strategy can take many forms. Its basic thrust is that a firm can succeed best by serving a narrow strategic target very well. Such a firm will achieve differentiation through better meeting the needs of the particular target, or lower costs, or both – it does this only from the perspective of its narrow market target. Once again when such a strategy is successfully followed then higher than industry average returns may be earned. An example of a focused low cost strategy is that followed by many Japanese suppliers of large companies, while an example of a focused differentiated strategy could be UK manufacturers of expensive hi-fi equipment. In spite of the dominant presence of Japanese giant electronics corporations these relatively small manufacturers have focused successfully upon a quality niche in the market.

As with the other generic strategies there are certain risks attendant upon focusing:

- The cost difference between the low cost producer competitor and the focused firm becomes more than consumers are willing to pay. Leica cameras may be in this category.
- The quality differences between the focused product and the low cost product become eroded. Japanese efforts at design and quality improvement have narrowed significantly the differences between expensive focused western cars and Japanese mass produced products.
- Non-focused large competitors may decide to target small market

segments and use their resources to cater for them in a 'focused' way. It could be argued that large multiple retailers who open specialist shops within a large shop are adopting this strategy.

Stuck in the middle

Porter claims that when a firm fails to develop satisfactorily one of the above three generic strategies it will become 'stuck in the middle'. Such a firm suffers from being too small to achieve a low cost position: it may lack market share and capital investment, i.e. it does not have the critical mass necessary to compete against the major competitors. It may also lack the differentiation necessary to charge premium prices as it may not have superior quality, superior reliability, chicness, or whatever attribute is necessary for differentiation.

Porter asserts that a firm in such a position is almost certain to have low profitability. It will probably also suffer from a blurred corporate culture and a conflicting set of organizational arrangements and motivation systems. When a firm is in such a position it must make one of two fundamental decisions: take the steps necessary to become low cost; or focus to achieve some form of differentiation.

STRATEGY SELECTION

Finally the strategy adopted by any firm will be formed through a combination of two elements: first, the overall strategy of growth, refocus, neutral or reduction; second, the generic strategy of overall cost leadership, differentiation or focus. The particular combination which is selected should be determined by the environmental prospects, the nature of the competition, the firm's resources, goals and culture.

NEW STRATEGIES: BUILDING SUPERIOR RESPONSES TO THE MARKET

So far this chapter has been concerned with developing strategy in fairly broad terms – growth, refocus, recovery, reduction and high volume low cost, differentiation and focus. Additional detail will now be given to the chosen broad strategy by relating it to specific marketing strategies which will enable the firm to build superior responses to the market. There are four major responses which are detailed below: pricing strategies; promotion strategies; distribution strategies; quality, innovation and service strategies.

PRICING STRATEGIES

Many managers, in spite of considerable evidence to the contrary, still cling to the view that the primary or indeed the only basis of competition is price. Indeed such managers will often speak despairingly in the following manner:

> 'If your price is the lowest you'll get the business. If it's not you won't.'

> 'This industry operates exclusively on the basis of lowest price. That's why there are no profits in it. No one makes any money.'

When these sorts of sentiments prevail in an unquestioned way they may cloud managers' vision of alternative, and often more robust and financially rewarding, approaches to building a superior competitive position in the market. It could be argued that price, which normally means low price, is the very worst strategy for most firms to pursue. This is often so for one or more of the following reasons:

- *Lower profits.* The lower margins often lead to lower profits. Although the unit costs stay the same, the lower unit price reduces the margins.
- *Disloyal buyers.* Low price strategies tend to breed disloyal buyers who will switch allegiance when a lower price is offered by a rival. They are quite rational to do this. If buyers only purchase on the basis of lowest price they will switch to any firm that offers it.
- *No managerial skill or knowledge is required.* Even a completely untrained person who is totally ignorant of the workings of a firm and its industry can formulate a highly effective strategy to increase sales through, say, a price reduction of 10 per cent. This type of strategy will boost sales but simultaneously may destroy profits.

- *Immediate retaliation.* Any price reduction can be matched immediately by rivals. If one firm makes a price reduction, rivals can instantly react by making similar or greater price reductions. Frequently, the effect of this type of retaliatory competition leads to a spiral of price wars which have the ultimate effect of passing substantial proportions of the profits of all the firms in the industry to the customers, with a consequent decrease in profitability for all competitors. An industry which has been plagued by this type of competition is petrol retailing.

Therefore it is argued that price is the worst possible competitive weapon which a firm can employ. Indeed, it is just one of the marketing tools or levers that managers have at their disposal when competing. For most firms a more comprehensive set of marketing levers includes: promotion; distribution; quality; innovation; service. The characteristics of these marketing tools are summarized in Table C3.12.Using any of these marketing levers rather than price is likely to generate robust superior profits.[10] Some examples of how these levers have been used successfully are now provided.

Table C3.12   Characteristics of the marketing levers

	Lower profits	Disloyal buyers	Managerial skill	Competitive reaction
Low price	Yes	Yes	No	Immediate
Superior promotion	No	No	Yes	Difficult
Superior distribution	No	No	Yes	Difficult
Superior quality	No	No	Yes	Difficult
Superior innovation	No	No	Yes	Difficult
Superior service	No	No	Yes	Difficult

Promotion

An aggressive strategic move based on promotion may lead to advertising battles, can actually expand the market for all competitors, enhance the level of product differentiation, build buyer loyalty and so preserve prices. For example, although the beer market in most advanced western countries is mature and therefore characterized by having low growth, low profit, commodity type products, in recent years the market structure has changed. Largely through promotion it has become more dynamic and certain niches have grown rapidly and been extremely profitable. Thus the overall beer market has become segmented as the brewers have sought, largely through promotion aimed at young, affluent, relatively price insensitive drinkers, to lever their products into high price, fast growing niches which are usually termed designer beers. The effectiveness of this strategy is demonstrated in Table C3.13 which shows the prices of off-licence packaged lager in a region of the UK in December 1995.

Table C3.13 Retail prices of packaged beers in a region of the UK, 1995

Beer	Retail selling price	Volume	Value
Miller	53.9	5.8	9.4
Harp	34.8	5.2	5.5
Budweiser	53.0	2.7	4.4
Tennents	30.4	2.1	2.0
Satzenbrau	52.3	1.3	2.0
Labatt	55.4	0.7	1.1
Carlsberg	44.9	0.5	0.7
Holsten	59.2	0.5	0.8
AO	46.8	0.4	0.6
Heineken	49.9	0.3	0.5
Rolling Rock	55.2	0.2	0.4
Becks	55.8	0.2	0.3
Tuborg	42.7	0.1	0.2
McEwans	31.5	0.1	0.1
Fosters	57.0	0.0	0.1
Carling	26.0	0.0	0.0
Michelob	63.0	0.0	0.0
Coors	47.9	0.0	0.0
Corona	66.7	0.0	0.0

Source: A. C. Nielsen Co. Ltd

Distribution

A superior form of distribution may permit businesses to earn superior returns. For example, in the beer and spirits distribution business it is not unusual for small regional distributors to coexist profitably and harmoniously with much larger lower cost national distributors. These much smaller regional players can enjoy superior returns because they are able to charge and justify a premium price on the basis of almost instant delivery.

Quality

Quality, or rather relative quality, can be used to build commodity products into premium priced differentiated ones. For example, in the hire car industry Hertz, Avis and Budget all charge significantly higher rates than most local or suppliers of hire cars. These companies have a reputation for quality, convenience and service which leads users, mainly business users, to conclude that even though their prices are the highest they still represent value for money because of the quality of their service.

Innovation

Product development through proprietary innovation may enable a firm to build a pricing structure which is not subject to the severe pricing pressures that more commodity type rivals suffer. For example, the world's leading manufacturer of notebook computers, Toshiba, continuously seeks to avoid the full competitive horror of price wars through relentless product innovation.

Service

Service is used in many industries to build differentiation. This is one of the key differentiators used by Hertz, Avis and Budget in the hire car industry.

Setting prices

Setting an appropriate price for a product is a complex and difficult process. Setting too low a price may cause profit potential not to be realized while setting too high a price may cause the firm to lose market share to rivals or even worse may stop sales from materializing. However, there is a number of influences which tend to predominate when setting prices:

- firm's marketing objectives;
- firm's unit costs;
- product's life cycle stage;
- product demand;
- degree of competition in market niche.

Each of these influences is now considered.

Firm's marketing objectives

In Table C3.14 there is a number of marketing-related objectives that firms often have and the consequences that these objectives tend to have in setting prices.

Table C3.14 How objectives influence pricing strategy

Objective	Likely price level	Rationale
Profitability	High	Emphasize differentiation
Gain market share	Low	Emphasize value for money
Deter or defeat competitors	Low[11]	Emphasize differentiation
Transform commodity into a branded product	High	Emphasize differentiation
Maintain a cartel	High	Don't rock the boat: every player is reasonably content
Sell profitable associated services	Low	No margin on product sales but make the margins on associated products
Send signals of quality	High	Consumers often assume that price is a clear signal of quality
Send signals of value	Low	Lower price than competitors often regarded as value for money

The firm's unit costs

How unit costs influence pricing strategy can be considered under the three main methods of how prices can be related to costs: cost plus pricing; target pricing; marginal cost pricing.[12]

Cost plus pricing

This involves determining the total cost per unit produced and then arriving at a price by adding to that cost a fixed percentage for profit margin. The total cost per unit is normally composed of the variable costs of production and marketing, plus an allocation of overhead to cover fixed costs. For example, if a firm had a pricing policy of always having a gross margin of 30 per cent and it found that the total unit cost of producing an item was £100, then it would charge a price of £130 to give the required margin.

Target pricing

The rationale of this strategy is that price should be calculated by meeting a predetermined return on the capital employed. For example, if a firm had a policy that its return on capital employed should be 20 per cent then all its products should be priced so that they generate this rate of return.

Marginal cost pricing

This occurs when a firm sets price by ensuring that it covers all the variable costs of production and marketing but the fixed costs are not fully covered. The fixed costs may be partly covered or not covered at all. This strategy may be appropriate when one or more of the following conditions prevail:

*   *Overcapacity*. To reduce investment intensity.[13] Seasonal fluctuation, for example, during the off season hotels often charge a marginal cost rate.
*   *Experience industries*. In certain industries, for example, electronics where unit costs are very strongly influenced by volumes (the larger the volume the lower the unit cost), the strategic imperative may be to accumulate as large a volume as possible – build mar-

ket share, rather than seek profit.

- *Multiple product lines.* When a firm has a multiple product line it may be appropriate to price select products in this fashion and cross-subsidize them from other products. In this way the lower price of the subsidized products ought to help them penetrate their markets.

Product demand

Demand is a fundamental influence on price and price is a fundamental influence on demand. The two are interlinked: as price rises, demand decreases, or as demand increases, price increases. The extent to which demand is influenced by price is expressed by the concept of 'price elasticity of demand' where this is the change in volume caused by a change in price. Some products such as food and other necessities tend to have a low price elasticity – the volumes consumed tend not to be influenced strongly by price. However, other products that are non-necessities such as jewellery and holidays tend to have higher price elasticities where price changes can have dramatic effects upon volumes. Bearing in mind the influence of price elasticities it will generally be the case that the greater the excess demand for the product, the higher will be the price that the firm will be able to charge.

Product's life cycle stage

The stage which a product has reached in its life cycle may have a strong influence on price (see Chapter B1).

Degree of competition in market niche

Most products must compete with other offerings and so their prices will tend to be related to those of competitors. For example, it is not unusual for the price of a product to vary from country to country and the variation to be caused not by the manufacturing or marketing costs but by the prevailing price regime. The differential between the retail prices of cars in the USA and UK is evidence of this influence. The influence of competitors' prices is often known as 'what the market will bear'.

Pricing new products or services

The pricing of existing products is generally a simpler task than the pricing of new products. Existing products have a pricing history and setting new prices is often merely an incremental adjustment to past price levels. However, when a new product that is unique is launched, setting its price tends to be much more difficult. There are no competing peer products. The 'rules of the market' in terms of growth rate, buyer behaviour and competitive reactions and strategies have not yet evolved. The only element known with certainty is costs.

Clearly, because of the uncertainties, the pricing of a unique new product presents problems. However, the following three-step methodology can help establish a price.

- *Step 1.* Assume that the price of the product will at least cover marginal costs.
- *Step 2.* Through market research – pilot test marketing, analysis of substitute products, assessment of competitive reactions – make estimates of the likely demand and likely returns for the new product with various prices, promotion methods and distribution methods.
- *Step 3.* On the basis of the market research decide upon a pricing level, plus promotion and distribution methods.

Often this type of analysis will lead to the adoption of one of the following archetypal new product pricing strategies: skimming or penetration.

Skimming pricing strategy

Skimming price means charging a premium price for a new product. The rationale is that the new product will be so attractive to buyers that they will be prepared to pay a premium price for it and the firm will be rewarded handsomely with extremely high profits. Underlying the adoption of this strategy is the assumption that the product is proprietary, i.e. cannot readily be manufactured by competitors and cheaper substitutes are not available.

Penetration pricing strategy

Penetration price means setting the price for a new product at a relatively low level, perhaps covering marginal cost but not covering all of the fixed costs. The rationale is that it will stimulate the market, cause very large volumes to be bought and the firm will gain something more durable than the shorter term profits likely to be earned by a skimming price. It will gain market share and, if unit costs decrease as volume increases, it will become a low cost producer which will help deter new entrants.

Table C3.15 summarizes the main conditions which ought to apply when a skimming or a penetrating price strategy is being considered.

Table C3.15 Conditions for employment of skimming and penetration pricing strategies

	Pricing strategy	
	Skimming	Penetration
Price level	High: signal of quality	Low: deter new entrants
Buyers	Price insensitive	Price sensitive
Product	Proprietary	Non-proprietary
Substitutes	Not available	Available
Cost	Not volume related	Volume related

Conclusion on pricing strategy

For most products relative price is the clearest signal of a product's position in its market segment. However, it is just one element in the marketing mix and for its influence to be maximized it should be integrated with the other marketing levers – promotion, distribution, quality, innovation and service – to meet consumer needs in a superior way and satisfy the firm's goals.

PROMOTION STRATEGIES

Promotion is the marketing lever which the firm uses to communicate with and influence its target market segments. It does this by positioning the firm and its products in the minds of existing and potential buyers and predisposing them to purchase. However, promotion is not just about generating sales or achieving superior prices for products, it often has additional more subtle goals.

Awareness

A firm often wishes its target audience to be aware of its existence. Thus, the sponsorship of sporting events, for example, the Dunhill Cup in golf, is not concerned with generating immediate sales. Rather it is concerned with reinforcing the Dunhill brand image. Similarly, a firm may wish to remind its current customers of its existence or the existence of a brand or a product through, for example, corporate diaries, pens, paperweights.

Attitude

Firms often wish their target markets and others to have particular attitudes towards them. For example, the major oil companies have, through their promotion campaigns, developed a much more environmentally aware image, with a consequent lower level of criticism than, say, mining companies.

Competitive signals

Firms often use promotion to signal to their stakeholders and indeed their competitors. For example, many publicly quoted firms trumpet their success through placing advertisements in the business press when their annual report is released. They are sending signals to their shareholders, bankers, customers, employees, society and competitors.

Action

Ultimately most promotion campaigns will lead to sales. However, the speed of sale completion will vary greatly. For example, telesales for CDs and tapes which are promoted on television fail if they do not lead to immediate sales whereas advertisements for house sales tend to have a much longer lag between advertisement and sale.

Promotion influences

The type and amount of promotion undertaken by a firm will tend to be a function of the following influences:

- The firm's overall goals and strategy, for example, growth rate ambitions, reputation, goals.
- The objective of the promotion campaign, i.e. awareness, attitude, competitive signal or action.
- The firm's position within the industry, for example, leader or follower, niche player or full range, high volume low cost or differentiated.
- The nature of the industry, for example, consumer or industrial goods, lag between promotion and sale, buyer behaviour and the role of promotion as a key industry success factor.

Effects of promotion

For certain industries, particularly consumer products, firms are often differentiated not on the basis of product, but rather on the basis of promotion. Promotion is used by firms in such industries to transform their products from inherently low margin commodities into high margin differentiated products. Industries such as distilling, food, carbonated drinks, shampoo, soap and fashion clothes are all inherently commodity industries and leading firms tend to use promotion as the primary lever to build distinctive brands. This is illustrated with examples from the grocery retailing industry in Table C3.16. As can be seen, the price premiums that consumers are willing to pay for the strongly promoted branded products is very substantial indeed and the commercial benefits are clear.

Types of promotion

Promotion can be divided into two major types: impersonal promotion, i.e. advertising; personal promotion, i.e. personal selling.

Advertising

The main media used for advertising are newspapers, magazines,

Table C3.16 A comparison between the market share values and prices of the leading brand and own label competitors in selected grocery segments in a UK region, December 1995

Product	Leading player		Own label		Price premium (%)
	Mkt share by value (%)	Price (pence)	Mkt share by value (%)	Price (pence)	
Yoghurt	Muller: 32.5	40.6	4.1	22.9	77
Carbonated drinks	Coca-Cola: 43.4	68.3	2.4	35.8	91
Dogfood	Pedigree: 57.9	125.7	3.5	54.0	133

Source: A. C. Neilsen Co. Ltd

posters, radio, cinema, television and the Internet. The medium which a firm uses will normally be influenced by the following:

- The firm's overall goals, for example, regional national or international scope.
- The promotion goals, i.e. awareness, attitude, signals or sales.
- The firm's resources, i.e. its promotion budget.
- The targeted segment's use of the various media. Some market niches are very medium specific while others can be influenced by a variety of media. Thus books tend to be promoted only in newspapers, magazines and specialist book periodicals while cars are promoted through magazines, newspapers, posters, cinema, television and radio.
- The audience quality where this means that the recipients of the message are likely to be interested in it, for example, promoting mountain bikes through a specialist magazine read by people deeply interested in the sport. This is a high quality audience.

Personal selling

As the name implies, personal selling involves generating sales through face-to-face contact, on the telephone or by letter. It is part of the process of promotion in that it is very directly concerned with promoting a firm's products in the psyche of potential customers.

Additionally, however, personal selling ought to include another important function: it should sensitize the firm to the changing conditions in its market niches and broader environment. Thus the selling task is probably a misnomer. It may be more appropriate to call it selling and reconnaissance.

Conclusion on promotion

Because promotion is in many ways less tangible than, say, product quality or channel of distribution it may not receive the attention it merits, especially from new businesses. But it is stressed once again that when used with the other marketing levers it can be an indispensable tool in hoisting a product out of a low margin fiercely competitive commodity niche into a burgeoning high margin differentiated one.

DISTRIBUTION STRATEGIES

Distribution activities determine where the product will be sold; the channels though which it will be delivered and associated decisions such as inventory levels. Superior distribution is another marketing lever by which a firm can gain a robust competitive advantage over rivals. The main means by which this can be achieved are now described.

Denial of access to new entrants

In industries such as food, the major incumbents will assiduously build exclusive routes to their retail market with guaranteed shelf space in order to prevent new entrants from gaining a foothold.

Locking in the customer

Major suppliers of large multiples often develop dedicated electronic inventory systems whose cost, speed and efficiency prevent rival suppliers from competing for the business. By this method they lock in the customer. To illustrate, in the clothing industry captive suppliers to the large multiples will install expensive IT systems which are integrated with the multiples' IT systems. This has the effect of locking in the multiples. It would be extremely difficult for them to find alternative suppliers willing to undertake the IT investment.

Meeting customer needs in a superior way

When producing commodity products which are widely available from many competitors, superior distribution may be a route to differentiation. For example, producers of plastic packaging materials tend to be in a commodity industry – many competitors, low barriers to entry and low switching costs. Differentiation may be achieved by focusing on customer needs and quality of distribution rather than the products. This can be reflected in the organizational structure. For example, if a producer of commodity plastic products had ten major commodity type product lines each contributing similar volumes of sales and one customer which contributed, say, 50 per cent of sales, it might help differentiate the firm's products if it were to define its business along two dimensions:

- *Dimension 1.* The 50 per cent customer.
- *Dimension 2.* All other customers.

A structure that would reflect this approach is shown in Figure C3.6.

Lowering unit cost of product or service

Altering the conventional method of distribution may lower the unit cost of the product below that of rivals. For example, in the retail industry centralized distribution and warehousing are increasingly pursued for this reason.

Difficult to replicate

Distribution methods that rivals cannot replicate tend to enhance differentiation. For example, the network of high street banks owned by the major UK banks would be extremely difficult and expensive for new entrants to replicate.

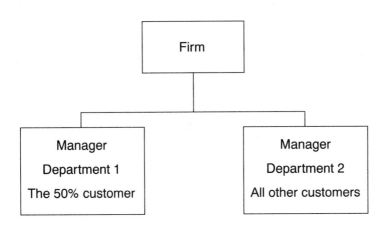

Figure C3.6   A structure which might help differentiate a commodity product firm on the basis of superior distribution to its main customer

Criteria used in deciding a distribution strategy

Among the more important influences in deciding a distribution strategy are: responsiveness to the customer; profitability; product pricing; promotion; relationships with distributing firms; control. These factors are now considered.

Responsiveness to customers' needs and wishes

The nature, quality and level of customer service will be often influenced by the chosen method of distribution. Generally, the longer the distribution chain, the less responsive the firm will be. For example, in the personal computer industry some firms, Dell and Gateway, conduct their distribution, not through retailers, but by direct dialling of the manufacturing plant and then direct shipping to the customer.

Profitability

The method of distribution chosen – in most cases there is usually a choice of method – usually involves a trade-off between the costs, which are significant in most industries, and the benefits, Christopher (14) indicated that, on average, distribution costs are about 15 per cent of sales turnover for a typical firm. Generally, the more focused and controlled the distribution system, the more costly it is likely to be.

Product

The characteristics of the product may be influenced by the method of distribution chosen. For example, a decision to distribute a product internationally may involve changing some physical aspects of it so that it conforms to international standard specifications.

Pricing

The pricing policy adopted will be influenced not just by manufacturing and actual distribution costs but also by the nature of distribution adopted. A decision by an organization to have broad, intensive, national distribution will tend to demand a lower price level than a decision to have limited distribution with a small number of exclusive high quality outlets.

Promotion

The promotional requirements for a product or service are also a function of the distribution methods employed. Thus the promotional requirements for intensive national distribution are very different from those required for smaller regional sales.

Relationships with distributing firms

The degree to which a firm outsources its distribution may have major long-term strategic implications. In many industries firms are continuously working on the equation for the optimal amount of distribution to be conducted from within and by outside contractors. The economics of outsourcing distribution is in a state of continuous change and must be monitored to assess the changing financial implications. For example, in the 1970s the major oil companies tended to take the view that they should control most of their shipping and consequently maintained large tanker fleets. But they did not believe that they should control most of their retailing forecourts and franchised many of them. In the 1990s their view tends to be that their tanker fleets should be considerably smaller, with the bulk of cargoes being carried by non-company tankers while they should run the retail forecourts rather than franchisees.

Control

The greater use a firm makes of intermediaries to carry out its distribution the less control will it have over the marketing of its products.

Innovative distribution and altering key industry success factors

In most industries there are accepted distribution practices that received wisdom within the industry asserts must be followed if a firm is to be successful. However, periodically, the accepted distribution rules will be challenged and new channels of delivery will be developed which, if successful, will confer significant competitive advantage on the pioneer and other early adopters. An illustration of an industry which is currently in the throes of this distribution revolution is retail banking.

Historically, one of the key success factors in the retail banking industry has been the quality of distribution as reflected by the extensiveness of the branch bank network, the high street branches. However, the role of this network is being challenged and its future role appears less and less important. Retail banking is being driven by technology and, as detailed in Chapter B3, this has had and will continue to have a major effect upon the costs of the various channels of distribution that are used to access customers: branch network; automated teller machines (ATMs) telephone banking; point of sale and other.

As shown in Figure C3.7, it is forecast that branch networks will shrink by as much as 50 per cent by the year 2000. Clearly the banks that most effectively adopt these channels of distribution are likely to enjoy superior returns based upon lower distribution costs, plus satisfying customer needs in a superior manner.

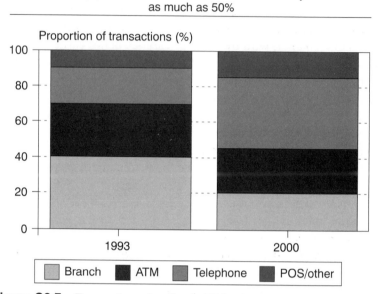

By year 2000 branch networks will shrink by as much as 50%

Figure C3.7   Transaction migration in USA, 1993–2000 (15)

Conclusion on distribution strategy

Clearly superior distribution is yet another marketing lever which can enable firms to build genuine and sustainable competitive advantage.

QUALITY, INNOVATION AND SERVICE

All industries are replete with examples of firms that are winners because of their quality. These successful firms charge premium prices and are recognized by purchasers as providing the best quality in the industry. Examples include:

- Automobiles: Mercedes.
- Food retailing: Marks & Spencer.
- Motor cycles: Honda.
- Personal computers: Hewlett Packard.
- Aircraft: Boeing.
- Aircraft engines: Rolls-Royce.
- Fashion: Versace.
- Vodka: Smirnoff.

Is quality industry specific or are there generic rules? The answer to this question is yes to both issues.

Quality is industry specific

It is impossible to state what are the key dimensions of quality without reference to the specific industry or market niche that is being considered. A key dimension of quality in one industry may be irrelevant in another. For example, in market niches such as vodka and carbonated drinks the underlying characteristics of the product offerings tend to be quite similar. The technology to make and deliver the products is widely available and the set-up costs of manufacturing modest in comparison with many other industries. Therefore, in these types of niches it is the quality of promotion and distribution, rather than the product itself, that is the key differentiator and is likely to be the most effective in deterring and defeating new entrants.

In contrast, in the aircraft manufacturing industry the quality of the physical product, as reflected in performance, safety, efficiency and durability, is the key differentiator. This is likely to be the most effective lever in deterring and defeating new entrants.

Quality is generic

The essence of strategy is to search for generic rules which can be applied irrespective of the industry. Some generic rules for quality do emerge when a strategic marketing perspective is taken. It could be argued that the elevation of the topic of quality to a major theme in the strategy literature and business practice reflects an attempt by the west to catch up with Japanese quality standards. When asked what quality is, many managers will often reply using phrases as:

- 'Achieving BS 5750.'
- 'Fitness for purpose.'
- 'Meeting or exceeding specifications.'
- 'Zero defects.'
- 'No wastage.'

While these comments are clear indicators of product quality they all take an exclusively internal and rather physical view of what quality, is. From a strategic marketing perspective, this view must be expanded to include an external – competitor and customer – perspective. The additional dimensions of quality can be considered as the following:[14]

Quality is not absolute but relative

Strategically it is more appropriate to consider quality, as a relative rather than an absolute measure. Rather than asserting that a certain firm's quality is the best, consider the quality of a firm's products relative to rival offerings. Thus a product can be considered as superior, equivalent to or inferior to competing products. For example, in the family saloon niche of the automobile industry any manufacturer can make a judgement as to whether its models are superior, equivalent or inferior by rivals using key buying influences such as space, economy, secondhand value, speed, durability, safety.

A consequence of adopting this relative view is that quality levels cannot be static – quality is dynamic. If one firm has a static level of quality while competitors are improving theirs, then the firm's quality is actually declining. For example, in the desktop publishing market niche there was an initial gap in quality between dedicated desktop publishing software and wordprocessing software. However, the gap has narrowed significantly as wordprocessing systems, and the associated hardware have improved in quality. The relative quality of dedicated desktop publishing is now often indistinguishable from good wordprocessing.

It is the customers' judgement, not the firm's

The right to judge quality does not rest with the firm producing the product: it rests with the customer. This must be so, as it is the customer who makes the purchase decision on the basis of competing offerings. Consequently when managers comment that their customers do not appreciate the quality of their products, this is almost certainly an erroneous view of the nature of quality. It is not for them to make the judgement, it is for their customers.

Product quality is too narrow: it should also include service

It is rare for customers to assess quality solely on the basis of the physical attributes of the product. Most customers will make their quality judgement on the basis of the physical attributes of the product plus its associated services.

For example, in a project undertaken by the author the client firm was supplying a complex major component to a foreign final assembler and serious discord had developed between the firm and the assembler over the issue of quality. The firm claimed that its quality was appropriate while the assembler claimed it was not. In the course of analysis it was found that the major quality issue was not the actual physical quality of the product, but rather the supporting service after the product had been delivered. Typically, after delivery, communication between assembler and supplier became very sloppy and difficult, reflected in telephone calls for technical assistance from the assembler either not being answered at all or being answered very late. The quality issue was resolved by improvement of the communication system – the associated service. Clearly in this case quality embraces both the product and the associated services.

Innovation

Innovation is often related to quality. Firms that are able to charge premium prices for their products and services on the basis of quality of engineering tend to be innovative in engineering. Those that charge premium prices basd on the quality of promotion tend to be innovative in promotion.

Although there can be many definitions of innovation, perhaps the PIMS definition is the most appropriate in a strategic marketing context. This measures innovation as the percentage of a firm's sales from products which it has introduced in the last three years.[15] Thus it is somewhat different from invention: invention is the idea and the prototype while innovation is the effective commercialization of the invention, i.e. when the invention results in actual sales. Although innovation has been used by many firms to differentiate themselves, for example 3M, Sony, Microsoft, Honda, it is a strategy that is fraught with risks. When a firm introduces an innovative product there is a number of risks:

- It is likely to be expensive to develop and there is no guarantee of success – it may not be accepted by the market.
- It may not be possible to protect the innovation and so, even if it

is successful in the market, it may be copied at much lower cost, by rivals who gain more from the innovation than the pioneer.

• There are considerable benefits in being a follower rather than a pioneer. The follower need only commit to the product and the market after it has become clear that there is a material market and that it will be able to develop a comparable or better product at a lower cost than the pioneer.

In general it could be argued that innovations can only confer sustained competitive advantage if they can be kept proprietary, and even then it may be difficult.

A clear example of the relationship between a pioneering company and an early adopter is provided by the strategies and behaviours of the Japanese electronics companies Sony and Matsushita. Sony has a reputation for being a highly inventive company frequently bringing to market products which are truly innovative – the video cassette recorder, the Walkman, the Discman. However, Matsushita has a reputation not for innovativeness but for re-engineering and improving innovations from other companies, especially Sony. Although the video cassette recorder was initially developed by Sony (Betamax system), Matsushita was successful in its commercial exploitation through the now world standard VHS system.

In spite of the caution necessary in the use of innovation as a competitive weapon, when it is applied in association with the other marketing levers it can be a major source of competitive advantage. Thus firms which have superior distribution, superior brands and high degrees of innovation are likely to prove successful.

Service quality

Because superior service is often not physically measurable it is more difficult to quantify. However, it still remains a major route out of horror commodity products. Superior service could be regarded as seeing to the heart of customer service needs and then fulfilling them in a superior fashion. For example, aircraft travel is an inherently commodity type business but there are niches in which superior margins can be earned and many airlines have sought differentiation through superior service reflected in:

- exclusive airport lounges.
- business support facilities, e.g. faxes, conference rooms.
- through ticketing and travel on the same carrier.
- limousine service to and from airports.
- superior inflight comfort, food and service.

Once again the provision of superior service tends to be industry specific.

DEVELOPING STRATEGIES

In this chapter the development of a new strategy was presented as the following cascading process:

- *At corporate level*:

  — Mission, goals or targets are set.
  — A fundamental strategy is developed: growth, refocus, neutral or reduce.
  — A generic strategy is developed: high volume low cost, differentiation or focus.[16]

- *At SBU level*: subject to conformance with corporate directives, for each SBU:

  — Mission, goals or targets are set.
  — A fundamental strategy is developed: growth, refocus, neutral or reduce.
  — A generic strategy is developed: high volume low cost, differentiation or focus.[17]

- *At product market level*: subject to conformance with SBU directives, for each product market:

  — Goals or targets are set.
  — A marketing strategy is developed to build, hold, harvest and divest.
  — The marketing levers to achieve the goals are selected: price, promotion, distribution, quality, innovation and service.

The type of firm in which this process typically takes place is shown schematically in Figure C3.8.

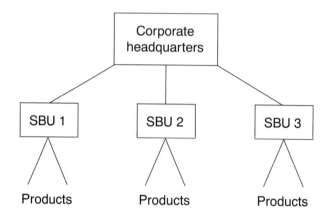

Figure C3.8   A hypothetical typical firm to illustrate how new strategies
are developed

Tying together the elements

Finally, Figure C3.9 ties together all of the elements in developing a
new strategy. The figure reflects the activities and strategies that would
be followed in a hypothetical firm:

Firm structure:

• Corporate headquarters.

• Three SBUs – SBU 1, SBU 2 and SBU 3 – reporting to headquarters.

• Each SBU has four product market groups
   — SBU 1 has product markets A, B, C, D.
   — SBU 2 has product markets E, F, G, H.
   — SBU 3 has product markets I, J, K, L.

Level	Corporate			Strategies
Corporate				
SBU	SBU 1	SBU 2	SBU 3	Fundamental strategy: Growth
				Generic strategy: Differentiation
				Fundamental strategy: Growth
				Generic strategy: Differentiation

Product market	A	B	C	D	E	F	G	H	I	J	K	L
Marketing strategies	Build	Hold	Harvest	Divest	Build	Build	Build	Hold	Hold	Hold	Build	Harvest
Marketing levers	Price, Promotion, Distribution, Quality, innovation and Service											

Figure C3.9 Tying together all the elements in developing a new strategy

Firm strategies:

- Corporate:

    — Fundamental strategy: growth.
    — Generic strategy: differentiation.

- SBU:

    — Fundamental strategy: growth
    — Generic strategy: differentiation.

- Product market:

    — Strategies: a variety depending upon each product market: build, hold, harvest and divest (see Chapter B1).
    — Marketing levers: price, promotion, distribution, quality, innovation and service.

CONCLUSION

This chapter provided a comprehensive methodology for developing a set of market-driven strategies which will enable any firm to achieve its goals. Although the process was set out hierarchically, i.e. driven from the top level in the firm, in practice although guidance will be given at this level, real creativity and seeing in unique ways to the needs of market niches will usually only be accomplished through the combined efforts of all levels of staff in the firm.

The tactics necessary to ensure that these strategies are actually implemented are considered in Chapter D1.

NOTES

1. This, of course, will be the preferred strategy for most firms.
2. A firm could become so small that it disappears. This case is not considered because it is assumed that this is not a normal managerial aspiration.
3. The industries are often known as experience related. For further details see (1).
4. Firms may of course employ a combination, i.e. growth coming from a combination of organic sources and also from acquisition. However, for the sake of clarity of exposition it is assumed that a firm will plump for one or the other. This observation would apply to all the strategies considered in this chapter, i.e. vari-

ous combinations are possible.

5. Relative market share, as explained in Chapter B2, is a fundamental determinant of profitability.
6. Specialist publications such as *Music Week* in the UK will confirm these trends.
7. In recent years, however, many tobacco companies have reversed this strategy and divested their CTNs.
8. For further information see (1), Chapter 3.
9. They may, of course, be sold as a differentiated product with a higher price, if they can be differentiated by a feature such as up-to-dateness which is unavailable elsewhere.
10. In practice, adroit firms will not simply use one of the marketing levers but a combination, for example: superior quality, superior promotion and superior service. In addition, for firms which are the largest in their market niches low price will tend to be an appropriate lever as they will have the lower unit costs.
11. The price may be low for relatively high market share competitors.
12. For the detailed calculations for each of these methods of pricing, see (12).
13. See (13) for further information on investment intensity.
14. These dimensions of quality reflect strongly the PIMS studies on the subject (11).
15. This definition may be somewhat arbitrary. In fast-moving industries, such as personal computers, three years might be an excessively long time span while in slower moving industries, such as heavy electrical turbine manufacturing, three years might be considered relatively short.
16. The balance of the group portfolio of businesses is, of course, also an issue.
17. The balance of the group portfolio of products is, of course, also an issue.

REFERENCES

(1) McNamee, P. B. (1985). *Tools and Techniques for Strategic Management*. Pergamon, Oxford.
(2) Yoshida Kogyo, K. K. (1982). In Stopford, J., Channon, D. and Constable, J., *Cases in Strategic Management*, p. 344. Wiley, Chichester.
(3) Extel.
(4) Davidson, W. H. and De La Torre, J. (1989). *Managing the Global Corporation*. McGraw-Hill, Maidenhead.
(5) Bombardier Inc. annual reports.
(6) Newbould, G. D. and Luffman G. A. (1978). *Successful Business Policies*. Gower, Aldershot.
(7) Leontiades, M. (1989). *Myth Management: An Examination of Corporate Diversification as Fact and Theory*, pp. 135, 159. Blackwell, Oxford.
(8) Donne, M. (1986). Aerospace: competition creates new turbulence. *Financial Times*, 30 August.
(9) ABB annual reports.
(10) Slatter, S. (1984). *Corporate Recovery*. Penguin, Harmondsworth.

(11) Porter, M. E. (1980). *Competitive Strategy: Techniques for Analyzing Industries and Competitors*. Free Press, New York.

(12) McNamee, P. B. (1988). Management Accounting: Strategic Planning and Marketing. Heinemann, London.

(13) Buzzell, R. D. and Gale, B. T. (1982). *The PIMS Principles: Linking Strategy to Performance*. Free Press, New York.

(14) Christopher, M. (1986). *The Strategy of Distribution Management*. Heinemann, London.

(15) Deloitte, Touche Tohmatsu International (1995). *The Future of Retail Banking: A Global Perspective*. Deloitte Touche Tohmatsu International, London.

D1

Tactics and Implementation

This chapter is about reality: it is concerned with ensuring that the strategic market plans which were set out in Chapters C1 to C3 do not remain unfulfilled aspirations but are turned into working practices. Achieving this can be rather difficult. When strategic market plans fail one of the most common causes is not the plan itself but failure to implement it. This chapter examines some of the major issues which are key to implementation.

Implementation can be considered at two levels: first, the overall and more general SBU-wide issues which must always be addressed; second, the detailed tactics, which vary from firm to firm, must be carried out to ensure that successful implementation does actually take place.

OVERALL SBU-WIDE ISSUES

Perhaps the most important consideration in implementation is the magnitude of change which is required to put the new strategy in place. Generally, the greater the degree of change, the greater will be the resistance to it. For example, when a new strategy calls for radical restructuring of the firm – say, from a production led to a marketing led organization – there will tend to be great resistance. In contrast, when a new strategy is merely an extension of the past, say, an incremental increase in sales, the resistance to the change can often be minimal. Consequently, a key issue in implementation is how to overcome resistance to change or, expressing it more positively, how to generate enthusiasm about change.

PROMOTING CHANGE

In studies of how firms effect change (1,2) the following method which always seems to end in failure is:

- *Stage 1.* Senior management set the new mission, goals and strategy of the firm. They provide a new vision of the future.
- *Stage 2.* This strategy is disseminated downwards through the hierarchy and with all the authority that senior management can muster the staff are required to follow it. After all, it is the future of the firm.
- *Stage 3.* After a period of apparent enthusiasm the 'new plan' withers and eventually the firm returns to the way it was, i.e. mission, goals and strategy, before the plan was developed.

This sequence suggests that it is not enough to have an excellent and logical plan to which all staff can relate and, having thought out how all staff can contribute, to bring about its implementation. The pure logic of the plan and the authority of senior management do not guarantee successful implementation.

More subtle approaches are needed which recognize that it is human nature not to welcome change. Indeed, if left to their own devices, most people would not wish to change at all. So the issue becomes what conditions can be set up that will lessen people's resistance to change or expressing this more positively, energise them into embracing change. When promoting change it is observable that often people do want the end result of change. What they resist is the process or transformation that must take place to achieve it. This is illustrated in Figure D1.1.

In Figure D1.1 a hypothetical firm has a current competitive position in which it has a low market share and earns average profits. In its desired competitive position it will be the highest market share competitor and will earn superior profits. Most people in such a firm would agree that the end result is highly desirable. However, what prevents them from achieving this result is the transformation that must take place, for example, in work practices, attitudes, behaviours, goals, in order to achieve this desired competitive position. Research (3) and observation indicate that the three main issues which tend to promote effective transformation are time span plus action and involvement.

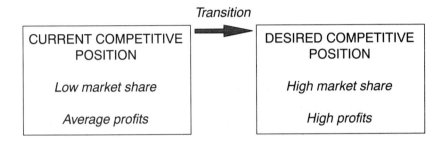

Figure D1.1   The transition process is the main impediment to change

Time span plus action

Implementation requires speedy and concrete actions. For example, if the desired goal is to have the highest market share in two years, talking about this goal and having a two-year time frame plan is likely to fail. Successful implementation is likely to be achieved by setting up small action teams with specific and immediate action targets. In this case teams could be required to: Target and then acquire one new major customer every four weeks for the next six months. One of the features of effective change is that ghost teams are set up to achieve these types of short-run tasks. When the task is completed the team is disbanded.

Successful firms will often achieve this type of transition by having, say, a monthly 'key implementation issue'. Meetings are held between key managers and all staff involved, plus perhaps a short newsletter detailing the tasks and actions for the month. An example of a key implementation newsletter on customer service is as follows:

Theme for the Month of April
'The Customer Only Rings Twice'

'*The Postman Only Rings Twice*' was the title of a successful film. '*The Customer Only Rings Twice*' is the title for our drive to provide the best telephone customer relationships in the industry. Currently on average our customers are answered after 10 rings and some after 20 rings. This is customer service way below what we can achieve. We believe that we can reduce the waiting to 2 rings and that is our target this month. We will log our performances and have a discussion at the end of each week for the next 4 weeks to see how we do and how we can achieve this target.

Involvement

Research (3) and observation show that the greater the degree of involvement in the process of change, the greater the chances of successful implementation. Involvement makes two major contributions. First, the greater the degree of involvement, the greater the degree of ownership. People who have ownership tend to defend it. Second, high levels of involvement will help build the critical mass of supporters of the plan necessary to ensure its implementation.

Beer, Eisenstat and Spector (1) have suggested that there are six major steps to ensuring effective strategic change.

Step 1: Generate commitment through joint diagnosis of the problems to be overcome

The wider the realization of the need for change, the greater will be the pool of people who will support it. This implies that the responsibility for developing change does not lie only with senior managers, but rather with as wide and varied a group as possible. The belief that the idea of the need for change emanates from senior management is not always reflected in practice. Thus it is not unusual for a particular department or group of people to change their approach or method of working. The benefits of this change are noted by senior managers and then copied in other parts of the firm.

Step 2: Develop a communal view of how to gain competitive advantage

When a communal diagnosis – all levels and all functions – is supported by a communal strategy of the competitive benefits of change, this tends to create a critical mass of supporters for change.

Step 3: Develop agreement about the new vision
and develop the skills to implement it

Once again when staff at all levels and all functions forge a common view of the strategies to be undertaken, implementation is facilitated. However, having a vision is not sufficient. Existing staff may need to develop new skills. New staff may need to be appointed. Additional resources may be needed.

Step 4: Extend the new vision through the actual people involved

Exhortations by senior managers on the necessity and rightness of change tend to have much less effect than face-to-face communication of the new agenda by people at all levels who are actually involved in the day-to-day tasks. Such people play a vital role in extending the vision throughout the firm. Communicating the new strategy and vision is often best achieved by small group meetings addressed by staff deeply involved rather than a mass meeting addressed by senior managers or, even worse, a 'letter to all staff from the senior management team'.

Step 5: Develop formal structures out of the embryonic

The informal structures set up initially to implement the new strategy should, as it takes hold, be changed into formal ones which support it.

Step 6: Monitor progress

Progress should be monitored to ensure that the change taking place is the one needed for the new strategy.

The effective promotion of change to bring about long-term goals requires communication, short-run actions and the involvement of as many people as possible in the process (see Figure D1.2).

ROLE OF LEADERSHIP IN IMPLEMENTATION

Implementation cannot be effected without appropriate leadership at all levels. The attributes of effective leadership are discussed in Chapter

Figure D1.2 Short-run tasks drive the prices to achieve long-term goals

B4. In terms of implementation the key question about leadership[1] is: Does the current leader have the authority, skills and drive necessary to implement the new strategy? Clearly there are two answers: Yes, the current leader is appropriate and stays. No, the new strategy will not succeed under current leader and will need to be replaced.

It should be noted that it is often the case that when the incumbent leadership realizes that it will not be appropriate for the new strategy, then, rather than leave, it will cause the new strategy to fail, either by failing to give wholehearted support or by abandoning it.

STRUCTURE AND STRATEGY

As discussed in Chapter B4, in the strategic market planning literature there has been a long and unresolved debate about whether strategy follows structure or structure follows strategy. However, irrespective of the conclusion, there has always been agreement that for competitive advantage strategy and structure must be aligned. The structure must be suitable for the strategy and the strategy must be suitable for the structure. Achieving this congruence can be a major and extremely contentious issue in implementing a new strategy as almost invariably when there is structural change there are winners and losers. Examples of structural issues that arise in implementation include:

- A new strategy involving cost reduction and improved communication will often require that a layer of management is removed (delayering): an issue of great potential conflict.
- A new strategy in which the business has been redefined in terms of markets rather than production could move power from the production function to the marketing function with consequent internal tensions.

However, irrespective of the tensions generated through structural change, the issue of having a good fit between strategy and structure is so important that it cannot be shirked by senior management.

When the overall SBU-wide issues have been resolved, the new strategies can be disaggregated into detailed action tactics of the type described above.

TACTICS

The detailed action tactics tend to be firm specific and can be considered on almost any dimension. The principal ones which most firms would use would include tactics for: products; customers; territories; pricing; promotion; distribution; quality; service; innovation; productivity; unit costs; human relations; information technology.

Rather than detail all the tactics for a firm, a pro forma which could be used for any dimension of tactics is presented in Table D1.1. Examples of tactics are provided in the Alban Chemicals strategic market plan in Chapter 5.

Tactics will normally involve: a specific task; a completion date and a person or group responsible.

CONCLUSION

Implementation is the interface between the plan and its reality. In practice it is the weakest part of the strategic market planning process

Table D1.1 Product tactics and implementation schedule

No	Task	Completion date	Action by
Product 1			
1	Building or holding or harvesting or divesting with specific target figures	Actual date	Named person
Product 2			
2	Building or holding or harvesting or divesting with specific target figures	Actual date	Named person
3	Say, a promotion campaign	Actual date	Named person
4	Say, a change in distribution	Actual date	Named person
Product 3			
5	Building or holding or harvesting or divesting with specific target figures	Actual date	Named person
6	Say, additional features	Actual date	Named person
Product 4			
7	Building or holding or harvesting or divesting with specific target figures	Actual date	Named person
Product 5			
8	Building or holding or harvesting or divesting with specific target figures	Actual date	Named person
9	Say, additional member of staff	Actual date	Named person
10	Say, acquire a rival firm	Actual date	Named person

and a major cause of failure. However, as long the process of implementation is pursued using an appropriate framework, which this chapter provided, it should be implemented.

Finally there are two caveats about implementation. First, the implementation process has a rather short life. After the development of the strategic market plan, if real action in implementation has not occurred within weeks then it is likely that the plan will 'drift' and fail to be implemented.

Second, in practice, it is unlikely that all the detailed tactics pro formas would be completed. This would be a rather time-consuming exercise requiring continuous revision. What tends to happen is that, using the pro formas as a template, tactics are agreed verbally by implementation teams.

NOTES

1. The leader is not just the chief executive, but also all the other leaders or managers – senior managers, middle managers and lower managers – in the firm.

REFERENCES

(1) Beer, M., Eisenstat, R. A. and Spector, B. (1990). Why change programs don't produce change. *Harvard Business Review*, November – December 1990, 158–165.
(2) Burnes, B. (1992). *Managing Change*, Pitman, London.
(3) Tom McConnologue. Unpublished PhD Thesis. Irish Management Institute, Dublin.

D2
Resources

Assuming that the strategic market plan is about expansion rather than contraction, then it is likely that additional resources – people, fixed assets and current assets – will be required. This brief chapter sets out templates which can be used to calculate the resources needed.

The additional resources can be considered at three levels: the overall additional corporate resources; overall additional SBU resources; additional resources by product line.[1] In addition to these assessments it can be useful to compute the additional net profit before tax that the additional resources will provide. (From this the payback period of the additional resources can also be computed.)

OVERALL CORPORATE ADDITIONAL RESOURCES

This is computed from accumulating the additional resources for each SBU and can be recorded in a pro forma such as Table D2.1.

OVERALL SBU ADDITIONAL RESOURCES

This is computed from accumulating the additional resources for each product line and can be recorded in a pro forma such as Table D2.2.

Table D2.1 Overall corporate resource implications of implementing the strategic market plan

Total firm	This year	One year ahead	Two years ahead	Change (%)
Staff (£k)				
Fixed assets: plant and equipment (£k)				
Current assets (£k)				
Other expenditures (£k)				
Total (£k/				
Net profit (£)				
Net profit (£)/ total expenditure (£) (%)				

Table D2.2 Overall SBU resource implications of implementing the strategic market plan

SBU	This year	One year ahead	Two years ahead	Change (%)
Staff (£k)				
Fixed assets: plant and equipment (£k)				
Current assets (£k)				
Other expenditures (£k)				
Total (£k)				
Net profit (£)				
Net profit (£)/ total expenditure (£) (%)				

PRODUCT LINE ADDITIONAL RESOURCES

These are the additional resources for each product line and can be recorded by means for a pro forma such as Table D2.3. Note that in practice it will often not be possible to have as fine a level of aggregation as product line. In such cases the lowest level of aggregation may be a group of products or only the SBU.

Table D2.3 Resource implications of implementing the strategic market plan for Product X

Product line X	This year	One year ahead	Two years ahead	Change (%)
Staff (£k)				
Fixed assets: plant and equipment (£k)				
Current assets (£k)				
Other expenditures (£k)				
Total (£k)				
Net profit (£)				
Net profit (£)/ total expenditure (£) (%)				

CONCLUSION

This completes one cycle of the strategic market planning process. In practice, when the cycle has been completed once, with the assumption that environmental conditions and the firm's goals and capabilities remain roughly the same, then the strategic market planning process can, say, for the next two years be more of a rolling plan in which the goals and targets are updated rather than being fundamentally reappraised.

The author has used this approach to strategic market planning in a considerable number of firms and found that after being introduced to the concepts managers can apply them regularly without outside help.

NOTE

1. Of course, additional resources could also be computed on the basis of customer group, territory or manufacturing site.

Index

Index of Names